IMAGES
of America

DUNLEITH

On the Cover: This May Day celebration was held at the Elbert School in Wilmington, Delaware. From left to right are Naomi Ruth, two unidentified people, Loretta Dryden, Arlene Boardley, and ? Moody. At top is Marion Dryden.

IMAGES
of America

DUNLEITH

Victoria James

ARCADIA
PUBLISHING

ISBN 978-0-7385-4205-8

Published by Arcadia Publishing
Charleston, South Carolina

Printed in the United States of America

Library of Congress Catalog Card Number: 2005930922

For all general information contact Arcadia Publishing at:
Telephone 843-853-2070
Fax 843-853-0044
E-mail sales@arcadiapublishing.com
For customer service and orders:
Toll-Free 1-888-313-2665

Visit us on the Internet at www.arcadiapublishing.com

Contents

ACKNOWLEDGMENTS

This book has been an incredible historical journey. Dunleith was documented in order to preserve its history and its legacy. Three generations helped to tie this book together, starting with the post–World War II matriarchs and patriarchs who purchased their first homes in Dunleith Estates. A relentless effort was conducted in terms of interviewing people and researching the history of Dunleith. Every person who contributed to this book did so from their perspective and because they sincerely desired to be a part of Dunleith history. Those reasons contribute to the uniqueness of this book. Nevertheless this book includes only a portion of Dunleith history. I am extremely grateful to everyone who helped with this project. Thank you for allowing me to use your family photographs for this project. Furthermore I am humbled by the support and the encouragement that I received from all of you. I would like to thank the following individuals: Jessie Carter, Thomas Carter, Maxine Davenport, Florence Foddrell, Emma Furrowh, Ricky Gaines, Robert Grinnage, Minister Glenn James Jr., Cherron Pindell-Miller, Rev. Dr. Maurice Moyer, Henrietta Nelson, Wayne Portlock, Marvin Prophet, Hazel T. Quarles, Sheena Quarles, Janice Rodgers, Ruth Slade, Eugene Stallings, Margaret C. West, Rev. Naomi Gaines-Winchester, Sue Wisher, and Dunleith matriarchs Dorothy Orr and Marion Perkins. I would also like to thank the following organizations: Rhonda Allende, Wilmington Institute; Martin Berger, Berger Brothers; Robin Bodo, State of Delaware Historical Preservation Office; Cameras Etc. Inc.; Colourworks Photographic Services; Delaware Public Archives; Connie Douglas, National Association of Home Builders, Washington, D.C.; Nancy Hadley, American Institute of Architects, Washington, D.C.; Barbara Hall, Hagley Museum and Library; George Kent, State of Delaware Mapping; Jaime Kinsey, Delaware County Department of Land Use; Marjorie McNinch, Hagley Museum and Library; Ronald Whittington, University of Delaware; and Jon Williams, Hagley Museum and Library. I would like to especially thank my daughter, Prophetess Sonja Hill, who gave me confirmation about this book three years ago. Thank you, Sonja, for extending yourself in the role as a consultant. I also would like to especially thank my husband, Rev. Glenn James, for his unconditional love, encouragement, and support throughout this project. Thank you, Lord.

INTRODUCTION

The Dunleith community was one of the first subdivisions in suburban New Castle County that offered homes to African Americans. From the late 1940s to the 1970s, the home ownership dream became a reality. Establishing this unique African American community did not start with the blueprints of men. The planning started in the hearts and minds of the men and women who desperately wanted equal opportunities in the housing market that could result in a better quality of living.

Living in Millside Federal Housing was just a stepping stone before better housing became available. One challenge in particular was finding good, affordable, and decent housing. The Housing Act of 1949 was put in motion to eliminate inequalities that arose from racial prejudice. Gradually the African American dream of being a homeowner became a reality.

In the 1950s, men such as Leon Weiner, housing developer; Don A. Loftus, contractor; and W. Ellis Preston, architect, helped to make visions become realities. Many World War II veterans, blue-collar workers, and teachers became homeowners for the first time. The community was named after the Rogers estate, called the Dunleith Mansion. This mansion was formerly held in the Rogers Trust under the Annie Rogers du Pont will. The house was called "The Castle" by residents from the area. The land for was released from the du Pont trust on December 23, 1949, to Delaware Community Homes. Helen Rogers Bradford, sister of Annie Rogers du Pont, lived in the Dunleith Mansion, situated in the New Castle Hundred in New Castle County. Leon Weiner developed the community. Most of the 85 acres owned in Dunleith by the du Pont family were released from their trust specifically for the building of Dunleith Estates.

Dunleith homeowners took pride in their homes. Dunleith property was maintained by painting and remodeling the exteriors and interiors as well as modest landscaping. By the early 1960s, one could see the many major home improvements throughout the community.

The churches were the pillars of the community. The churches helped the community to have a sense of balance. The routine of daily living was carried out with a purpose and plan to succeed in life. These houses of worship functioned as formal mentoring centers for the community. The Coleman Memorial Methodist Church provided a myriad of resources to help educate youths and families in their spiritual walk, home life, and with social issues as well.

The Community Presbyterian Church started a day nursery for pre-school children of working mothers in 1956. These children were brought to the Community Presbyterian Church basement nursery school. Both of the churches role-modeled family living. Neighbors knew each other and consequently found themselves sitting on church pews together. Strong morals and values were taught. For the most part, families stayed intact.

Julius Ryland served as principal of Millside School for six months in 1952. The *Delaware Educational Directory 1953–1954* recorded Dr. George Miller Jr. as state superintendent and Earle C. Brown as the principal of Millside School. The new Dunleith Community School was completed in 1956. The school eventually provided education to students in grades one through nine. Benjamin C. Rogers joined the Dunleith faculty as elementary school principal in 1957.

Teachers were highly qualified and dedicated to molding and shaping individuals. The school was an educational setting where students were expected to achieve academically. The teachers were an extension of the family. Teachers combined their teaching skills and their nurturing techniques in an effort to help students to become successful.

Family meal times usually took place in the home. Streetlight curfews were enforced by parents who kept track of where their children were. Next-door neighbors were extended family members also. Many neighbors acted as substitute parents in the absence of a child's biological parent.

There were a variety of celebrations. Special occasions with family members were rituals that were practiced by the entire family unit. Parents and children took pride in attending and celebrating many major events together. A wholesome community managed to navigate through the stressful times of the post–World War II era successfully. As a result, the lives of many African Americans have been impacted positively because of a community named Dunleith.

One

Early Establishments

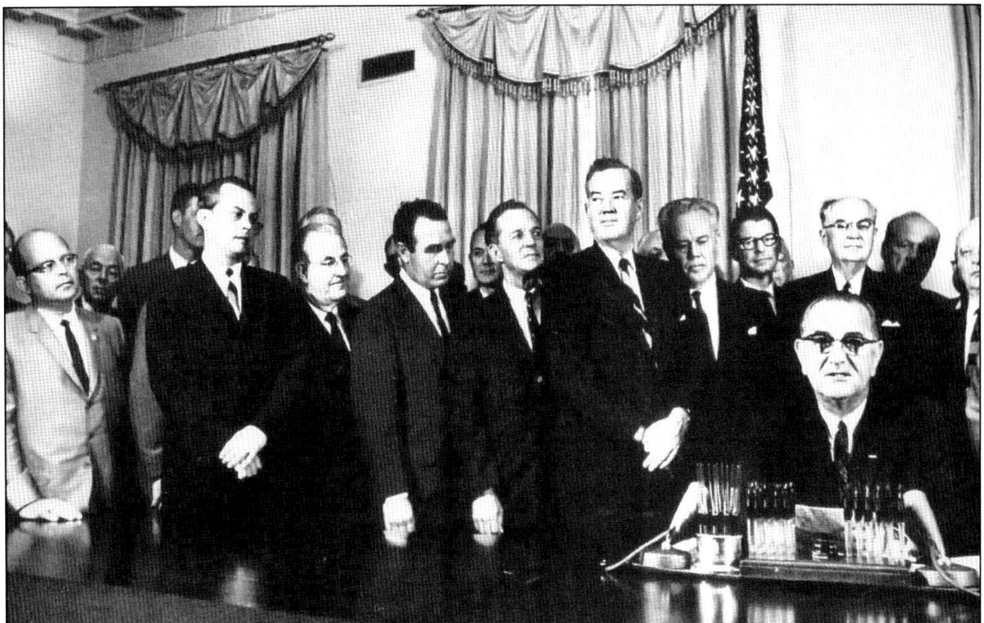

Lyndon B. Johnson, president of the United States from 1963 to 1969, is seated at right. In 1968, President Johnson appointed Mr. Leon N. Weiner (far left) to the Kaiser Commission on Urban Housing, which led to the landmark Housing Act of 1968. The goal for every American to have suitable housing was set forth in the Housing Act of 1949.

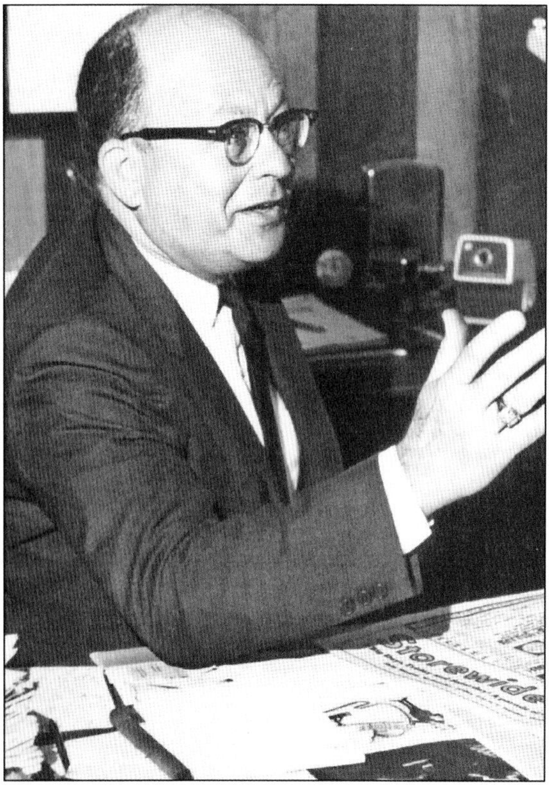

Leon N. Weiner, a builder and developer, was known by the National Association of Home Builders as the "conscience of the housing industry in America." Mr. Weiner was a third-generation builder. He was responsible for the construction of more than 5,000 homes and 10,000 apartments. One of the first communities developed by Mr. Weiner was Dunleith Estates, south of Wilmington, in the early 1950s.

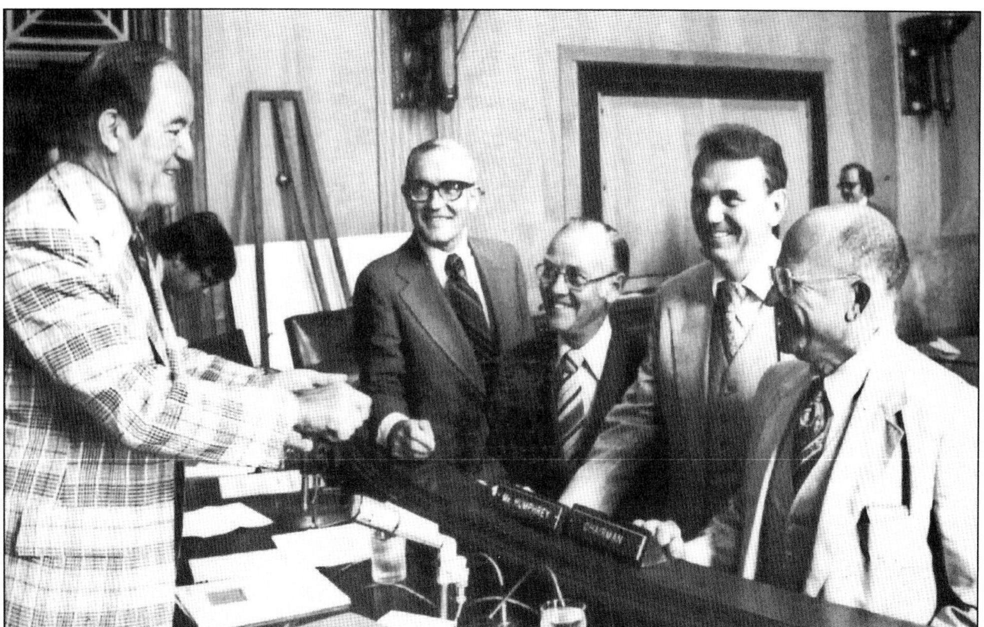

This is a picture of a congressional hearing on Capitol Hill in the 1960s. Mr. Weiner was congratulated for playing a key role in developing housing policy on a national level. His experience as a builder, a developer, and a hands-on executive brought him national acclaim. Behind the desk is Hubert Humphrey; at far right is Leon Weiner.

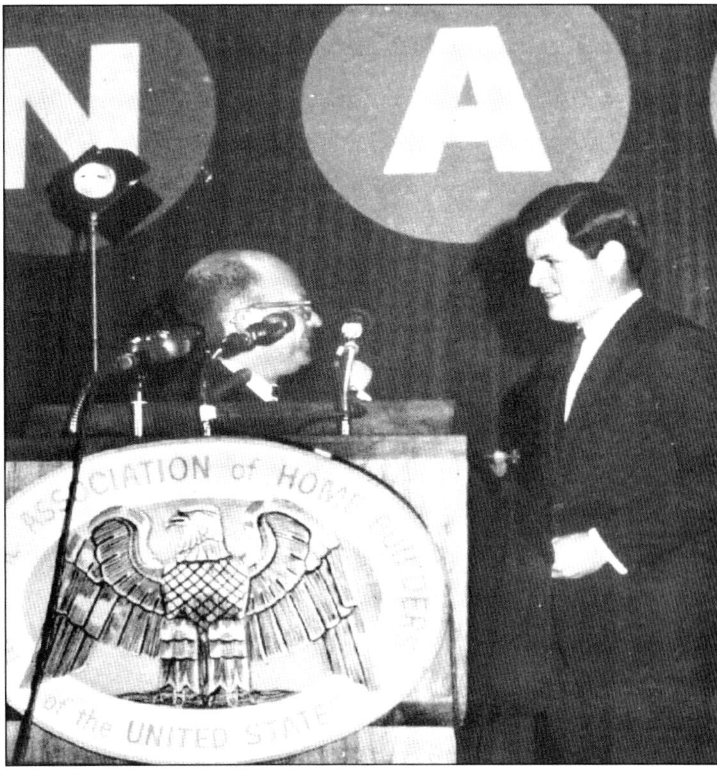

Here, Ted Kennedy (right) greets Mr. Weiner (behind the podium) following his speech before the National Association of Home Builders in the 1960s. Mr. Weiner was praised for being among the very best in the industry of home building. He was hailed as being an outspoken, enthusiastic, and effective advocate for every American family.

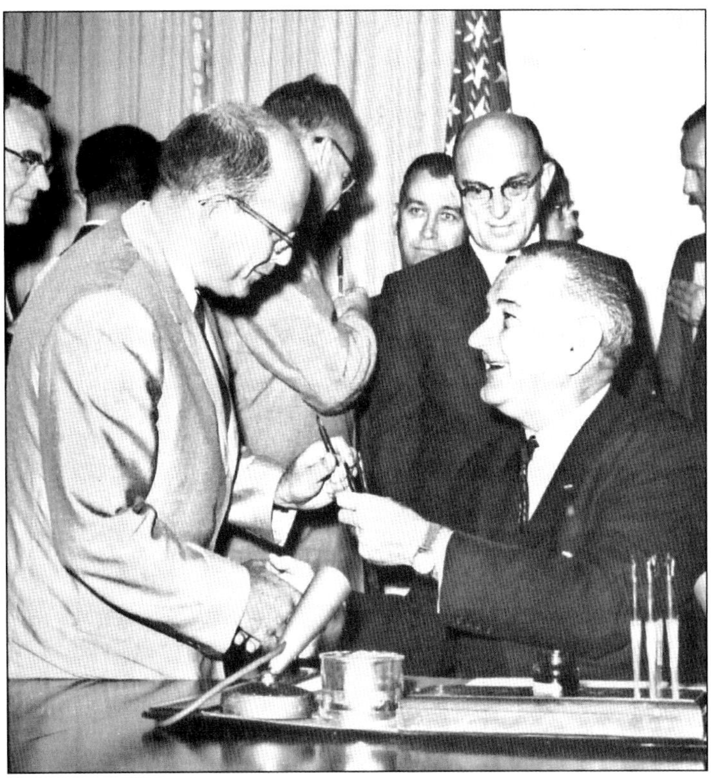

Mr. Weiner accepts the pen that Pres. Lyndon B. Johnson used to sign the landmark Housing Act of 1968. He received distinguished honors that related to the housing industry in America. Mr. Weiner was inducted into the National Association of Home Builders Housing Hall of Fame in the 1970s.

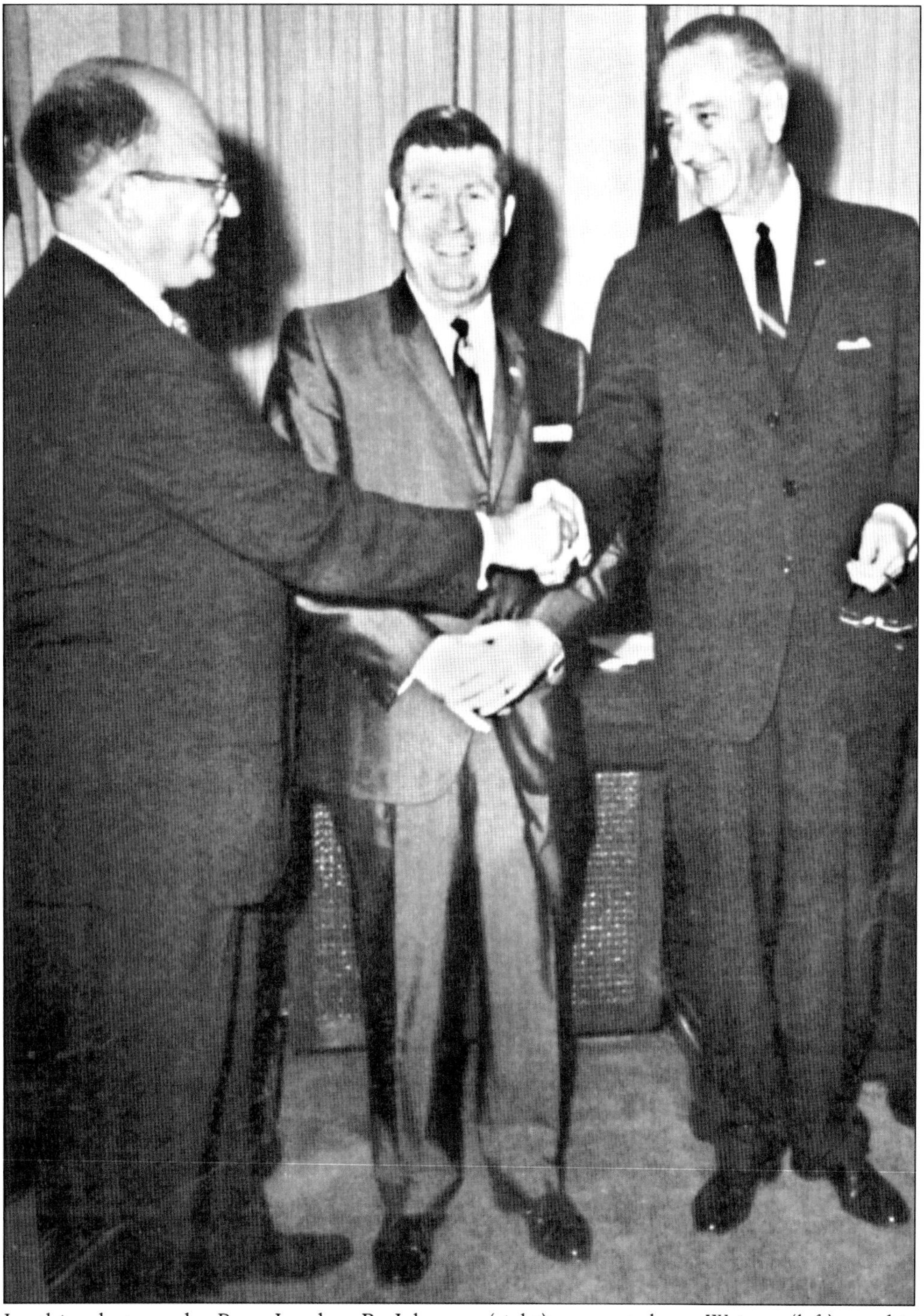

In this photograph, Pres. Lyndon B. Johnson (right) congratulates Weiner (left) on his developing and building accomplishments in the housing industry. Weiner's work in the 1960s included working with a consortium of developers to purchase over 1,000 acres to build the mixed-use development of thousands of townhouses, apartments, single-family houses, parks, and commercial centers in the Newark, Delaware, area.

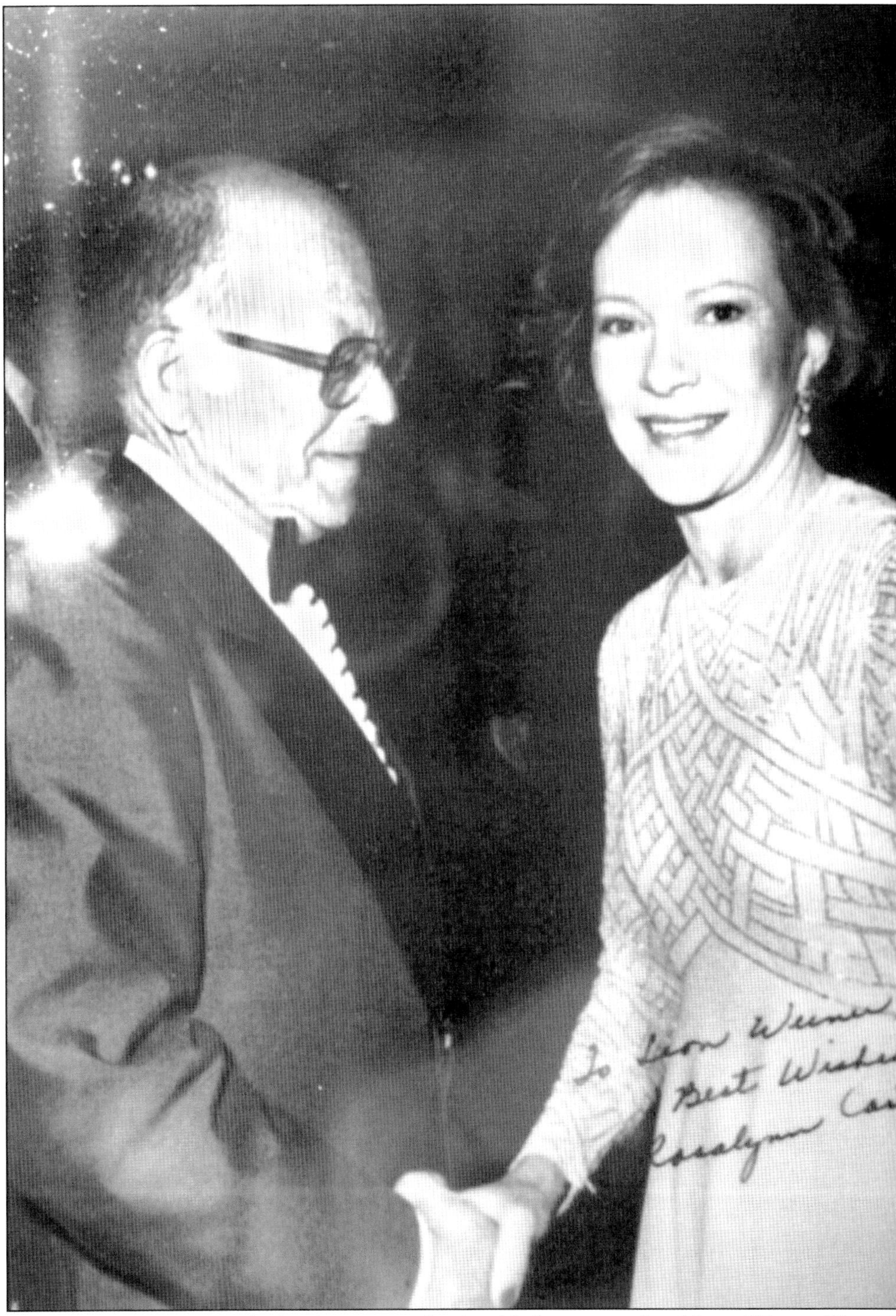

Rosalynn Carter, who worked on better care for the elderly, congratulated Leon Weiner. Weiner's efforts included providing affordable housing for low-income families and the elderly. His honors and awards included the National Housing Conference's Person of the Year in 1973, national recognition, and appointments to three presidential commissions on housing and related issues.

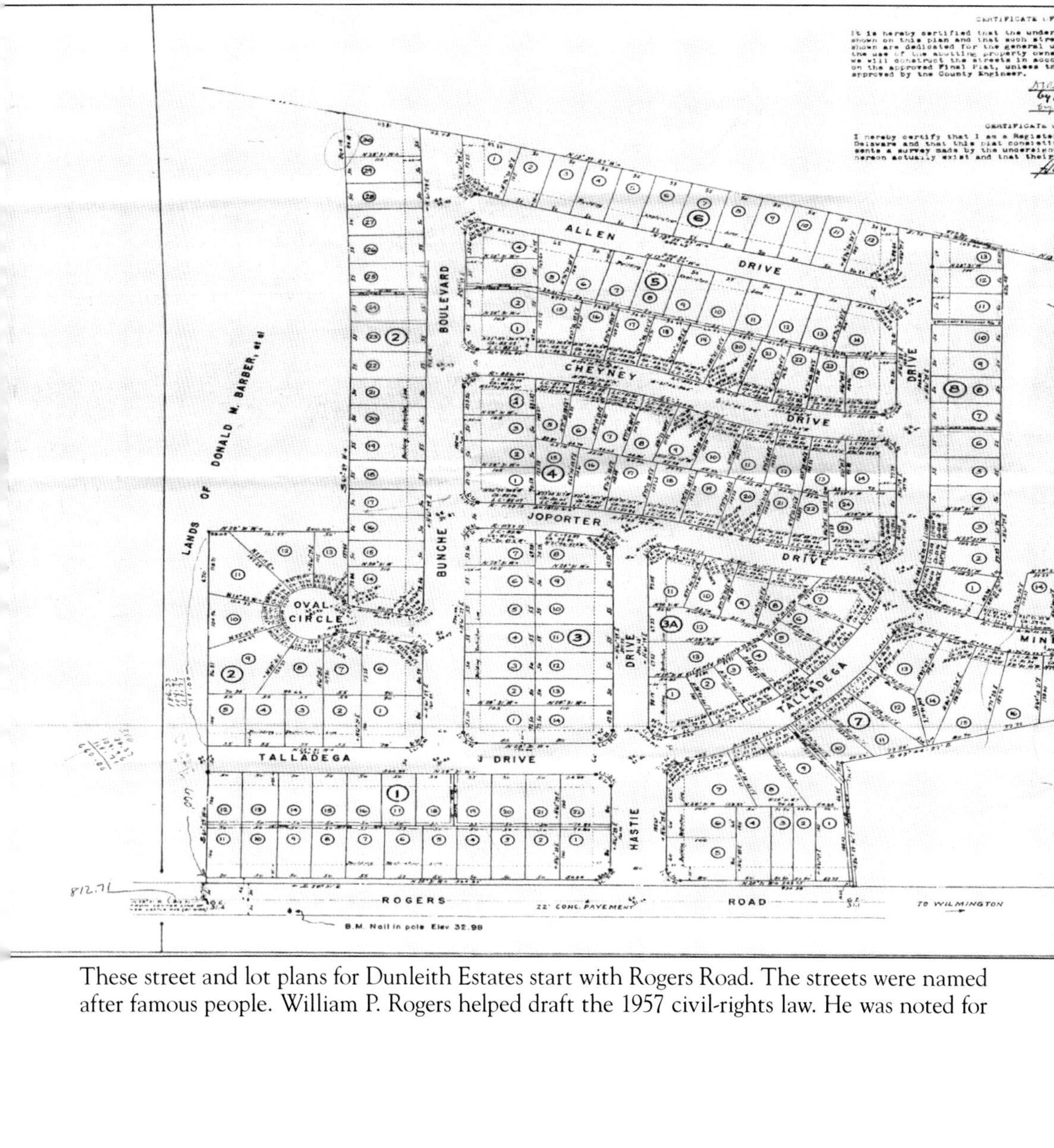

These street and lot plans for Dunleith Estates start with Rogers Road. The streets were named after famous people. William P. Rogers helped draft the 1957 civil-rights law. He was noted for

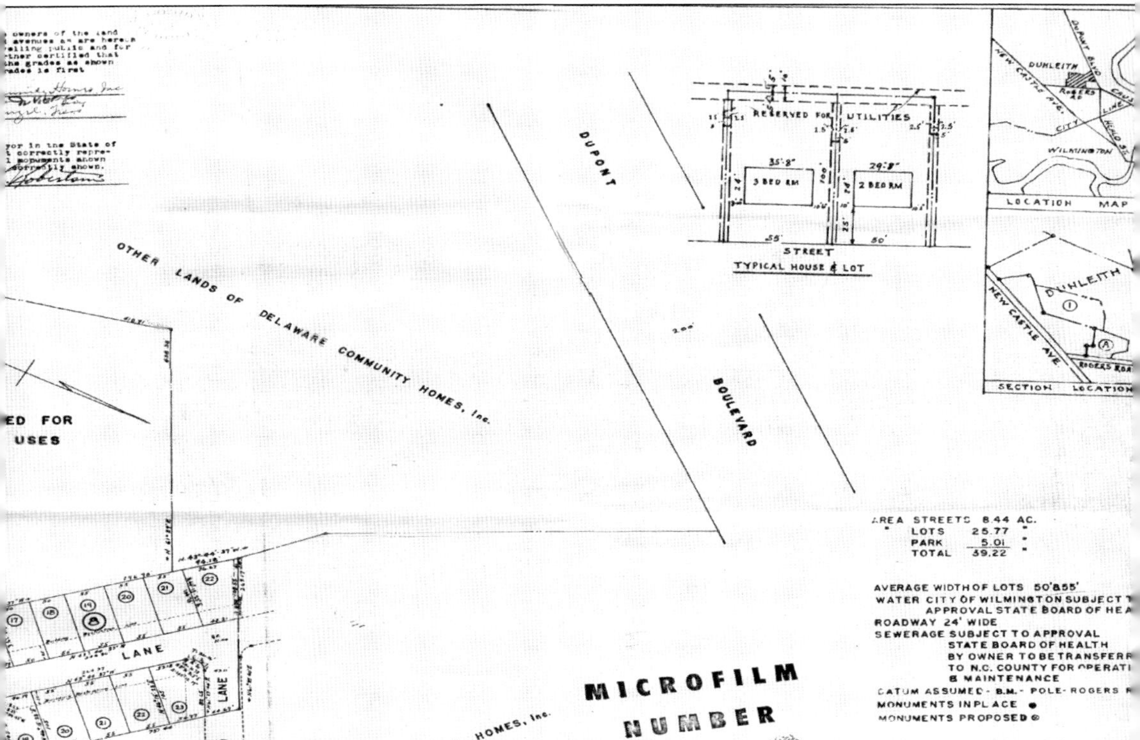

his prosecution cases involving violations of African Americans' civil rights.

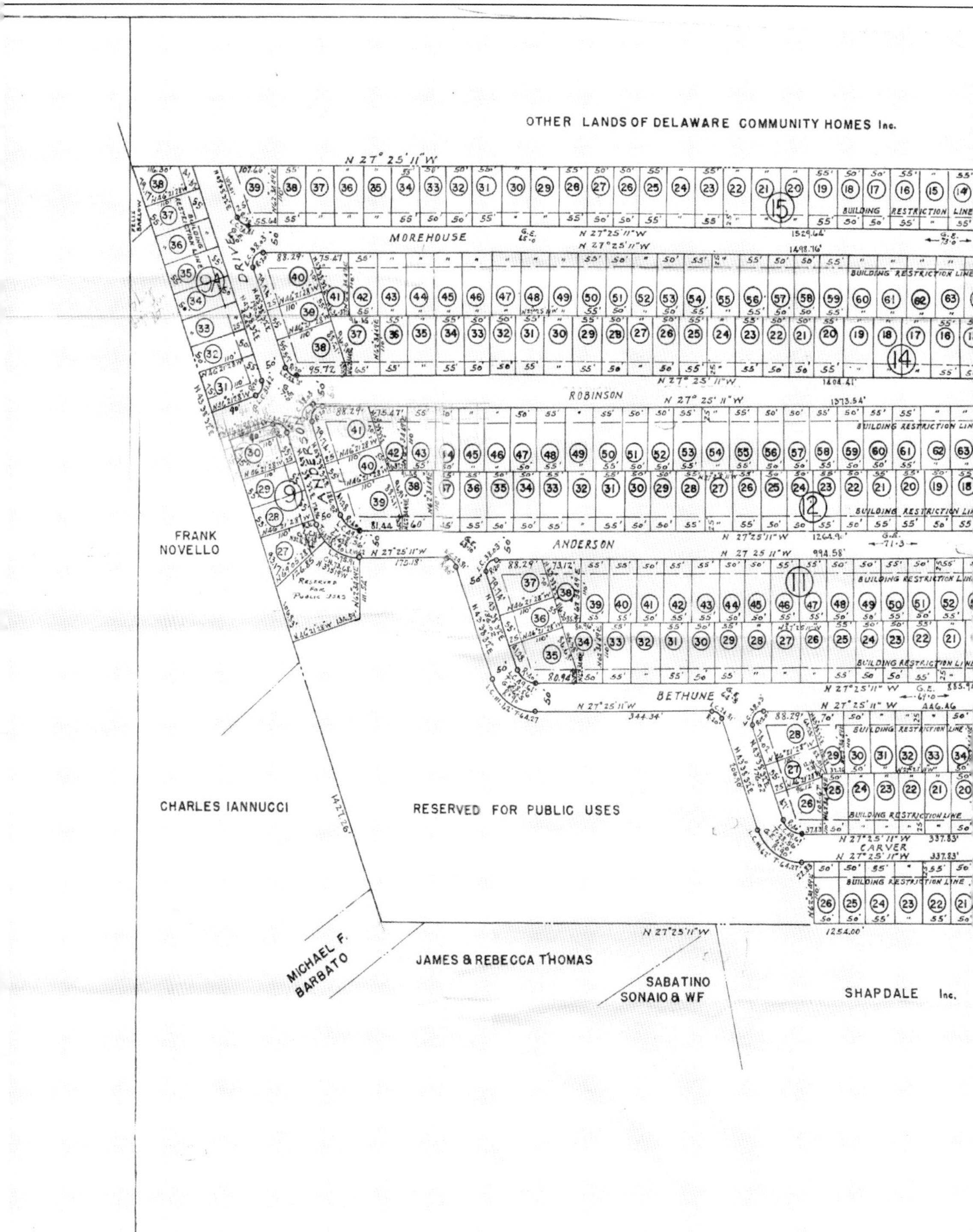

The street and lot plans for Dunleith Estates shown here start with Carver Drive. George

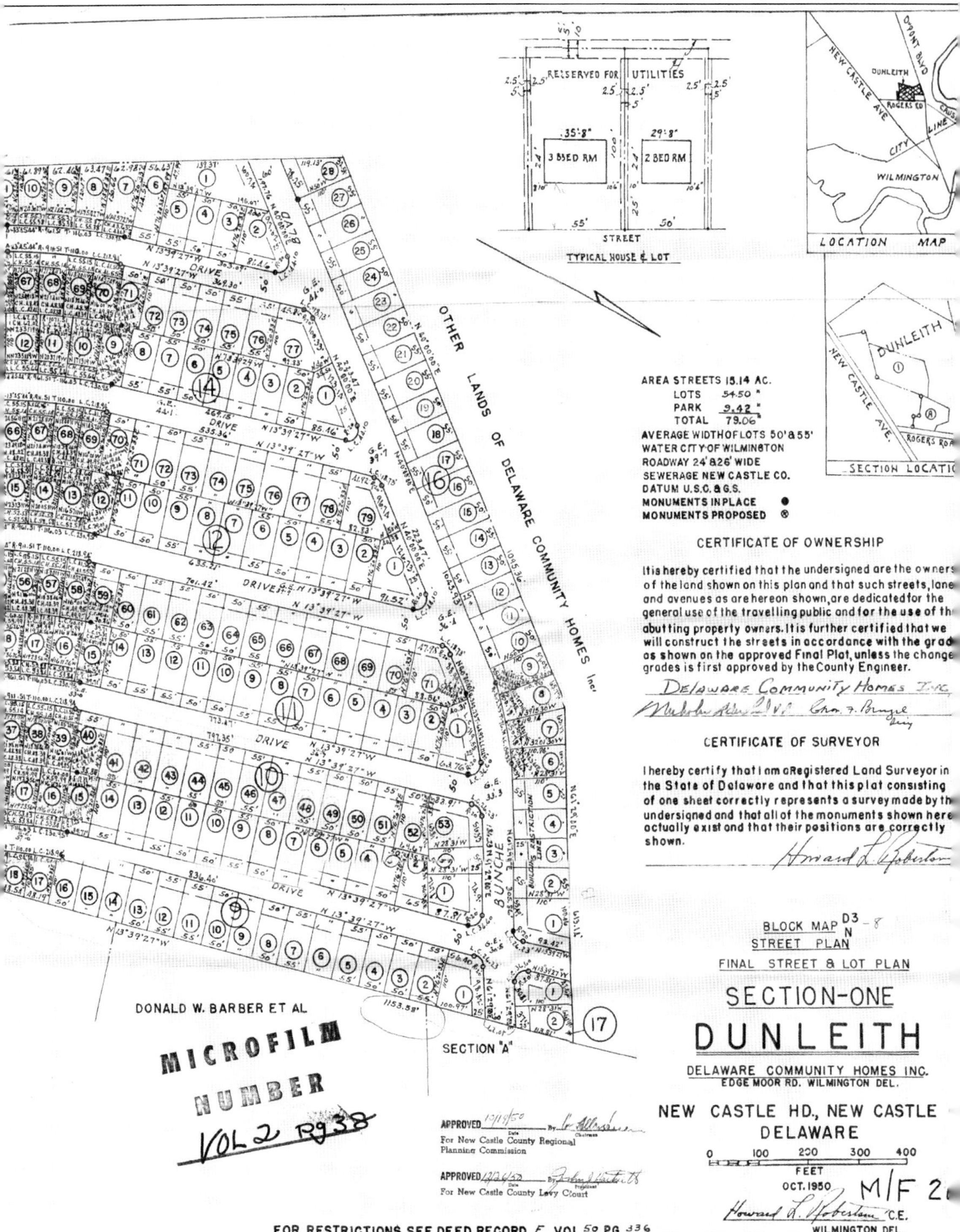

Washington Carver was an African American scientist and educator.

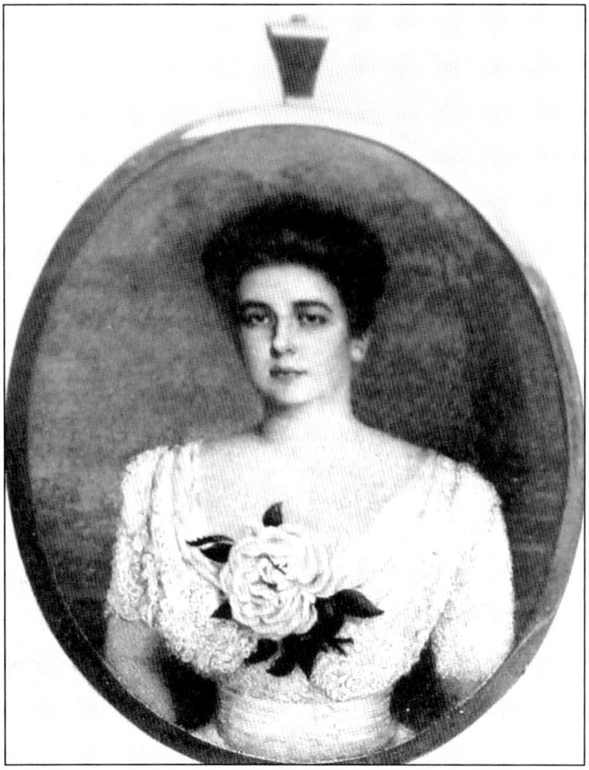

Annie Rogers (du Pont) was born May 4, 1858. Annie Rogers du Pont was the wife of William du Pont Sr. and daughter of Theodore and Mary N. Rogers. Upon the death of Annie Rogers du Pont in 1927, approximately 85.57 acres of Dunleith property and certain lots were held in the Rogers Trust. The acreage was divided into blocks and some of the land was sold. In 1933, the State Highway Department acquired land at Rogers Corner for the purpose of widening the highway.

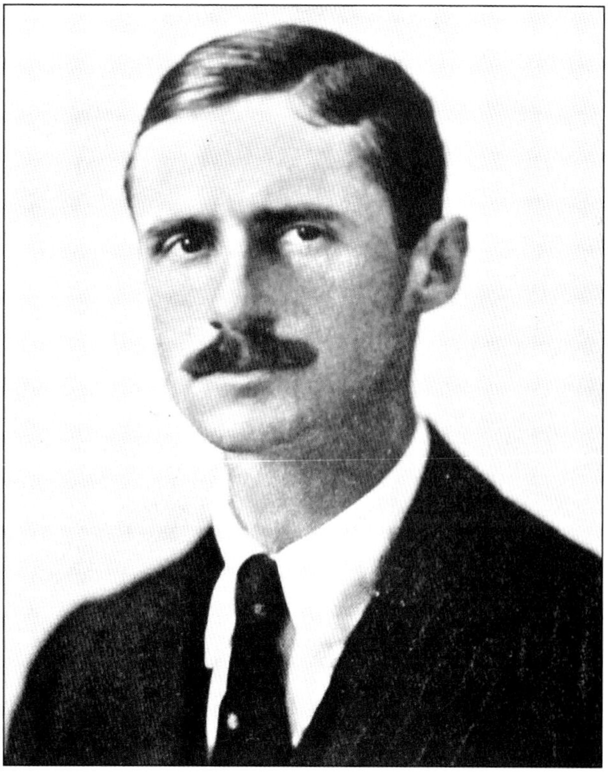

This picture is of William du Pont Jr., son of William du Pont and Annie Rogers du Pont. Dunleith lots were held for William du Pont under his mother's will.

Marion du Pont Scott, daughter of William du Pont and Annie Rogers du Pont, entered into an agreement of sale to sell her portion of land on April 20, 1949. The agreement conveyed that certain lots and parcels of land, including the mansion house known as Dunleith, were to be sold.

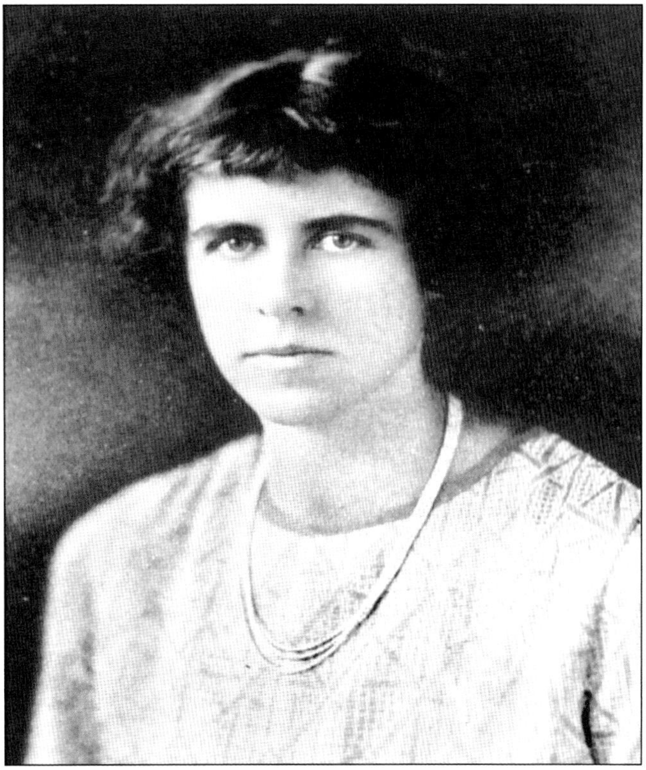

New Castle County Recorder of Deeds

Instrument: 194912230390740 **Volume Page:** M49 538 Purchase Copy
Recorded: 12/23/1949 **Pages:** 12 ParcelView
Document Type: DEED **Consideration:** 0
Grantor: SCOTT, MARION DU PONT / SHAPDALE INC /
DU PONT, MARGARET OSBORNE /
DU PONT, WILLIAM,JR / DELAWARE TRUST COMPANY-TRUSTEE
Grantee: DELAWARE COMMUNITY HOMES INC
Legal Description:
Marginal:

Instrument: 194912230863195 **Volume Page:** M49 550 Purchase Copy
Recorded: 12/23/1949 **Pages:** 1 ParcelView
Document Type: DEED **Consideration:** 0
Grantor: SHAPDALE INC
Grantee: DELAWARE COMMUNITY HOMES INC
Legal Description:
Marginal:

Instrument: 195004061859532 **Volume Page:** B50 258 Purchase Copy
Recorded: 4/6/1950 **Pages:** 5 ParcelView
Document Type: DEED **Consideration:** 0
Grantor: DU PONT, EMILY / DU PONT, HARRY B
Grantee: DELAWARE COMMUNITY HOMES INC
Legal Description:
Marginal:

Instrument: 195004270453118 **Volume Page:** A50 334 Purchase Copy
Recorded: 4/27/1950 **Pages:** 2 ParcelView
Document Type: DEED **Consideration:** 0
Grantor: DELAWARE COMMUNITY HOMES INC
Grantee: DELAWARE POWER & LIGHT COMPANY / DIAMOND STATE TELEPHONE COMPA
Legal Description:
Marginal:

This document from the New Castle County Recorder of Deeds is a deed indicating that Marion Scott du Pont, William du Pont Jr., and others sold their portion of land located in Dunleith in 1949. The land was sold to Delaware Community Homes Incorporated. The land was to be used to construct homes in and around Dunleith.

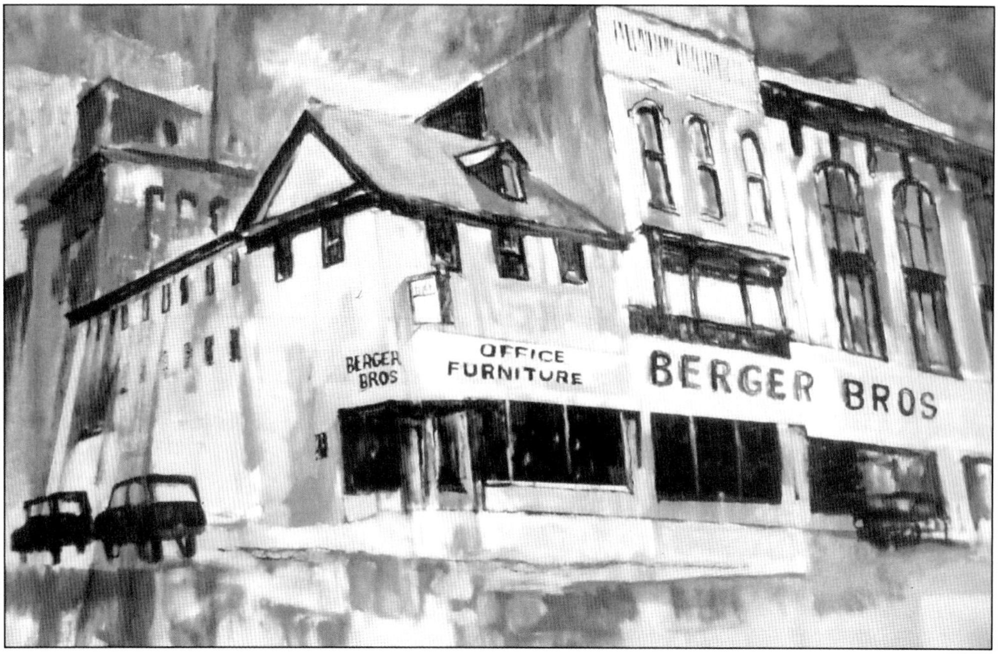

The owners of the first Berger Brothers Furniture Store, Samuel and Elizabeth Berger, came from Russia and started the business in the 1920s. The store was located at 103 East Third and Shipley Streets in Wilmington, Delaware. Furniture from this Berger Brothers store was used to furnish the model homes in Dunleith. There were four model homes. They were located at 308, 310, 312, and 314 Rogers Road. This is a painting of the store in the 1940s.

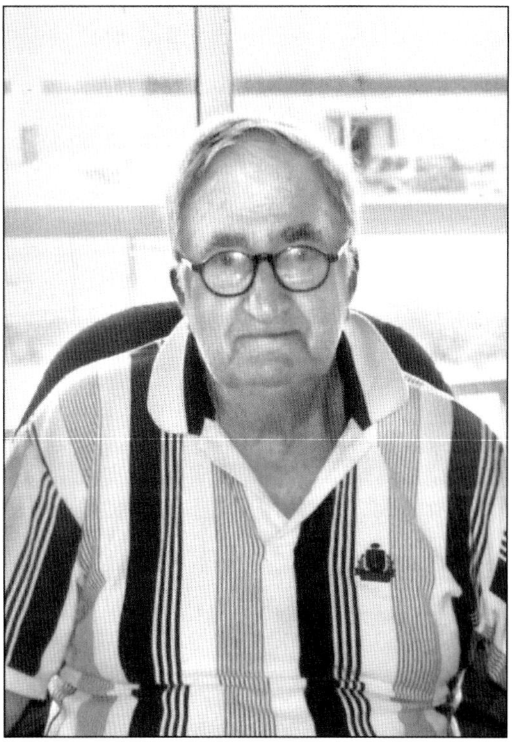

Martin Berger was born in the city of Wilmington and was the 11th of 13 children. Mr. Berger was a second-generation store owner. The business became successful, and another store was added on New Castle Avenue in Wilmington. Martin Berger was active in World War II as well.

Two

DUNLEITH ESTATES

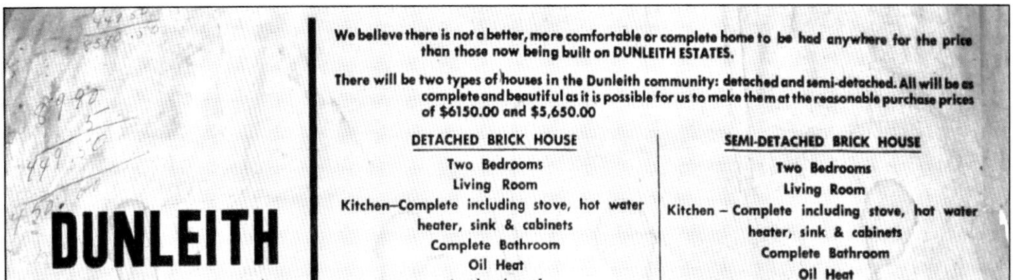

This is a picture of the original sign that was used to market homes in the Dunleith Estates community. The paper sign is enclosed in a two-by-two-foot glass frame. There were two types of brick homes that were offered. Veterans did not have to come up with any money down. The price of the homes was affordable enough for hundreds of African Americans to purchase. The mortgage was not more than $35 per month. This sign was designed in the early 1950s.

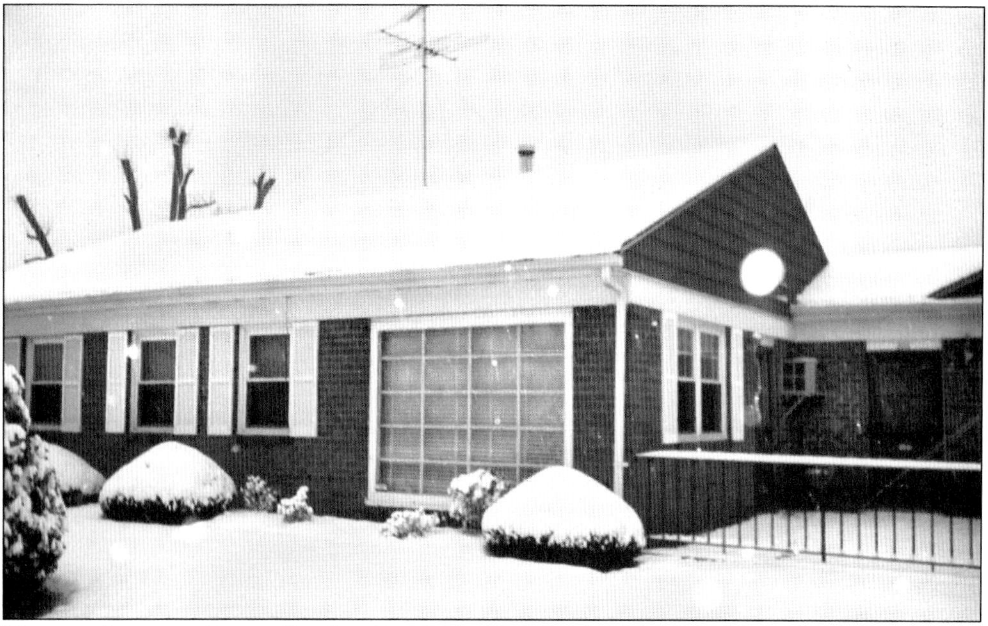

Here is a home on Rogers Road in Dunleith Estates. The exterior of this home has not been changed. The home was especially designed by the owner. Plans and specifications were for a two-bedroom masonry house. The home was presented for the occupancy of a paraplegic veteran. Special fixtures or movable facilities were added for the particular veteran to reside in the house. The home was also built with space provided for an exercise room.

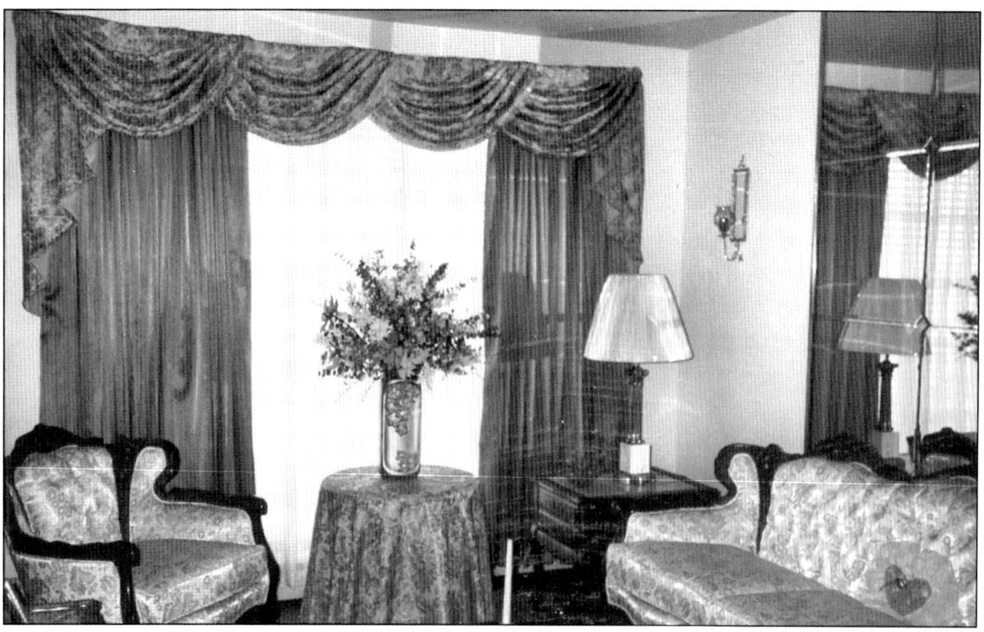

Only a few modern accessories were added. This masonry house has two bedrooms, a living room, a dining room/kitchen, a den, a bathroom with an oversized tub, and a garage. There is a small patio off of the living room. The du Ponts originally had a large iron gate on the front of the property before the land was developed. The owners had the gate removed. The interior of this Dunleith home, pictured in the 1950s, was exquisite.

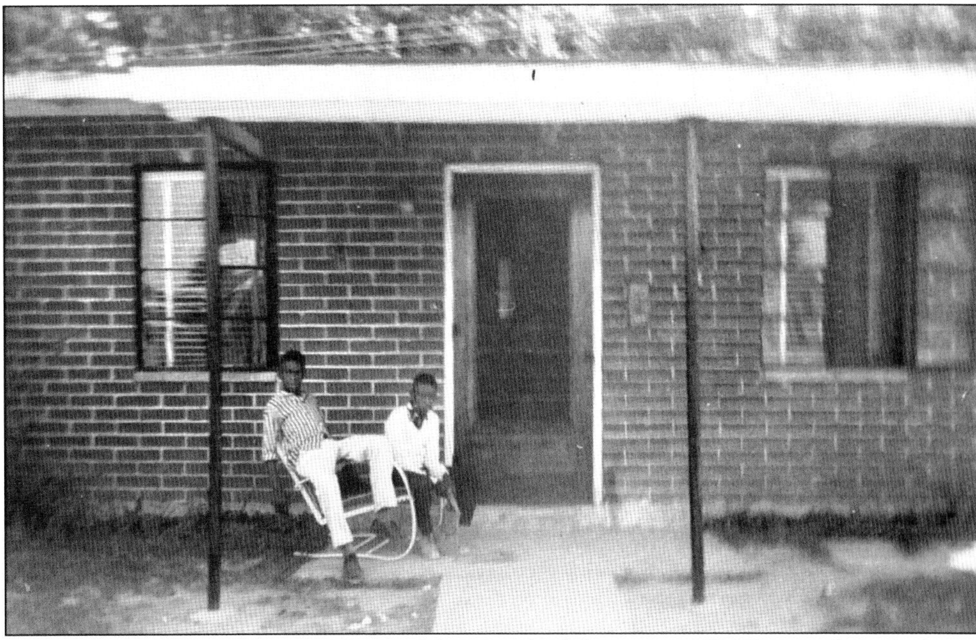

Bernard (left) and Bill Orr sit in front of their Dunleith house in 1957. This was how the house looked on Carver Drive before renovations. The red brick home had a flat-top roof. Many of the flat-roof homes like this one had poles out front. These poles were attached to a small trimmed overhanging. The home interior and exterior were basic.

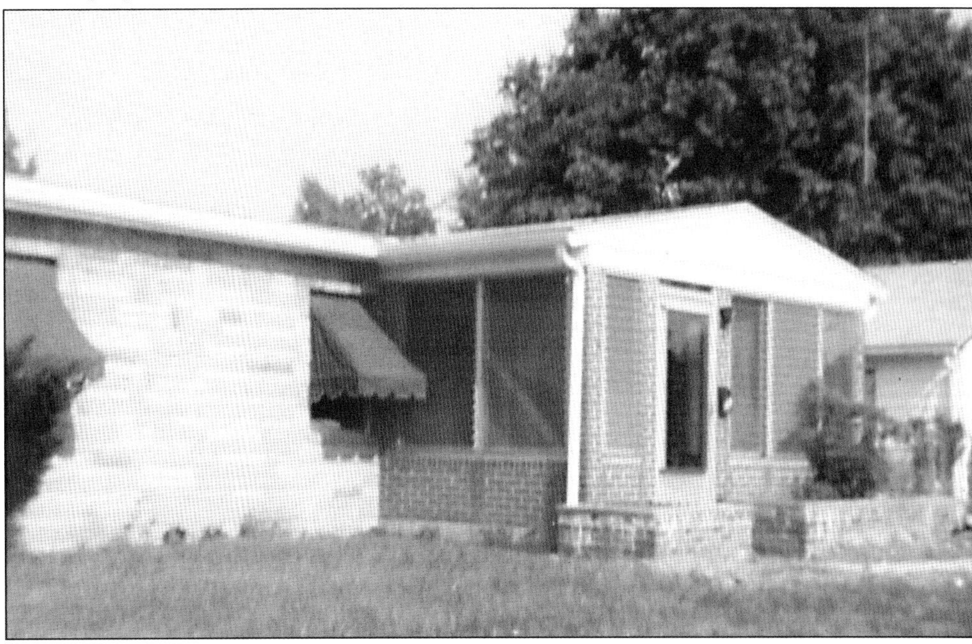

This is a picture of a home on Carver Drive in the 1960s. The home's exterior was renovated. This major improvement enhanced the exterior dramatically. An enclosed porch with adjustable jalousie windows added light to the house. It was also used as an outdoor sitting area. The light and dark stones replaced the brick front, and fabric awnings covered the bare windows. Landscaping was added as well.

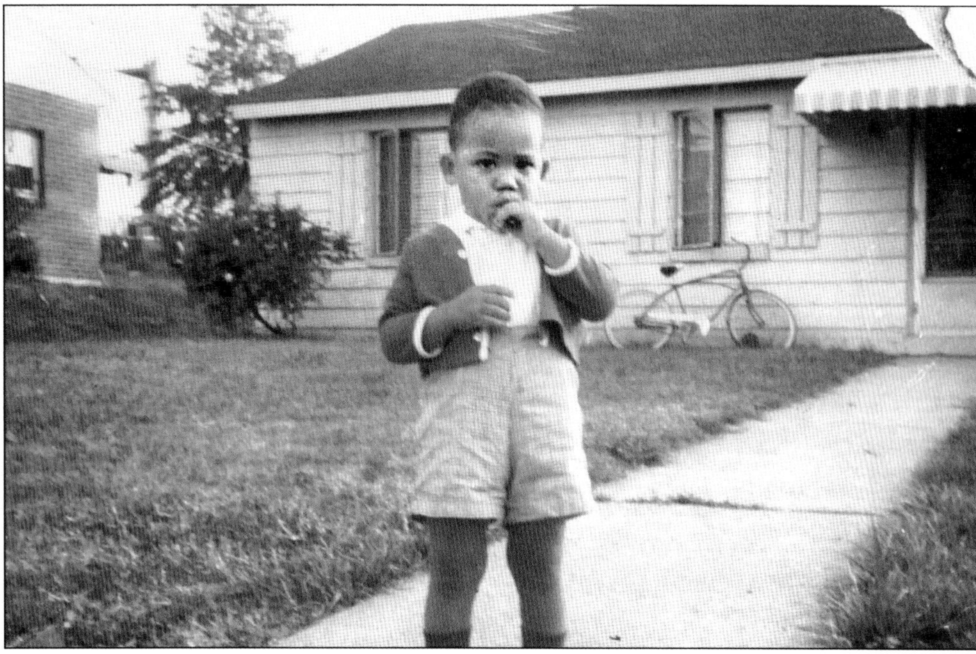

Timothy Perkins stands in front of his home on Talladega Drive in the late 1950s. This home was built with three bedrooms, a kitchen, and one bathroom. The roof is slightly pitched and trimmed in wood. Wood shutters frame the windows on the front of the house. The owners added a metal awning to enhance the front of the house. The sidewalk is cement. The thick carpet of grass helps the modest landscape.

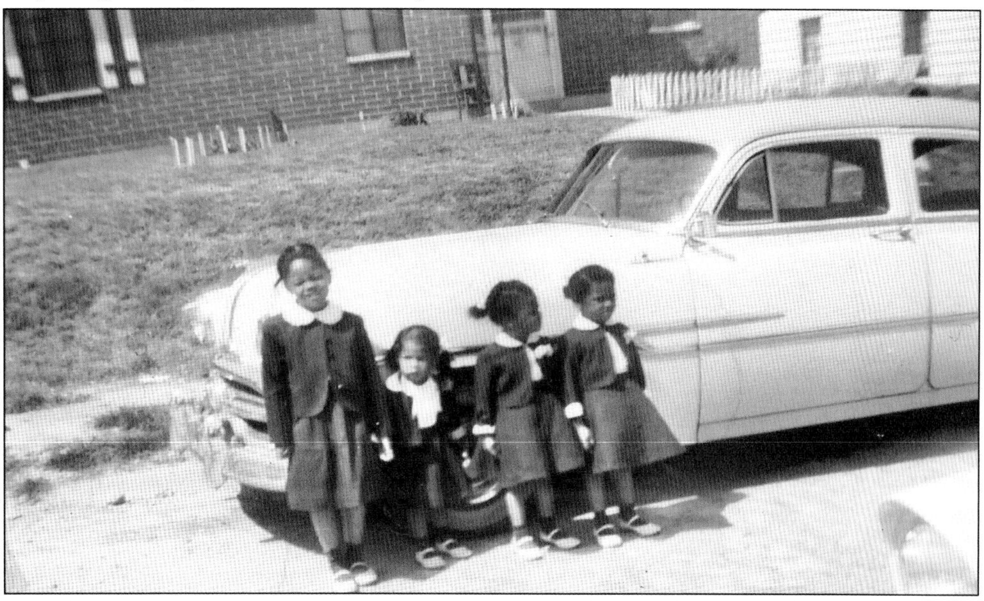

This Dunleith home was made with bricks and had a slightly pitched roof. The window on the far left is the only one framed with a shutter. The front door is enclosed with a storm door. The dark poles that frame the front door appear to be attached to the upper portion of the house. This homeowner added a small partial fence to help improve the property in the late 1950s. Pictured from left to right in front of the car are Darlene, Joyce, Penny, and Barbara Perkins.

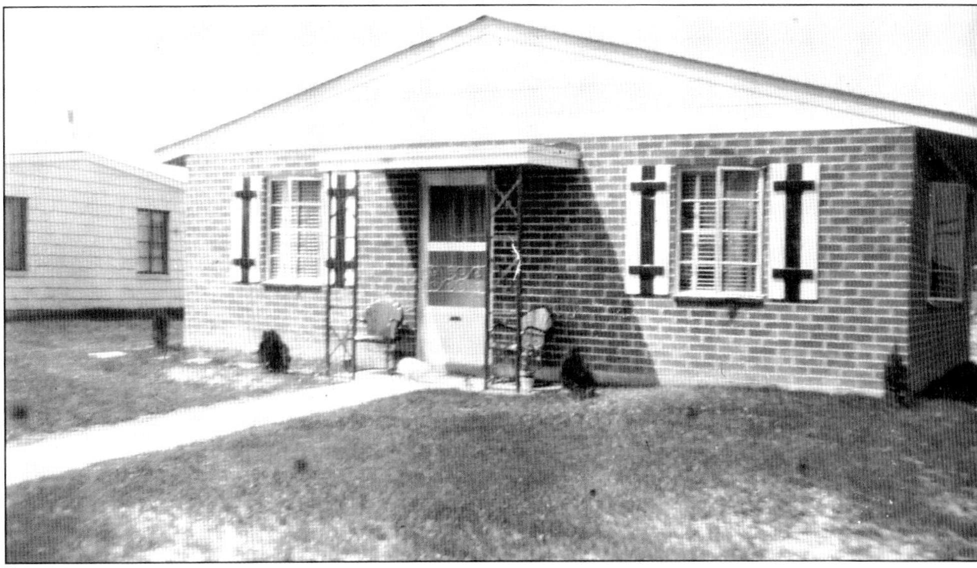

This is a picture of the home of Robert L. and Gertrude Grinnage. The home is located at 404 Bethune Drive. This was how the house looked when the owners moved in in 1951. The shutters were a familiar detail in many of the Dunleith homes. The brick home with a pitched rooftop is trimmed in wood. The double poles on each side of the front have an X pattern from top to bottom.

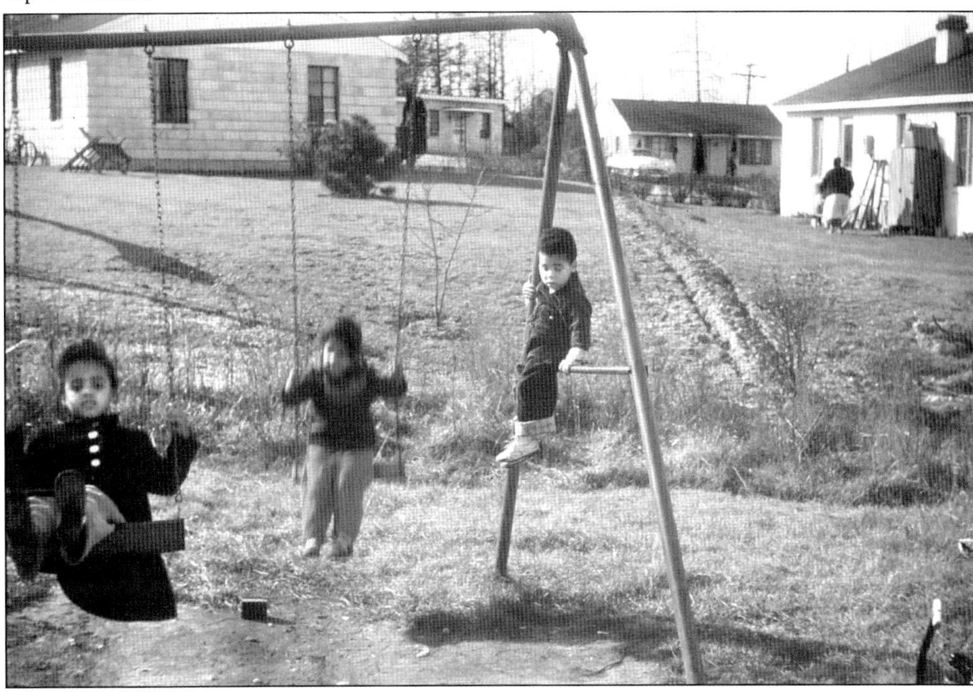

This yard backs up to Oval Circle homes. The masonry homes had a mixture of pitched and flat roofs. The windows do not have shutters on the backs or sides of the homes. The house on the right has a smoke stack on one side of the roof. Storage space was limited. Bicycles and other miscellaneous items were stored outdoors. The new lots were void of landscaping. From left to right in this 1950s picture are Barbara, Joyce, and Timothy Perkins.

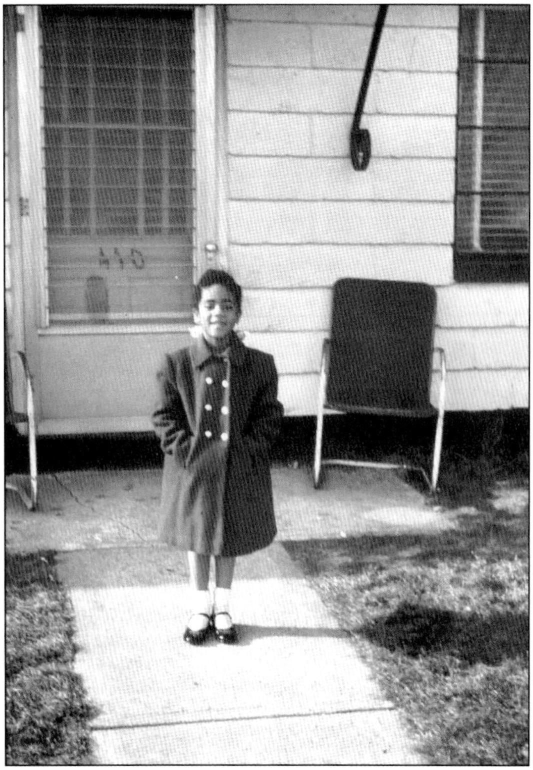

This is a picture of a masonry home that had a jalousie storm door. The small glass panels on the door could be adjusted for ventilation during warm weather. Instead of poles, a decorative metal scroll trim was attached to the front of the house. The metal chairs matched the metal house trim. Penny Perkins poses on the walkway in this 1950s photograph.

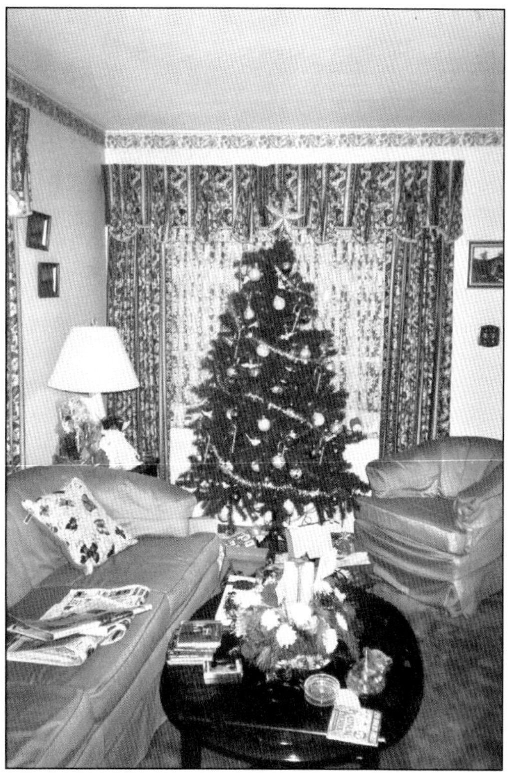

Pictured here in the 1960s is the living room in a home that was custom decorated. The solid walls were dressed up with a border that matched the window treatments. The inner window was covered with a lace curtain. Old chairs were covered to change the look of the room.

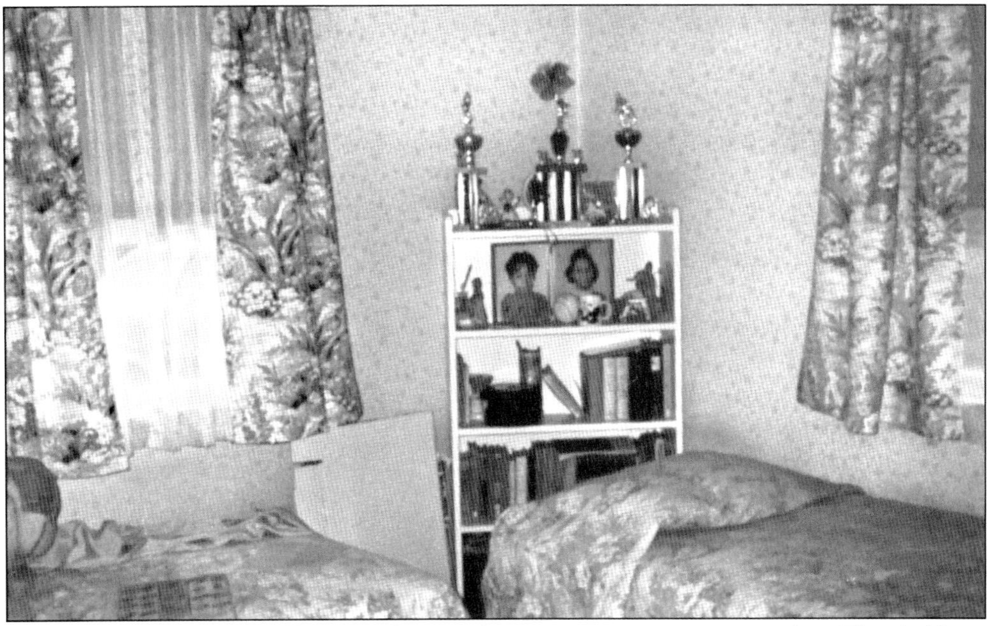

The hand-crafted bookshelf was used to tie this pretty teenage room together. The shelf was also used for decoration and for storage. The matching curtains and bedspreads helped give the room a pulled-together look. All of the curtains had to be closed by pulling them together by hand. This picture and the one below were both taken in the 1960s.

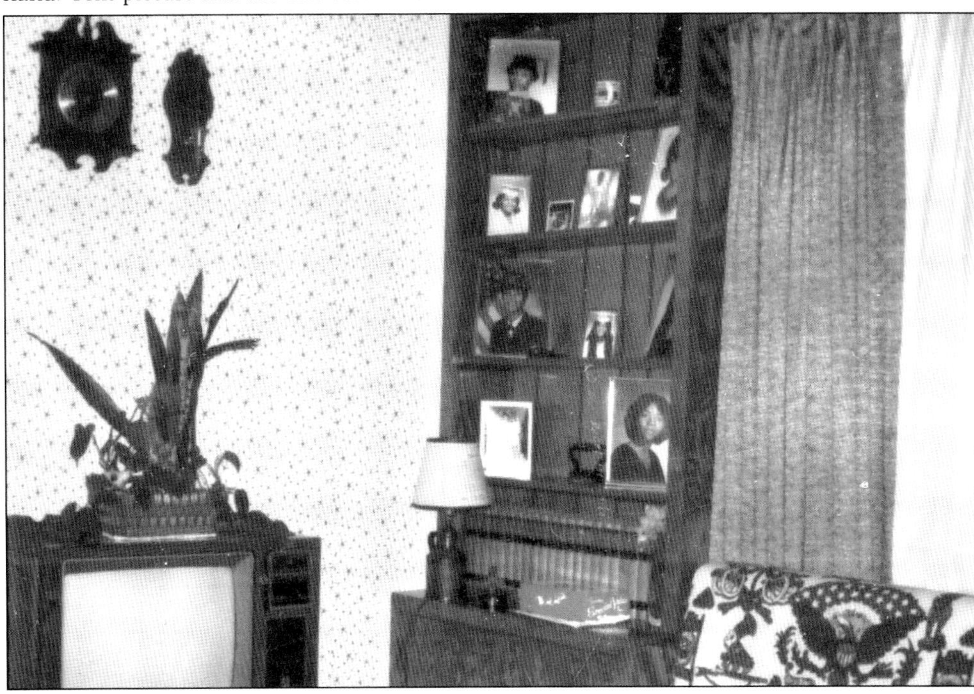

This den has an American eagle theme. The theme makes a patriotic statement in this Colonial-dressed room. The corner picture shelf was handmade. The walls were painted with a solid paint, and a design roller was used to go over the solid walls. The chair cover was handmade to match the room's décor.

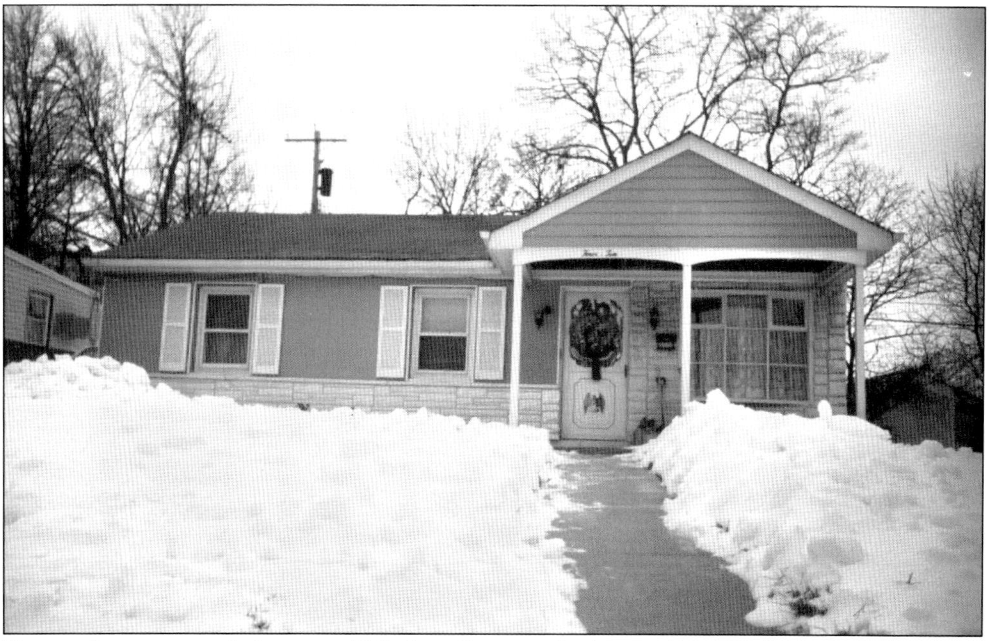

Here is the exterior of a home on Talladega Drive in the late 1960s. This home was completely renovated. The stone and siding were combined to blend together. New light shutters with small slats were added to complement the windows. A new storm door and bay window were added to replace a small overhang that was once there. Wooden stilts were added to the front of the roof.

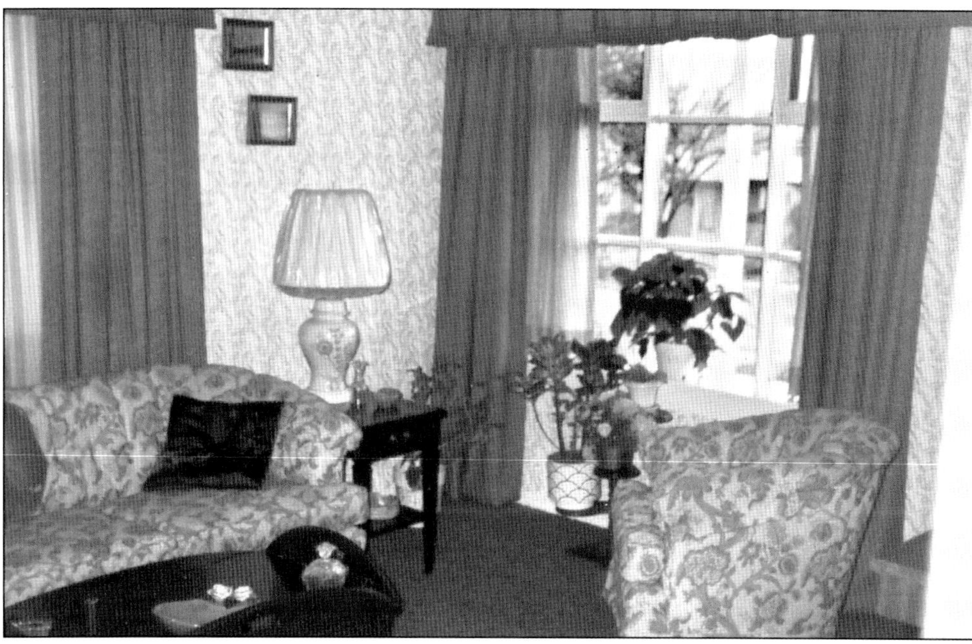

Window treatments and complimentary wallpaper were used to tie this designer living room together. The bay window had a sheer curtain that could be pulled to either side. The drapes could close completely. The matching sofa and chair were re-upholstered pieces. The plant stand in the bay window added a special touch to the updated late-1960s room.

Lynn Perkins is pictured in front of a Dunleith masonry home framed with shutters. The roof is slightly pitched. The striped metal awning adds interest to this 1960s home. The light trim on the bottom of the house was painted to match the window and roof trims. The landscape that lines the front of the house is barely visible.

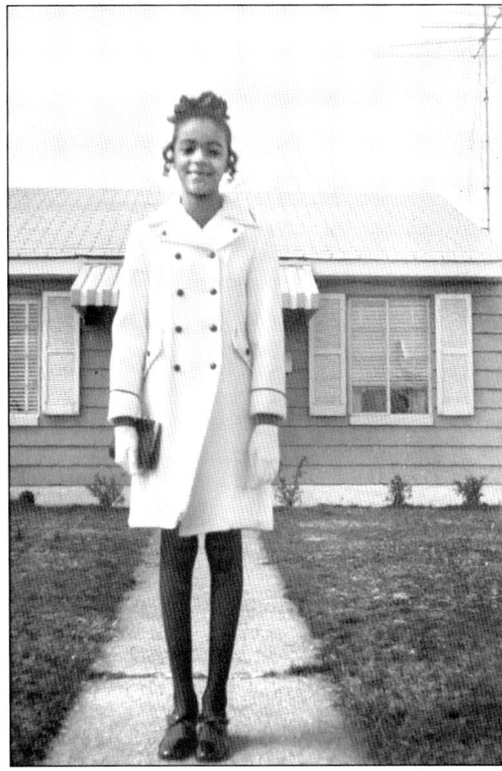

The flat-top roof of this two-bedroom home, seen in the late 1950s, is trimmed in a light wood. Two sets of shutters frame the front of the house. The cement walkway has a few trees along the sides. Both sides of the home have shrubbery for landscape. The front door is a combination of wood and window.

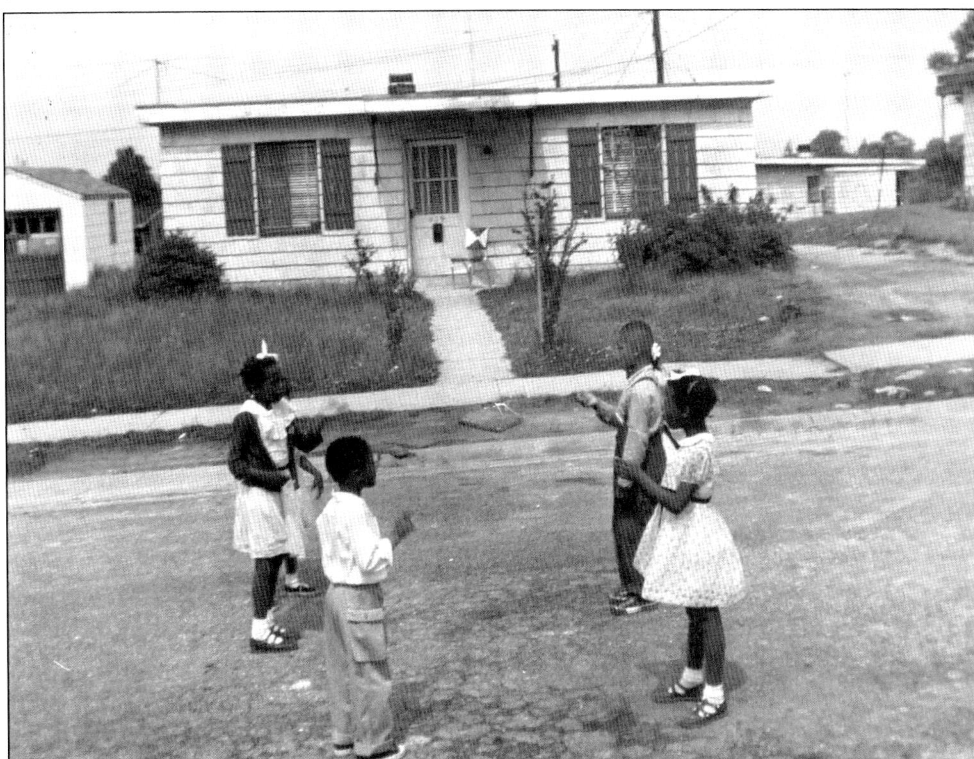

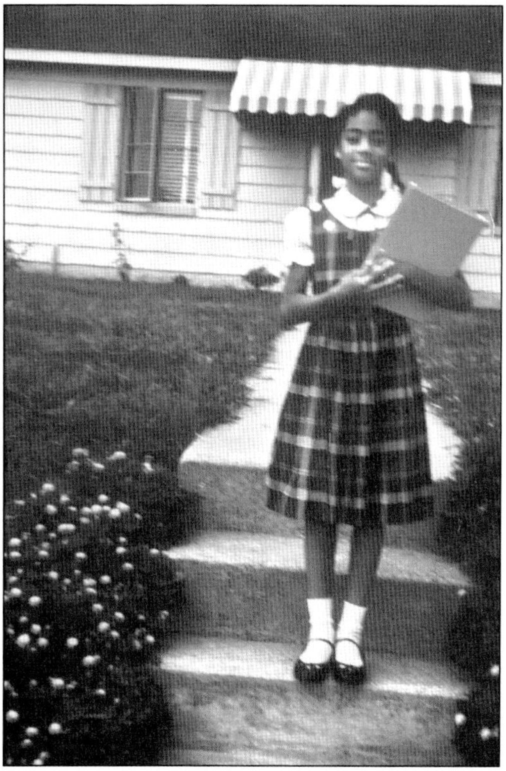

Here is a Dunleith house built with plain masonry brick. The flowering landscape along the steps gives this home a feel of hospitality. The two windows that frame the front door are given character with thick wooden slats. The trim along the edge of the roof matches the trim on the bottom of the house. The awning was made from a lightweight metal. Penny Perkins posed for this photograph in the 1960s.

Another flat-top roof home is the backdrop for Dorothy and James Orr in this 1960s photograph. The house was built with masonry bricks. The thick slat shutters were made out of wood. The roof trim and the porch trim were built with wood. The small porch was held up with dark poles. The yard has small shrubs across the front on both sides of the house.

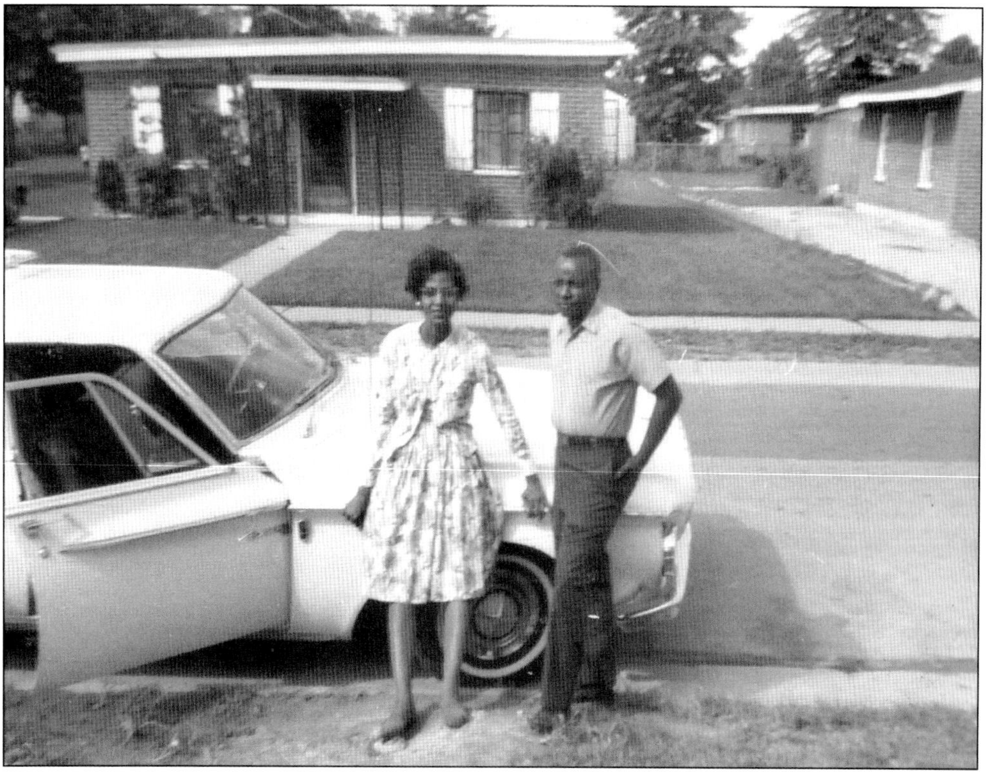

Three

MILITARY

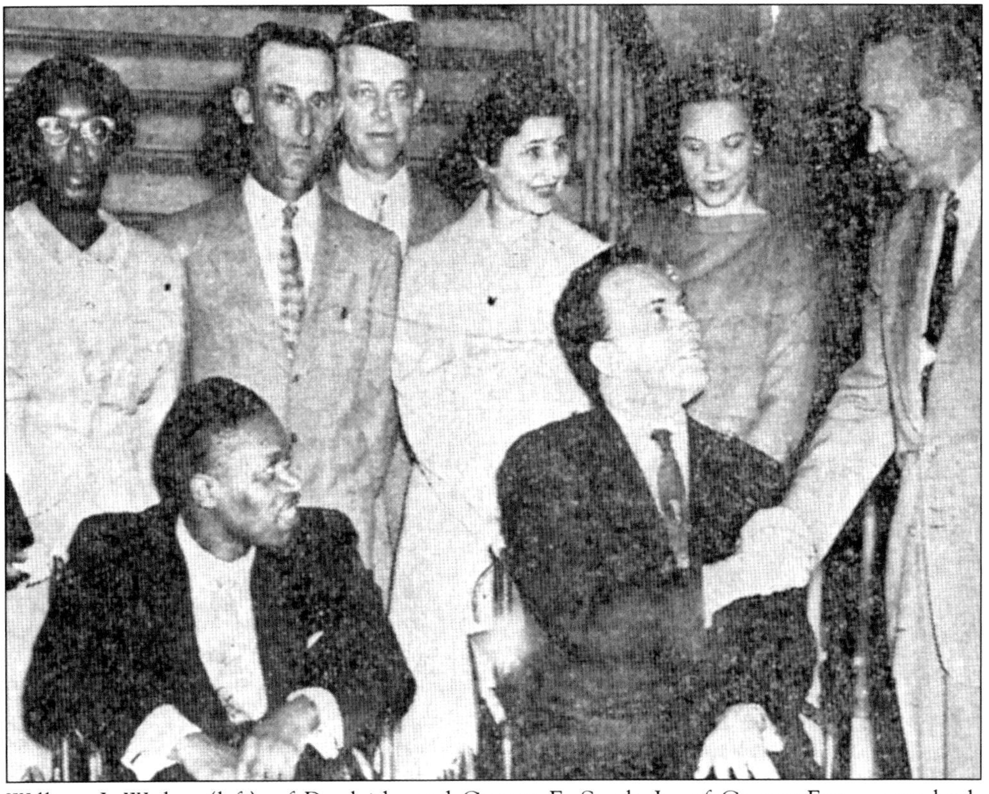

William J. Wisher (left), of Dunleith, and Garrett E. Steele Jr., of Cooper Farm, were both paraplegic veterans who, previous to this picture, received $600-a-year bonuses under the provisions of a bill introduced in the general assembly in 1957. They were welcomed to Legislative Hall by Gov. J. Caleb Boggs. In the rear are, from left to right, Wisher's wife, Sue; state representative Elmer L. Betts (D-Felton), one co-sponsor of the bill; Joseph Micker, national service officer of the Disabled American Veterans; state representative Margaret R. Manning (R-Marshalton), another co-sponsor of the bill; Steele's wife, Bertha; and Governor Boggs.

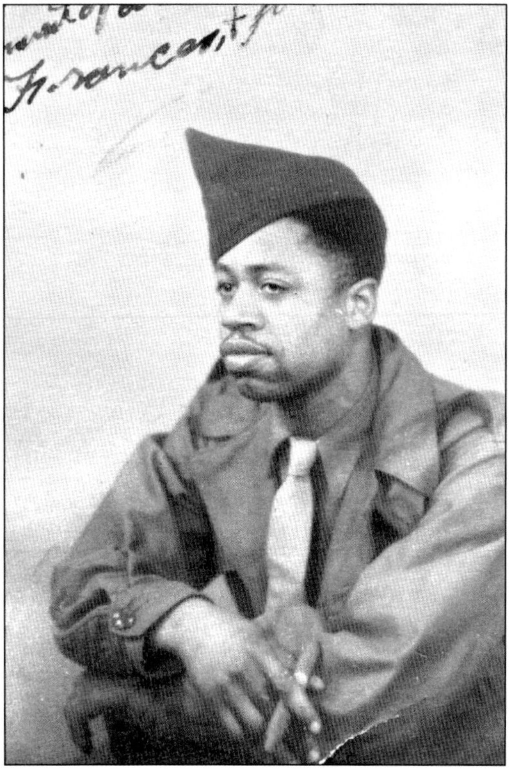

William J. Wisher came home from World War II a paraplegic. The Veterans Administration loan guaranty officers made a determination about his medical feasibility. The government gave him plans to have a specially adapted house for paraplegics. His deed was recorded on December 26, 1950.

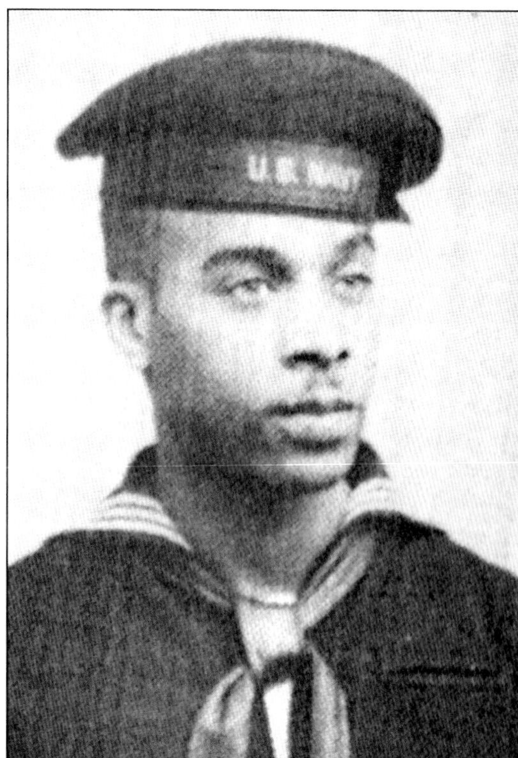

Howard F. Dobson and his wife, Gloria Dobson, were among the first homeowners in Dunleith. They purchased their first home on Rogers Road. Their deed was recorded on November 13, 1950.

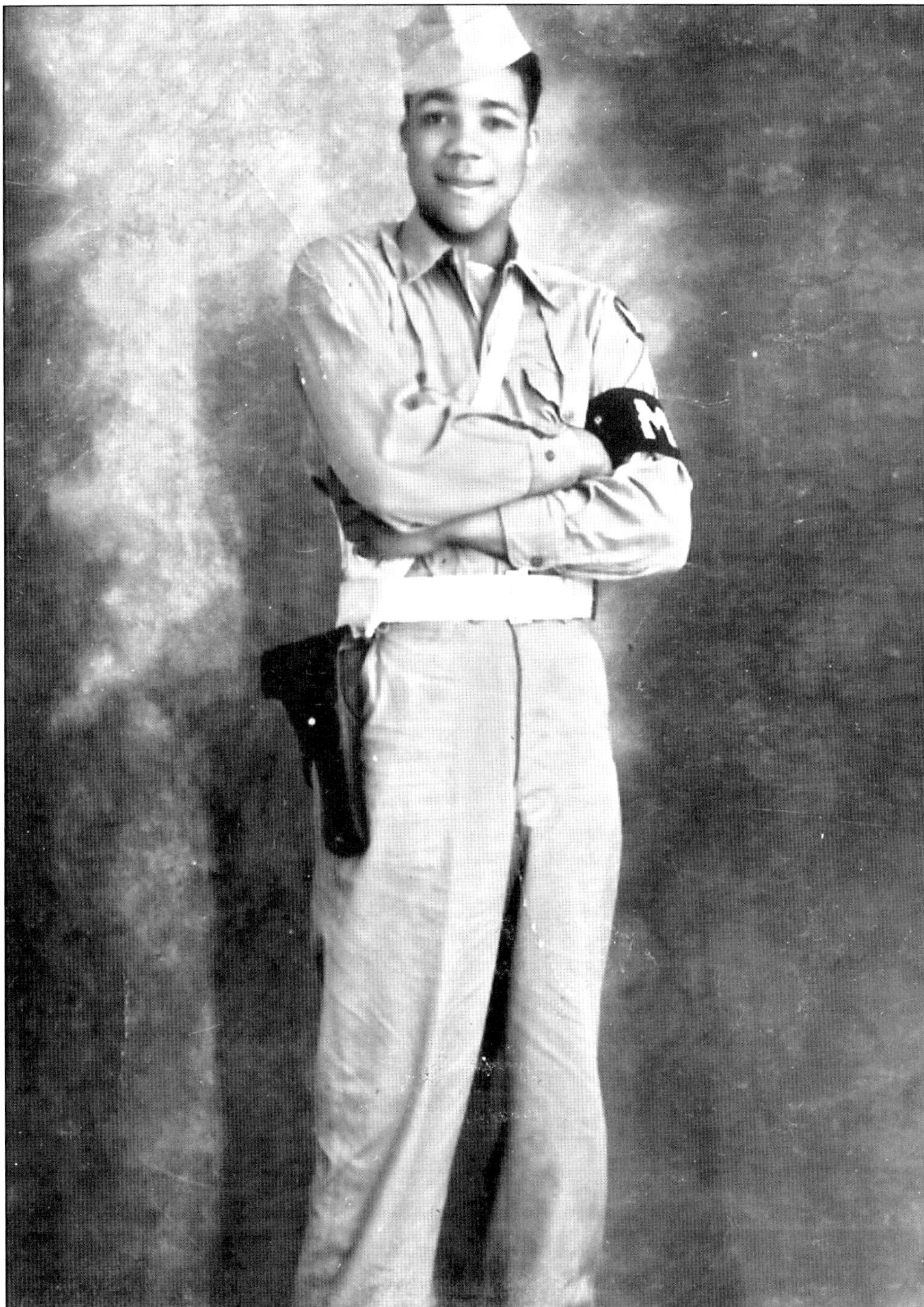

Matthew Perkins and his wife, Marion, lived in Millside. After serving in the military, Perkins purchased a home in Dunleith on Talladega Drive. He worked for the U.S. Postal Service as a letter carrier. He also worked part-time for the home-based Tex Taxi-Cab Service, which was located on Rogers Road. His deed was recorded on December 4, 1950. This picture was taken in the late 1940s.

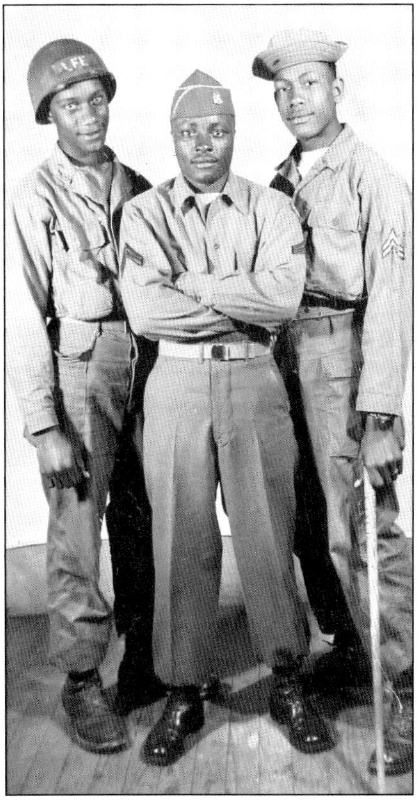

James Orr is impressively flanked by his military buddies, who are unidentified.

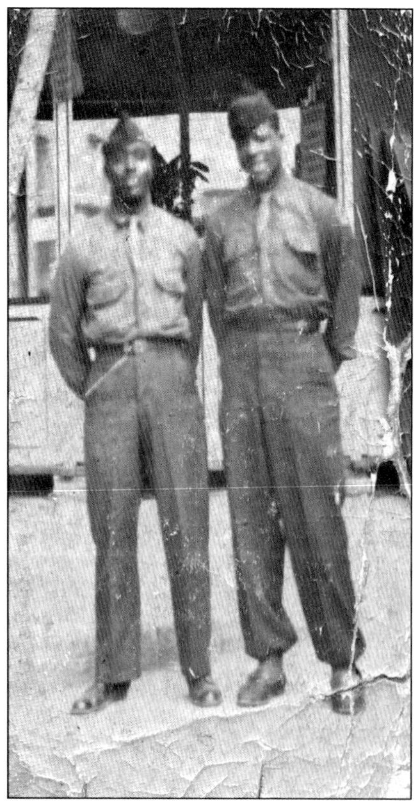

Pictured here in the 1940s are two unidentified soldiers who were military friends of Matthew Perkins.

Maurice Moyer, pictured here in the late 1940s, became the Reverend Dr. Maurice Moyer of the Community Presbyterian Church in Dunleith Estates on Rogers Road. He and his wife, Vivian, had two sons, Thomas and Norman. Reverend Moyer and his family lived on Morehouse Drive in Dunleith.

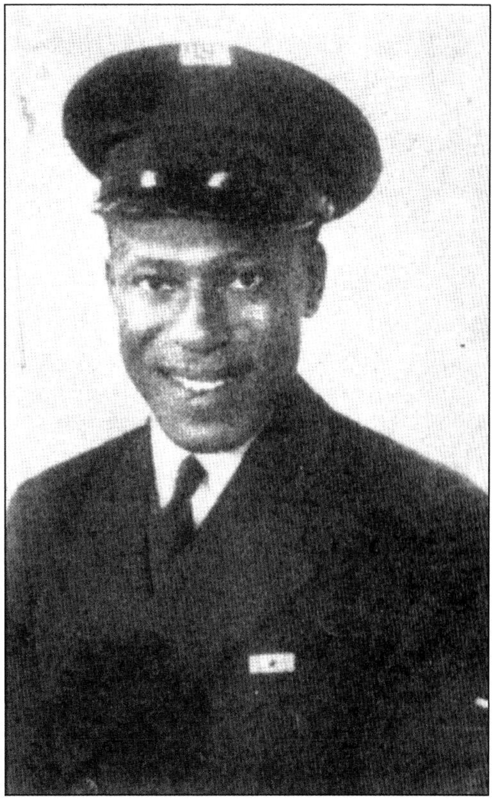

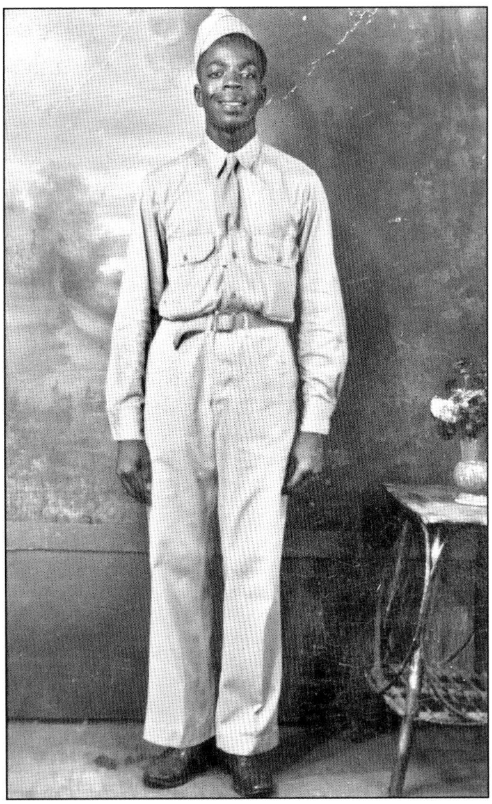

James Furrowh, seen in the late 1940s, was married to Emma Juanita Blackiston. After he served his time in the military, he and his wife purchased their first home in Dunleith. Mr. and Mrs. Furrowh had 10 children. He was a layperson at Coleman Memorial Methodist Church. Mr. Furrowh became Rev. James Furrowh later in his ministry career. Their house was located on Carver Drive. The deed was recorded on June 19, 1951.

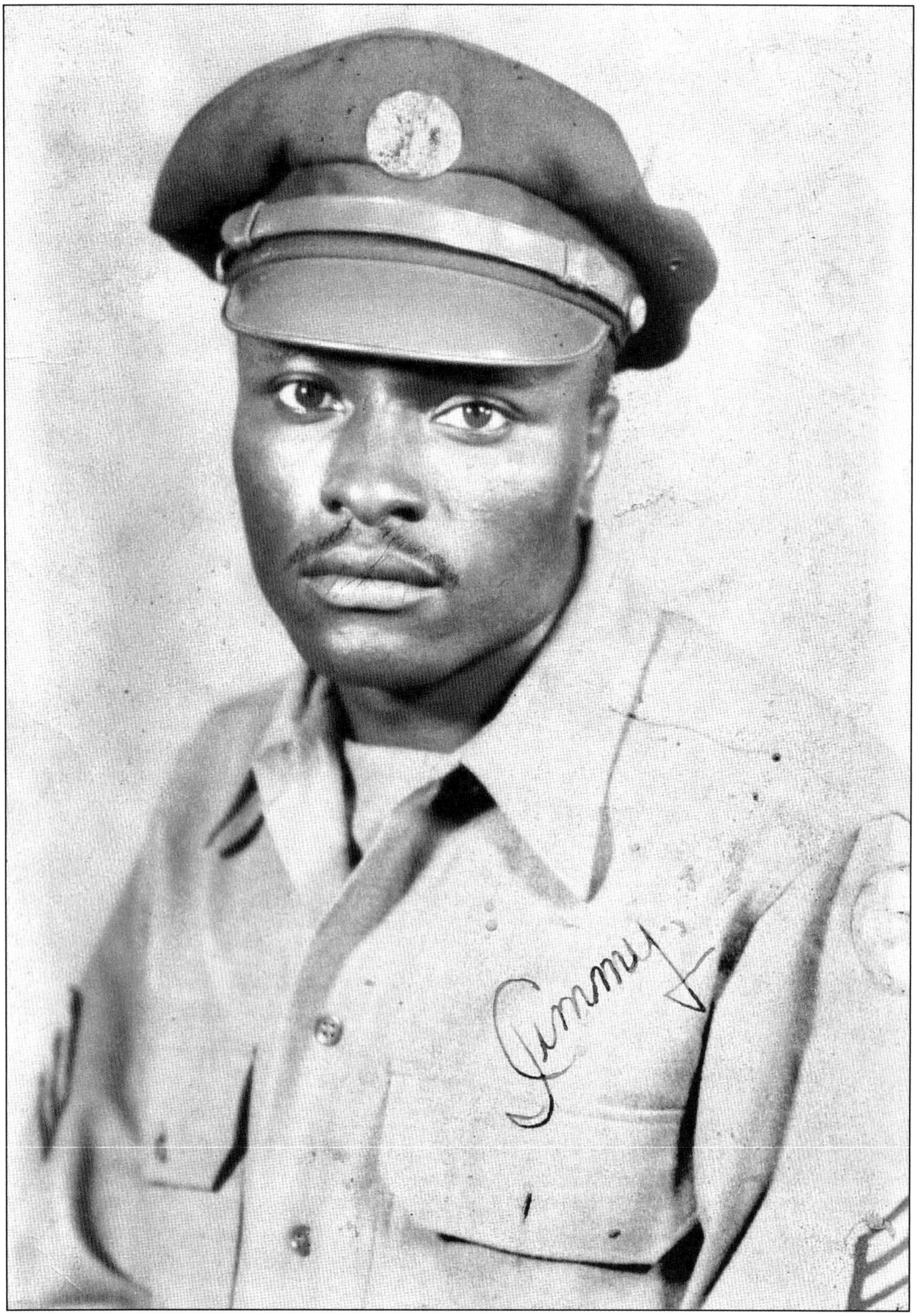

James Orr and his family lived in Millside before they moved to Dunleith. Their home was located on Carver Drive. James and Dorothy Orr had five children: Bernard, Bill, Bruce, Brenda, and Dianne. Mr. Orr was an entrepreneur. He owned a package goods store in the city of Wilmington. Their deed was signed on January 29, 1951. This picture was taken in the late 1940s.

Four

MILLSIDE

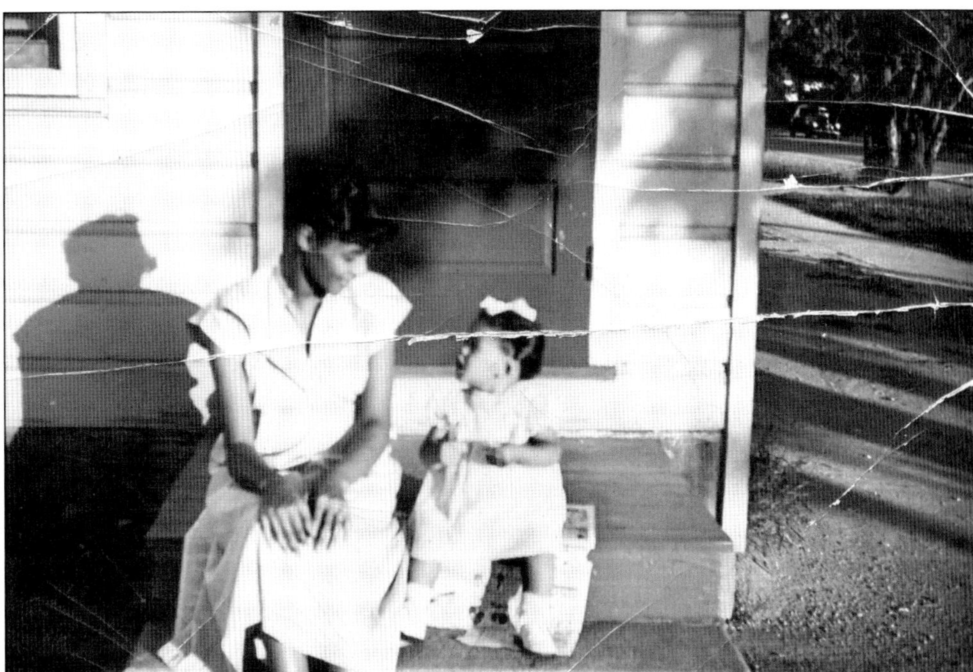

Marion Perkins sits on the front steps of her apartment with her daughter Darlene in the late 1940s. This tiny two-bedroom dwelling on Schoolhouse Lane was home for a year. The dwellings were low-income housing. Mrs. Perkins was extremely neat. She arranged newspapers on the steps to keep her clothes from becoming soiled.

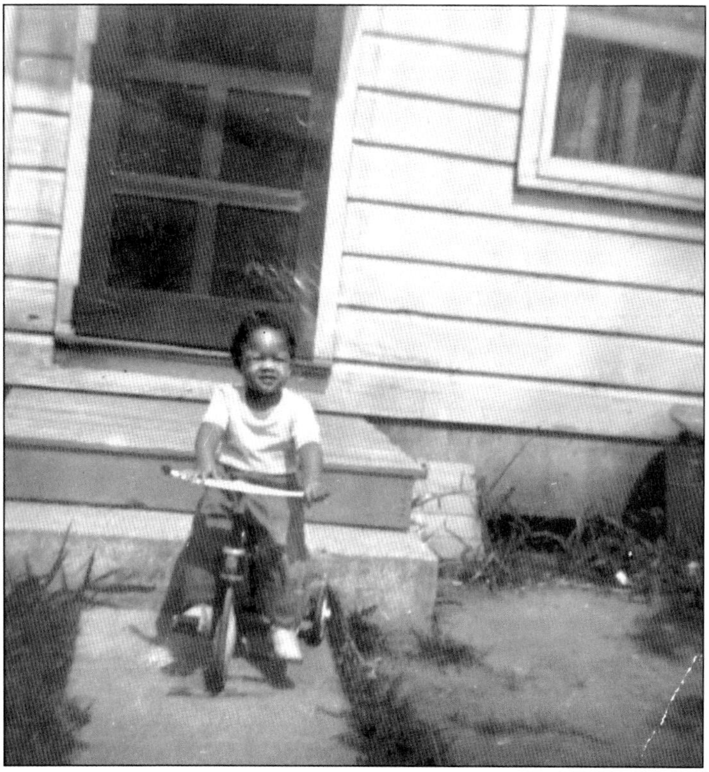

The small, dreary dwellings were home to many children like Darlene Perkins. She enjoys her tricycle in front of the Millside home. The screen door was heavily covered with wide wooden slats. The windows were small, but they had screens in them. Grass was allowed to grow along the sides of the walkway.

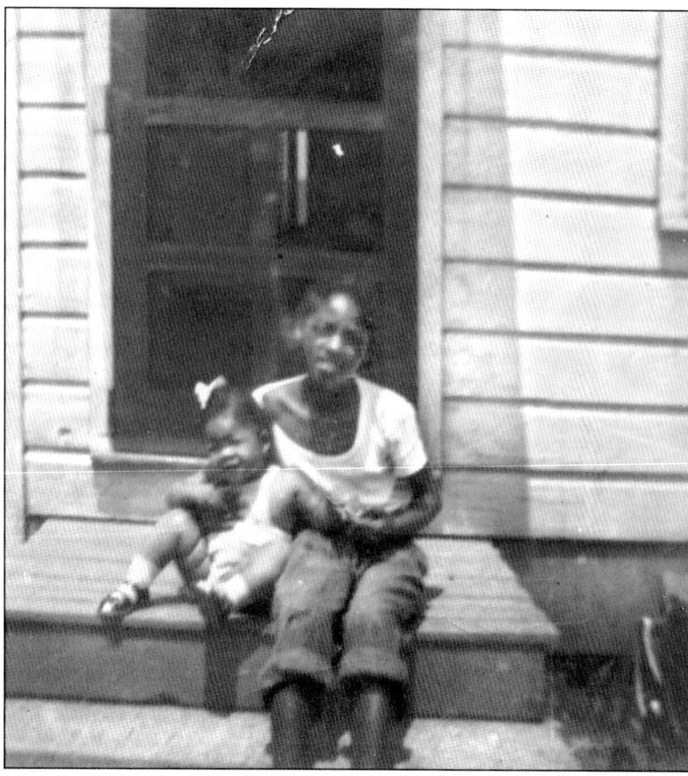

Pearl Dryden sits with her niece Darlene Perkins on the front steps of a home in Millside in the late 1940s. Peal is babysitting for her sister, Marion.

Bill Orr enjoys riding his bike on the Millside grounds in the 1950s. The houses were built in rows. The land was void of any trees and the grass was sparse.

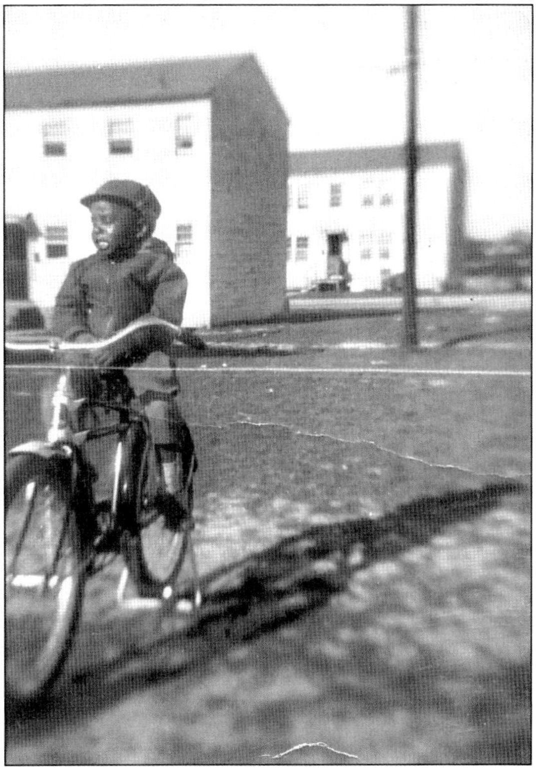

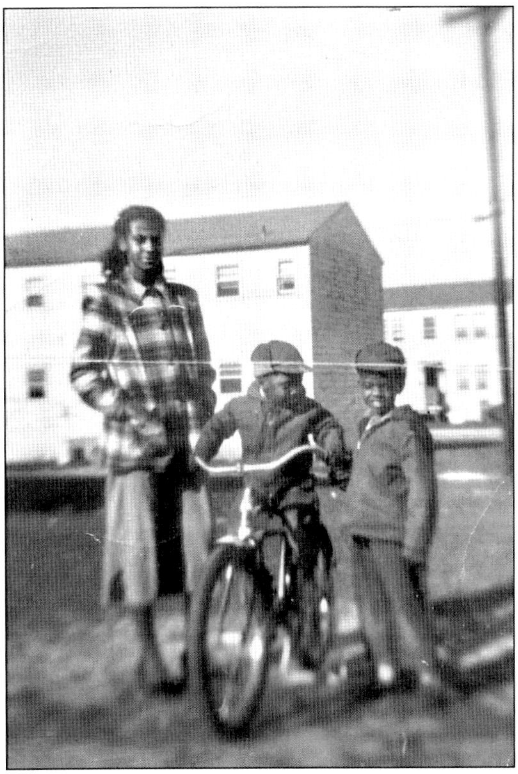

Dorothy Orr watches her sons as they take turns riding their bike in the 1950s. The yards were used as a neighborhood playground. Children played with their siblings in their front yards.

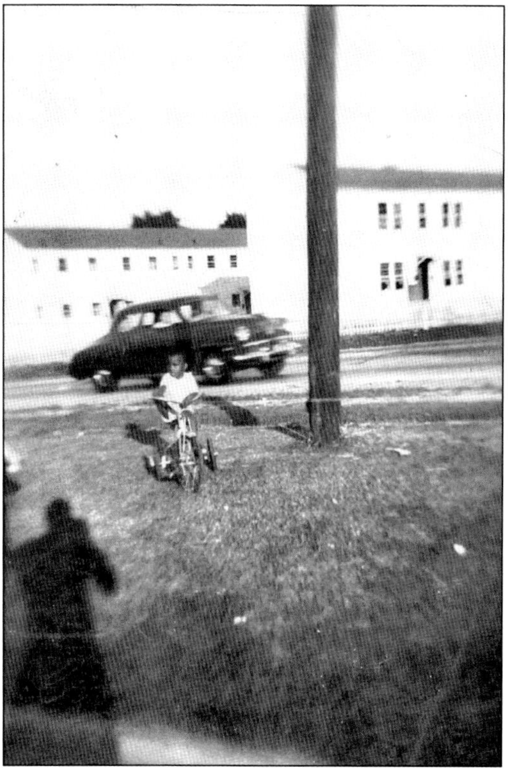

Bill Orr rides his tricycle around his neighborhood in Millside in early 1948.

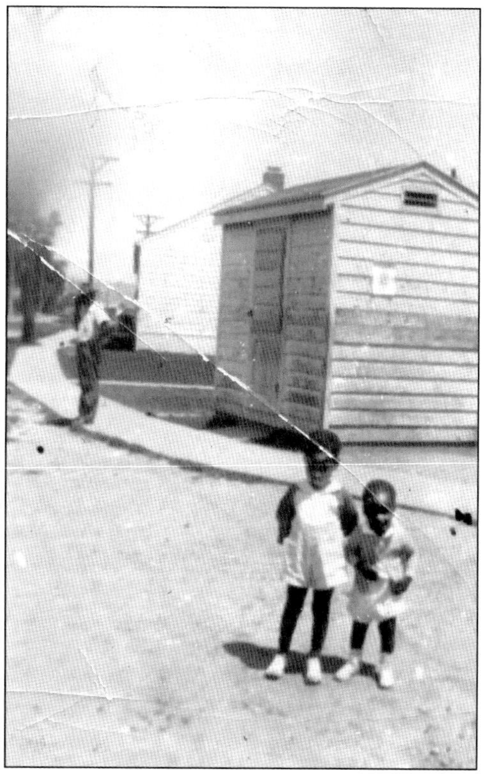

Pictured here are two unidentified children from the Millside housing complex in the 1940s.

Five

Church History

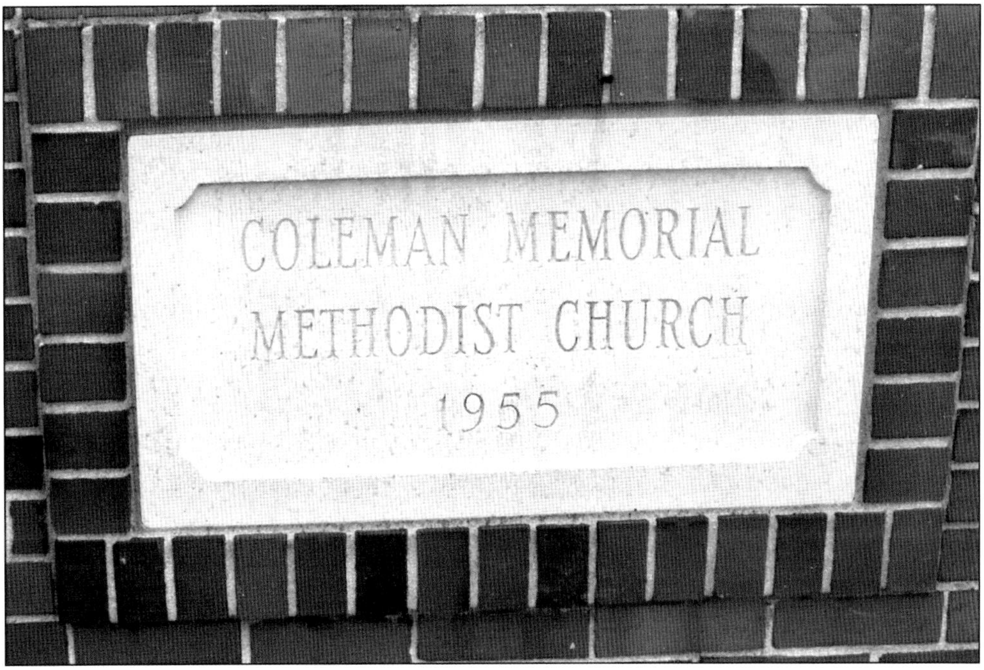

This is a picture of the cornerstone of Coleman Memorial Methodist Church. The Colonial brick church located at 465 1/2 Anderson Drive, Dunleith Estates, was built in 1955. Many congregation members took time from their busy schedules to help construct the church. The congregation celebrated its anniversary in June 1966 with a mortgage burning.

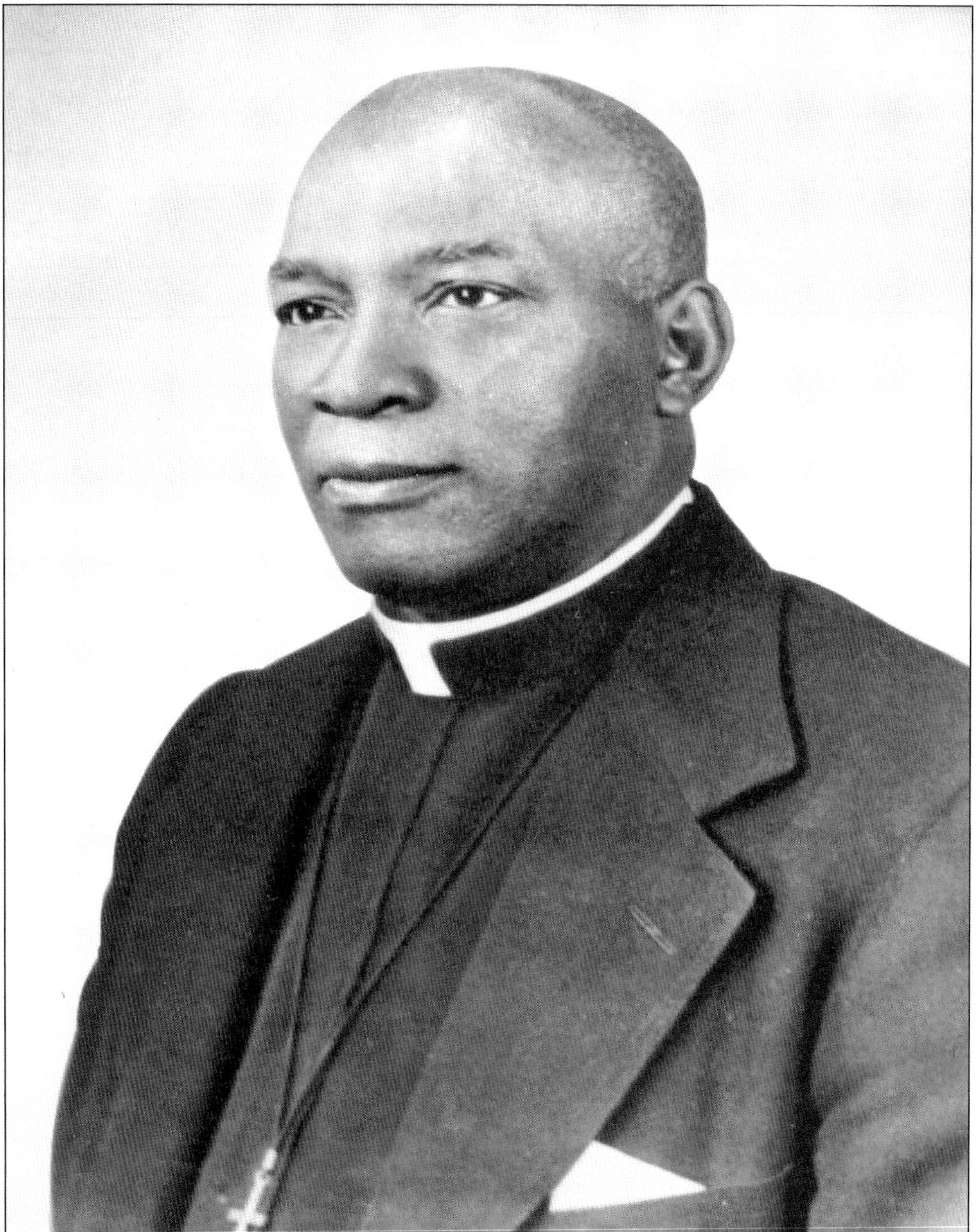

Pictured here is the Reverend Howard R. Coleman in 1951. The district superintendent of the Wilmington District investigated the building of a Methodist church in Dunleith. However, while working on his project to build a church, Reverend Coleman was killed in an automobile accident. The work was continued, and in May 1952 at the annual conference, a proposal was made to name the Coleman Memorial Church in memory of Rev. H. R. Coleman.

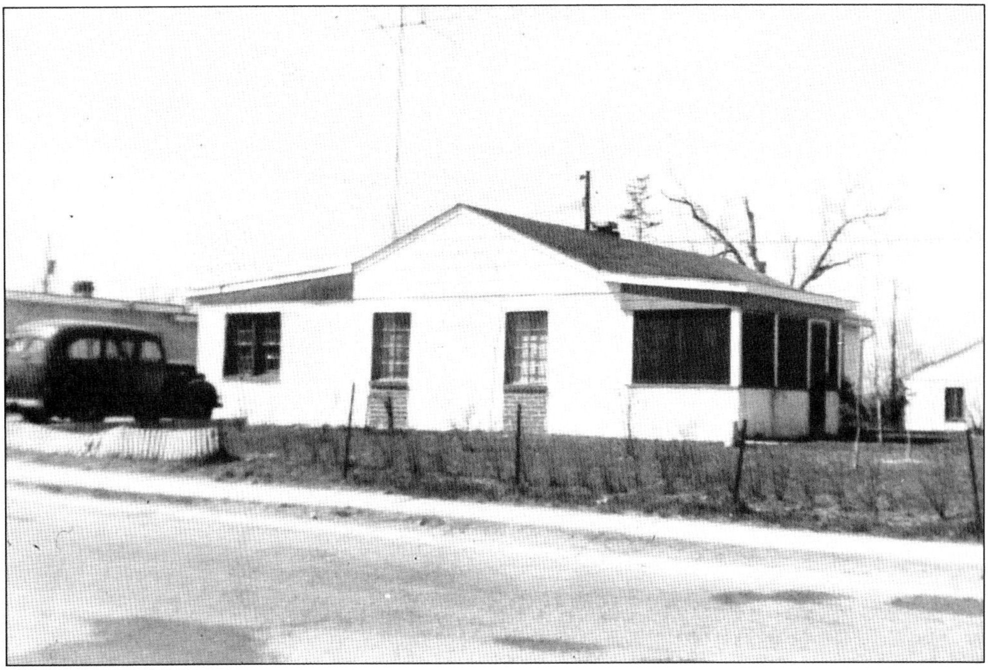

This is a picture of the first church home. Prior to the first church service, the work in Dunleith was conducted on a part-time basis and was known as the Ezion Mission. The first church service was held on May 25, 1952, at the home of Mr. and Mrs. William Jenkins at 402 Talladega Drive. There were eight adults and one child in attendance. Rev. Daniel L. Williams was the minister.

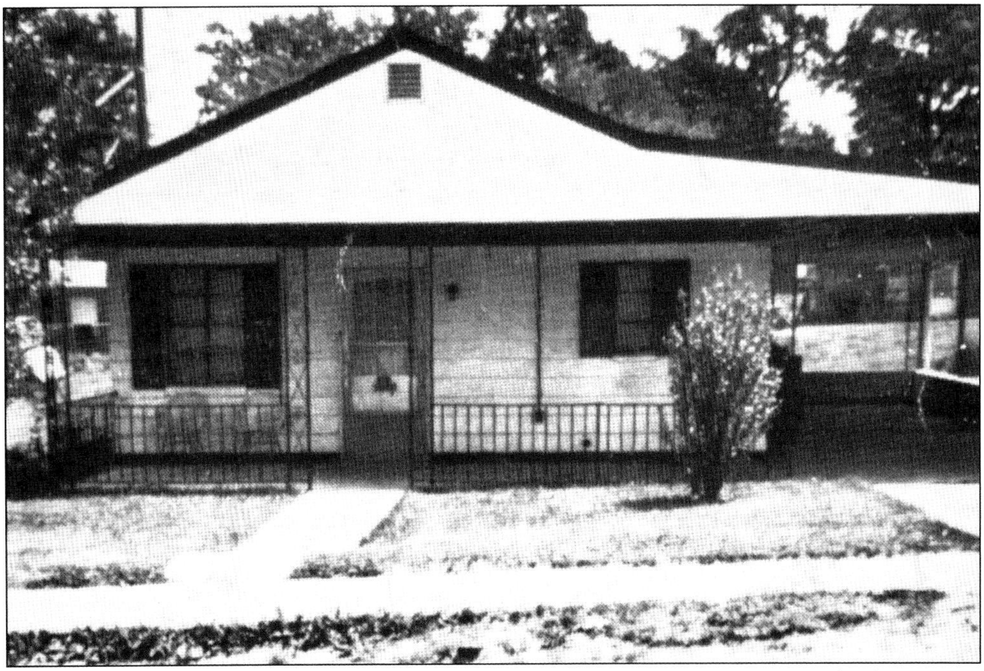

The first church parsonage was located in Dunleith at 425 Bethune Drive. This house was purchased by the Delaware Conference for parsonage use. The house was also used as a temporary worship center. The parsonage was used from 1952 until 1955.

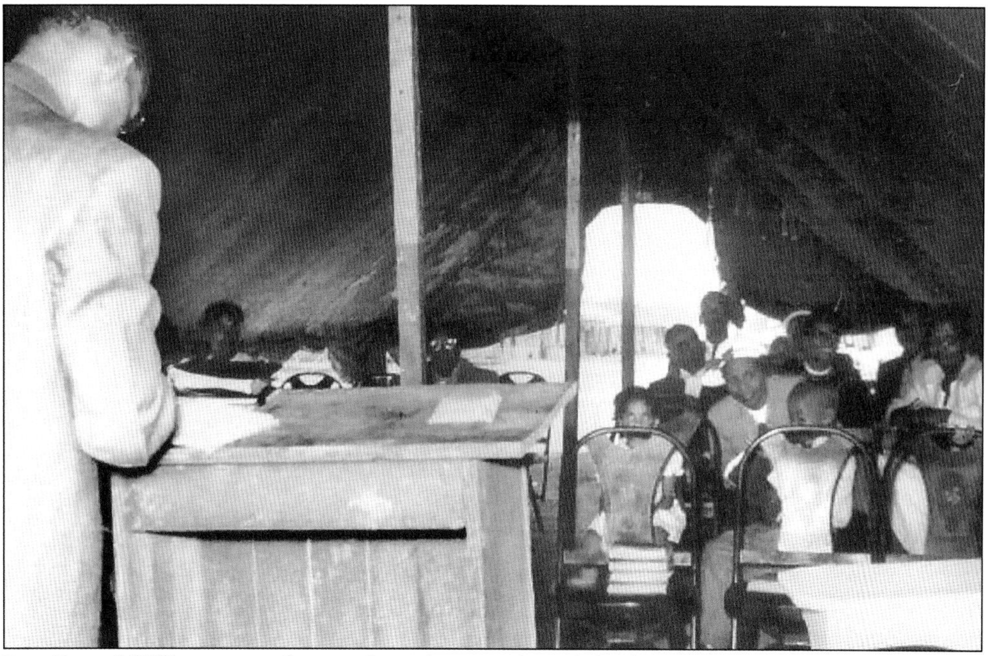

Rev. Daniel Williams, standing at the pulpit, conducted the first tent meeting on the corner of Bunche Boulevard and Anderson Drive. The tent meetings were conducted during the summer and fall of 1952.

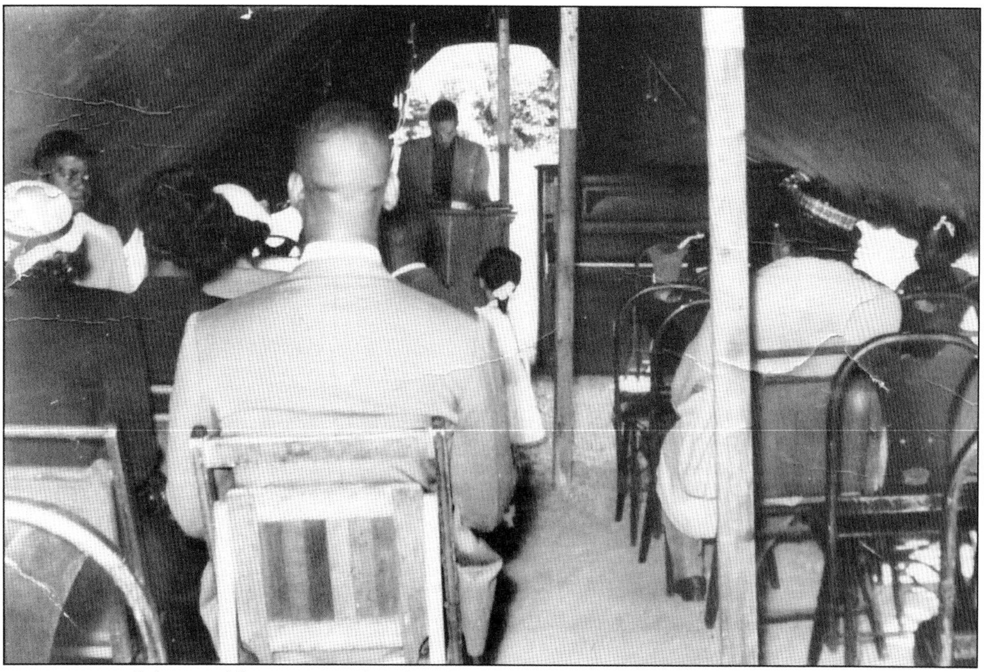

Mr. Lewis Tilghman (the man in the chair) was a member of the first finance committee that was formed at Coleman Memorial Methodist Church.

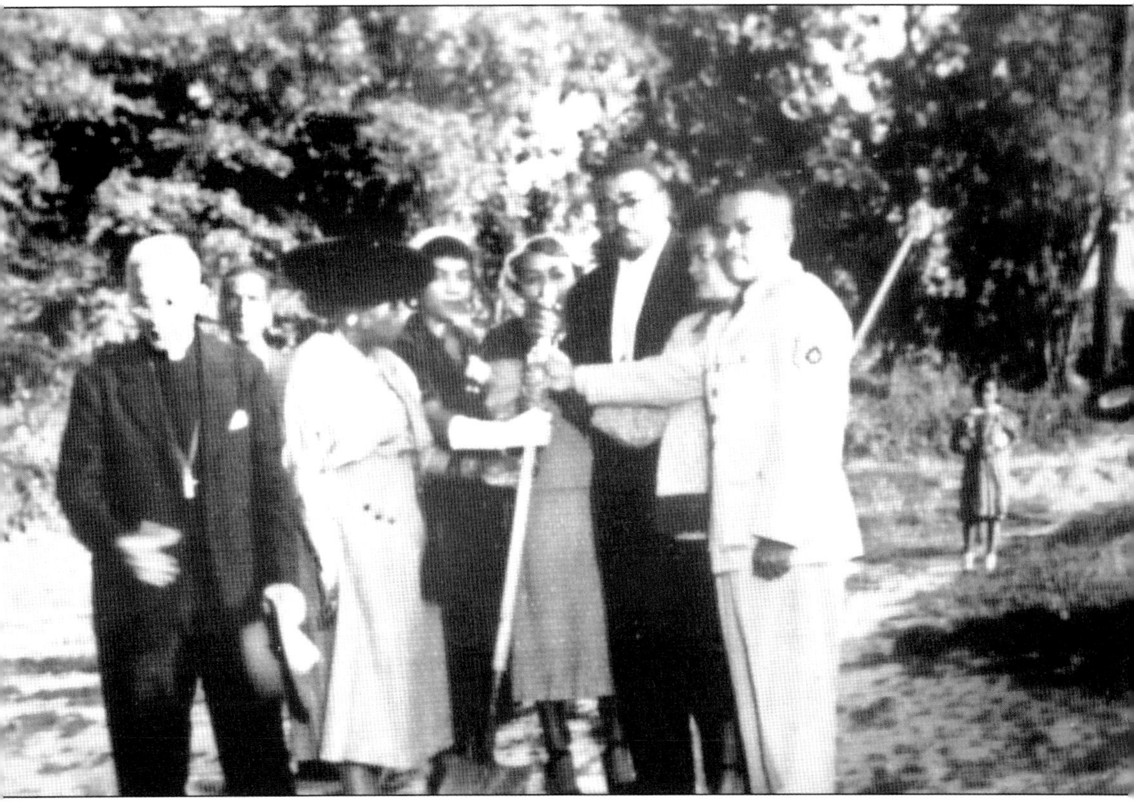

This is a picture of Coleman Memorial United Methodist Church's 1954 groundbreaking ceremony. From left to right are district superintendent Rev. Wears, Charles F. Johnson, Mrs. Ada Coleman Jenkins, L. Frances Collick, Anna B. Coleman, Rev. John W. Coleman, Mary Coleman Cuff, and Rev. William F. Coleman.

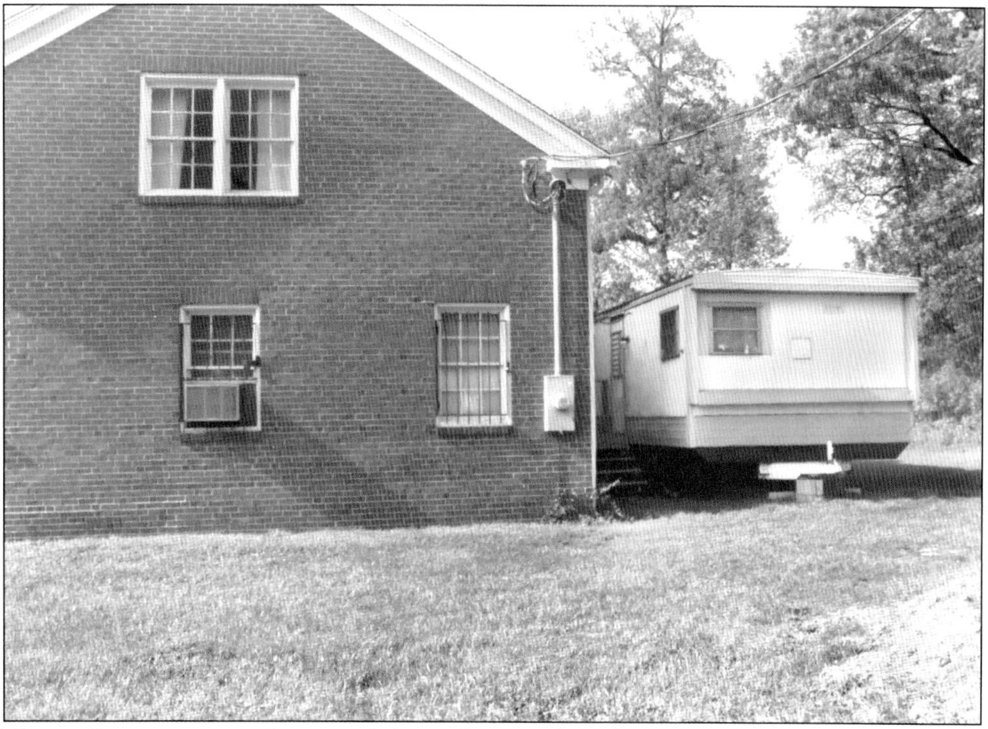

This trailer was positioned next to Coleman Memorial Methodist Church to provide additional space that was needed while construction was taking place on the church in the 1950s.

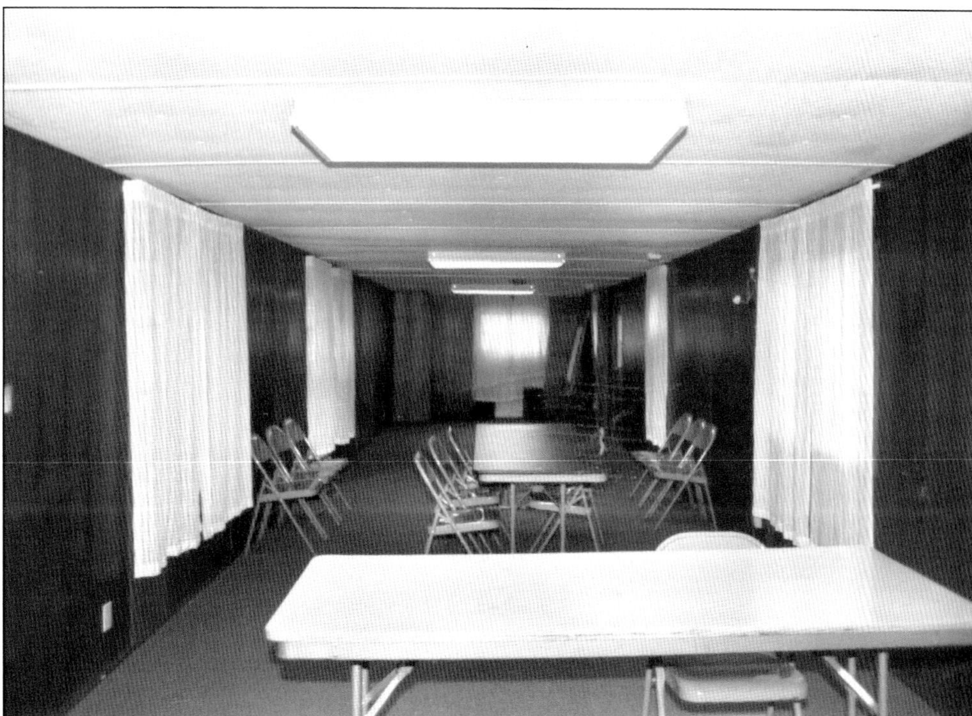

The inside of the trailer was used for bible study classes and church meetings in the 1950s.

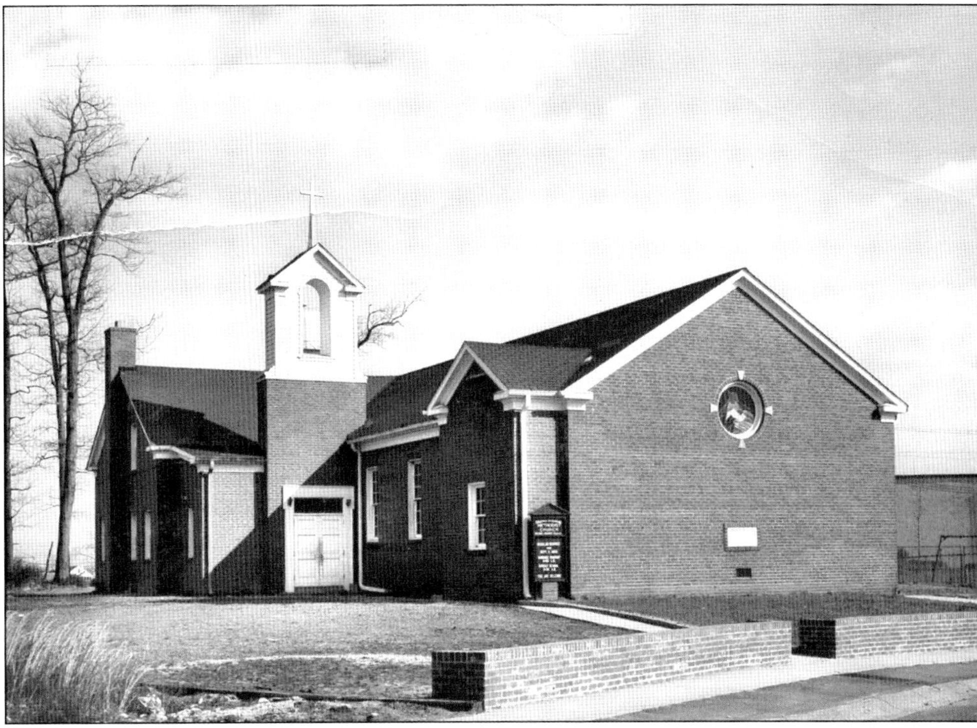

This is a 1955 picture of the newly constructed Coleman Memorial Methodist Church. The brick wall was built free of charge by Brother William Alston.

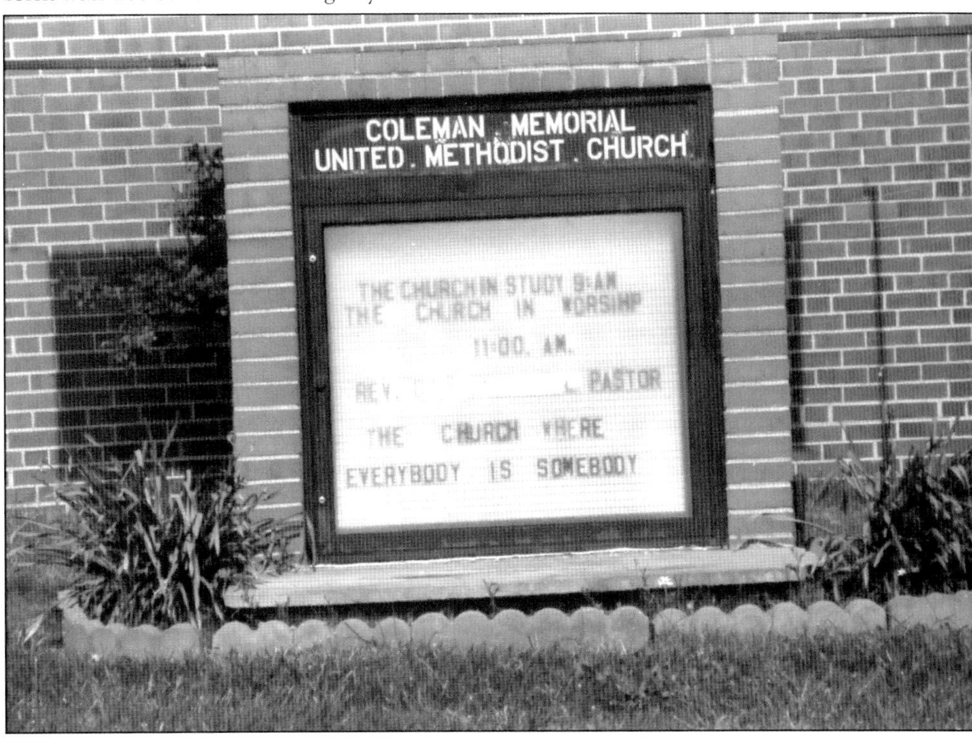

This enclosed glass church bulletin board replaced the original wooden one from 1955.

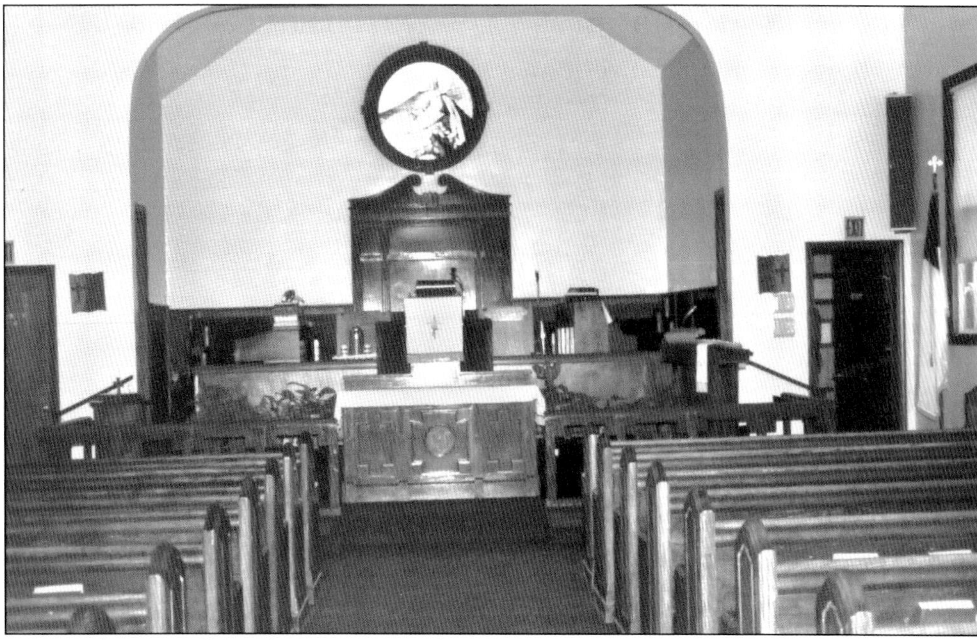

Here is the beautiful Coleman Memorial Methodist sanctuary as seen from the rear of the church. The picture of Jesus is in the round stained-glass window on the rear wall. On either side of the pulpit area, there is seating for the choir members. The center podium is for the pastor or the main speaker. The congregation's wood pews, refinished in 1969, are stained a medium brown.

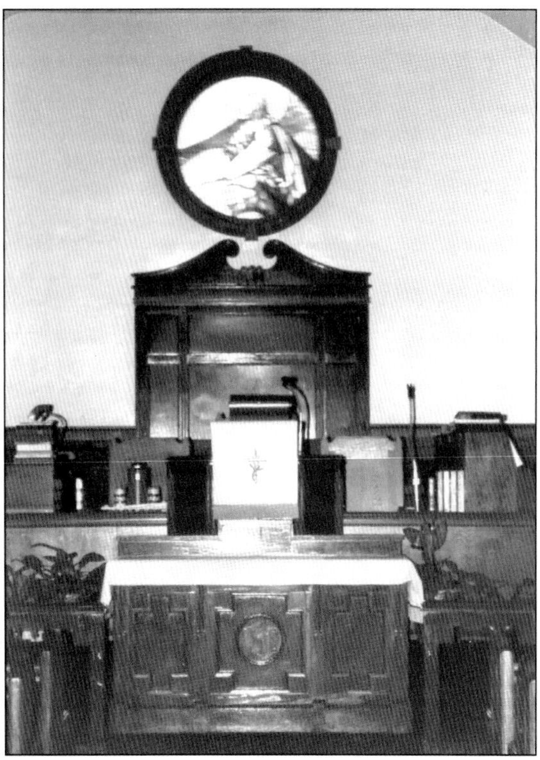

This is a picture of the wood altar furniture in the 1950s. The stained-glass picture of the Lord remains from the original construction. The intricately carved wooden altar is dressed in white.

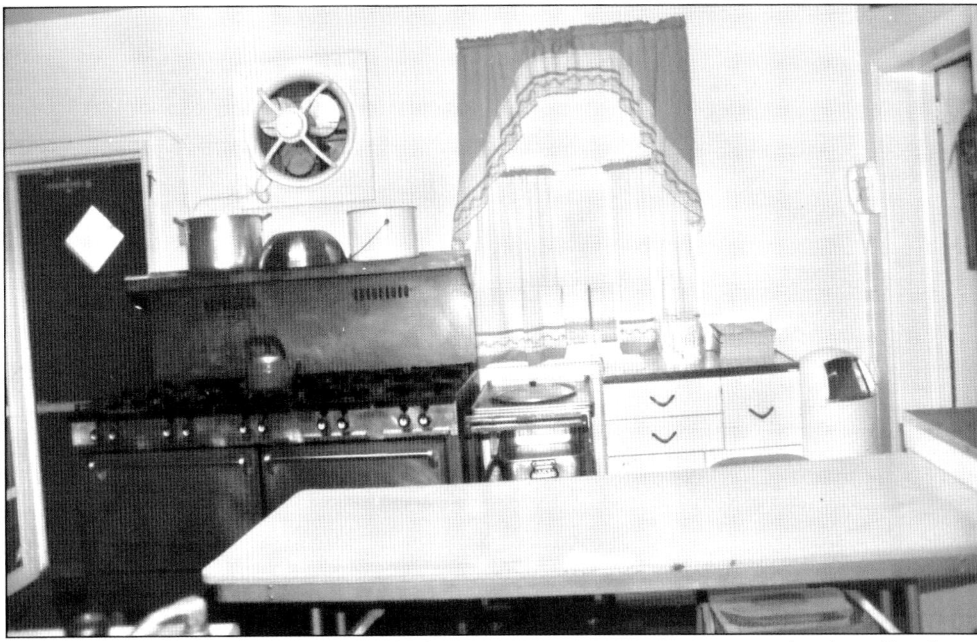

Here is the original church kitchen before major improvements were made. A wall exhaust fan was used to pull out cooking odors. A huge metal stove with multiple burners was used to cook for hundreds of people. The old stove had a back splash to keep the walls clear. On the top of the stove was a storage unit for cooking equipment and utensils. A warming table can be seen next to the storage drawers. There was also a huge food preparation table. The church purchased the 10-burner, two-oven gas stove in the 1970s.

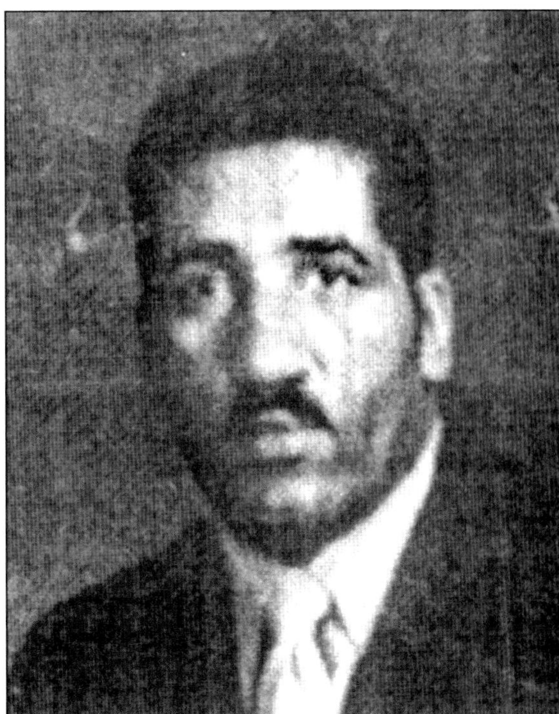

Mr. William Benson, pictured in the late 1950s, has worn many hats in the church. Besides being on the church choir, he has provided catering for the church. He has owned and operated his own catering business. Benson has organized and planned numerous church events. As a wedding consultant, he has coordinated and prepared menus for weddings of church members and clients. Mr. Benson was also chairman of publicity.

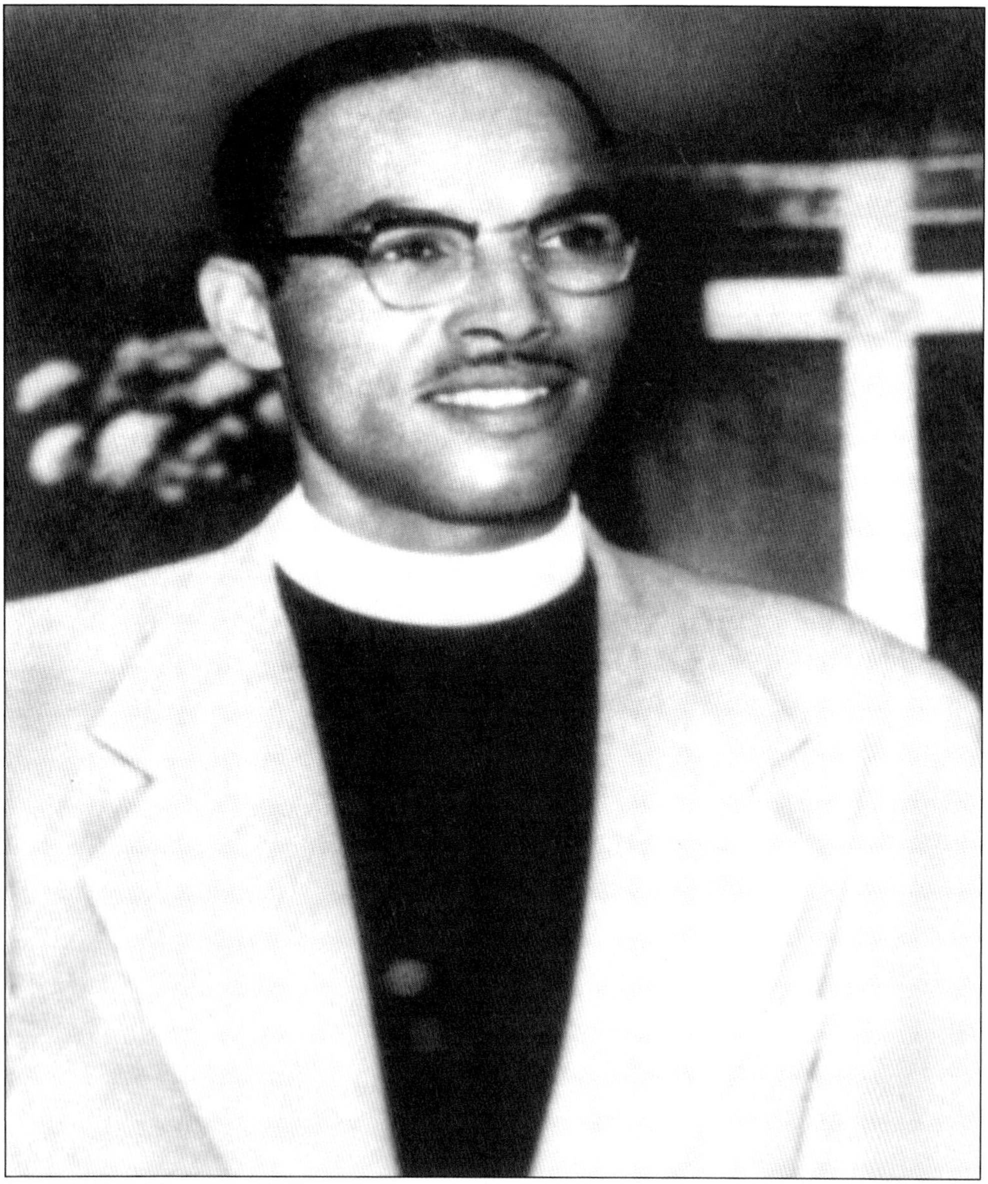

In 1952, Rev. Daniel L. Williams Jr. became the first pastor of Coleman Memorial Methodist Church. Reverend Williams was called to administer the work for the Methodist church. Before becoming the pastor, he was a student at the Drew University Seminary. Through the newly appointed district superintendent, Rev. W. H. Mears, Reverend Williams was appointed assistant pastor of Ezion Methodist Church.

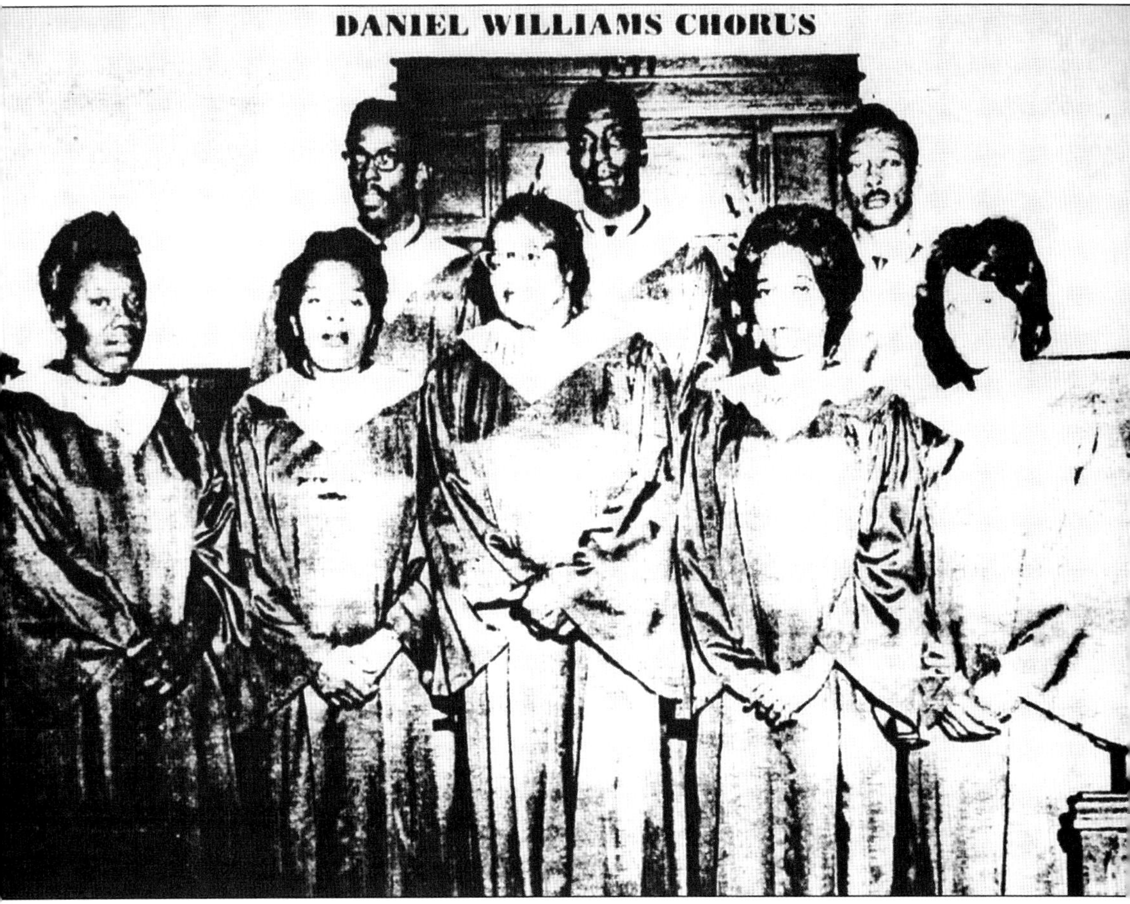

The Daniel L. Williams Chorus was the first choir group formed at Coleman Memorial Methodist Church. Shown here from left to right are (first row) Dorothy Broadway, Emma Simmons, Catherine Snead, Doris Lambert, and Georginia Lucas; (second row) Fletcher Morgan, Ernest Lambert, and William Lucas. Absent when the picture was taken in the 1960s was William Benson.

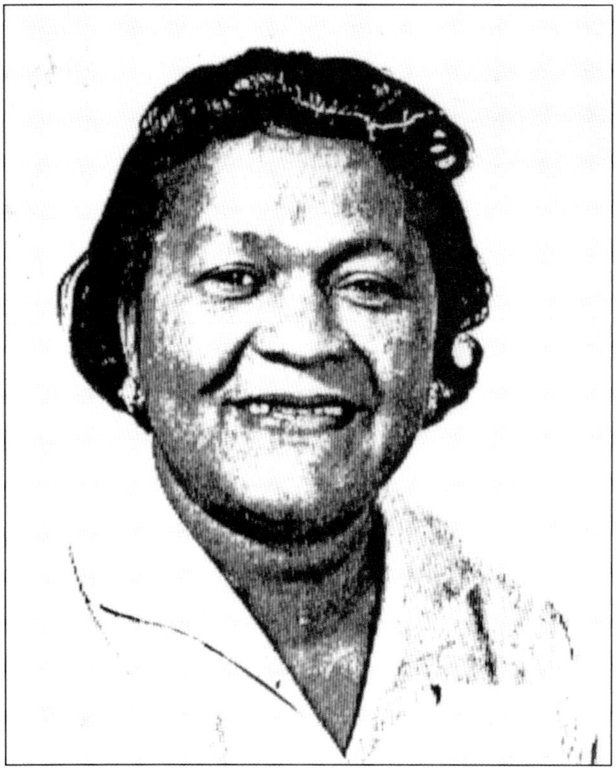

Mrs. Violet A. Jenkins was a founding mother of Coleman Memorial Methodist Church. She was the historical committee chairman, and she served on numerous other committees as well. She was communion steward, a member of the flower committee, annual fall rally captain, and planner for special events. These committees were started in the early 1950s. This picture was taken in the 1970s.

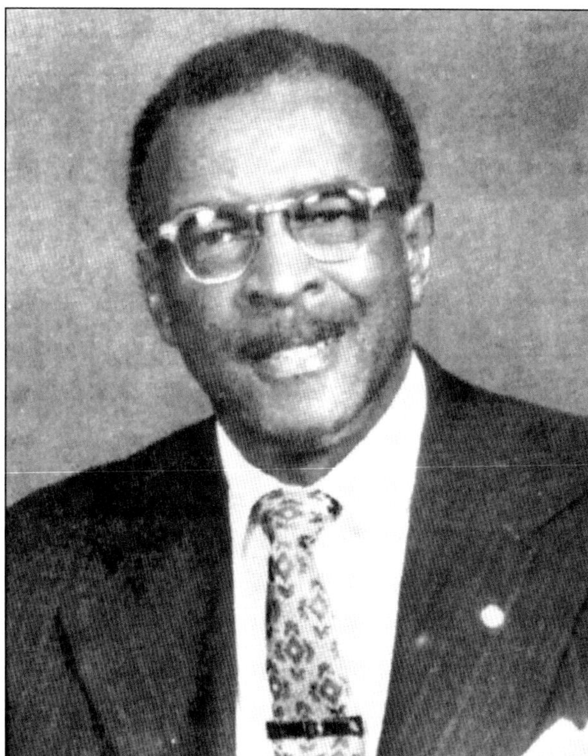

Mr. William E. Jenkins, pictured in the 1970s, was a founding father of Coleman Memorial Methodist Church. Jenkins was a unit leader and served on a variety of committees such as the historical and finance committees. He also assisted with interior church construction and with the upkeep of the church building.

Arlington O. and Ruth Miller have been members of Coleman Memorial Methodist Church since the 1950s. Mr. Miller became a church lay speaker in the 1960s. This picture of the couple was taken in the 1970s.

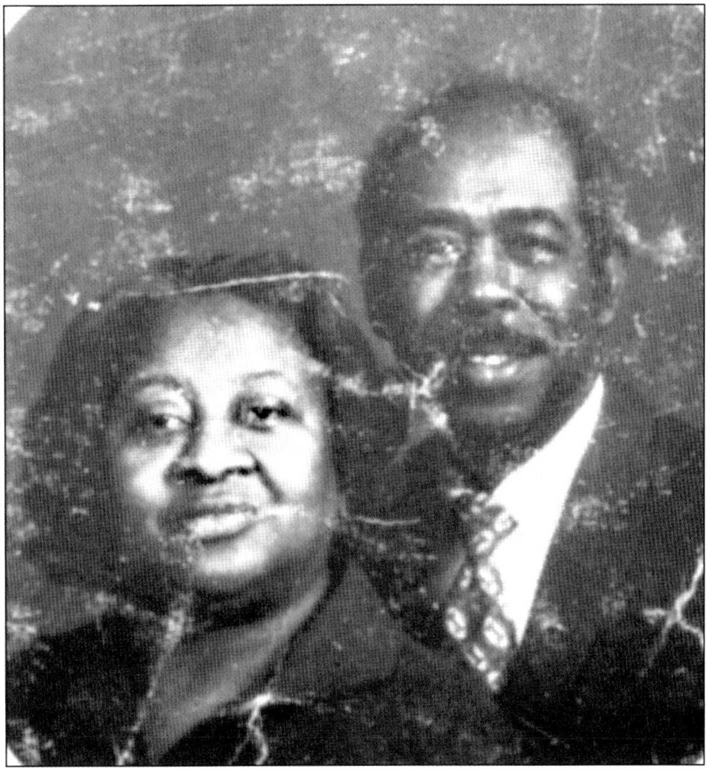

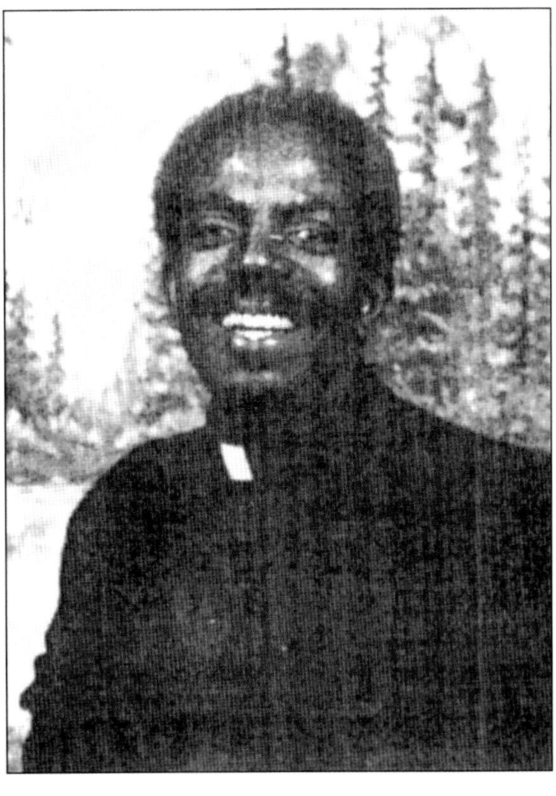

Rev. James Linton Furrowh received Christ at an early age. He joined the Coleman Memorial Methodist Church, where he was a Sunday school teacher and a lay speaker during the 1950s. This picture was taken in the 1960s.

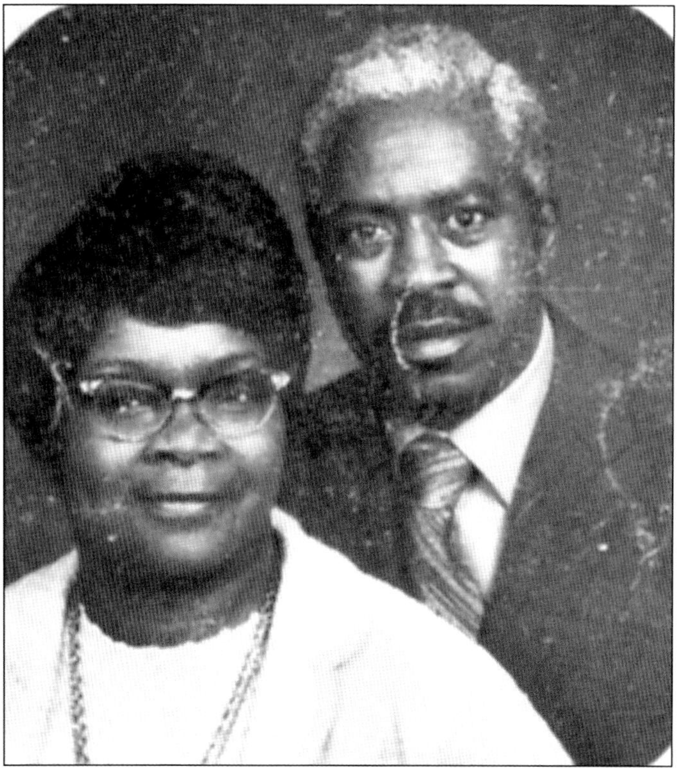

George and Sula Wilmore were among the first elected officers of Coleman Memorial Methodist Church for 1952–1953. George Wilmore was a trustee and president of Methodist men. Sula Wilmore served on the historical committee, was the recording steward, and served on the church board of education. They became Dunleith homeowners in 1950. This picture was taken in the 1970s.

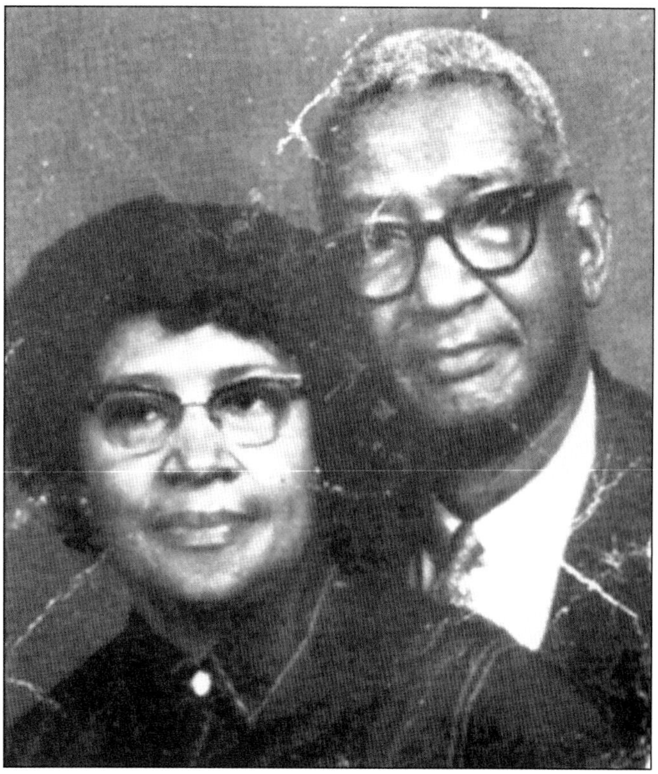

Lewis and Marian Tilghman were both actively involved as members of Coleman Memorial Methodist Church. Mr. Tilghman helped to construct the prayer room and other areas of the church. He did many odd jobs and assisted with the church maintenance. Mrs. Tilghman was a member of the finance committee and a speaker in the 1950s. This picture was taken in the 1970s.

Hazel Tyler-Quarles was a Sunday school teacher and a Methodist Youth Fellowship leader. She was responsible for planning a variety of activities for the students that she taught. Mrs. Tyler-Quarles also took an active role in mentoring and nurturing the students. She is pictured in the 1960s.

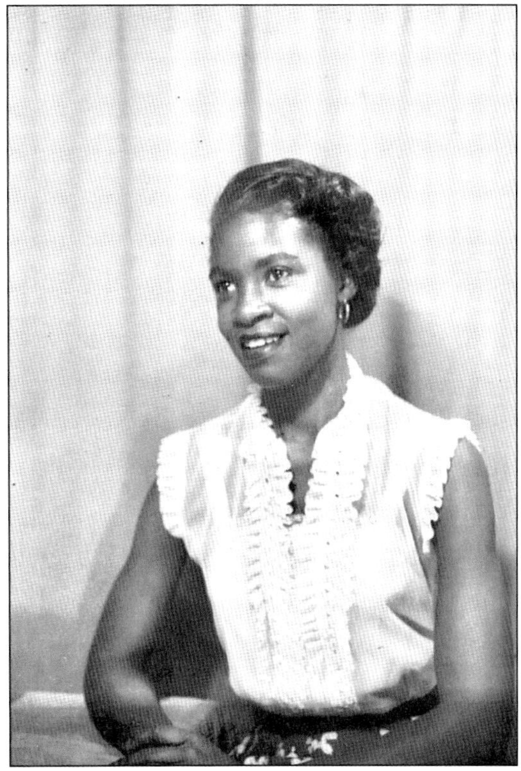

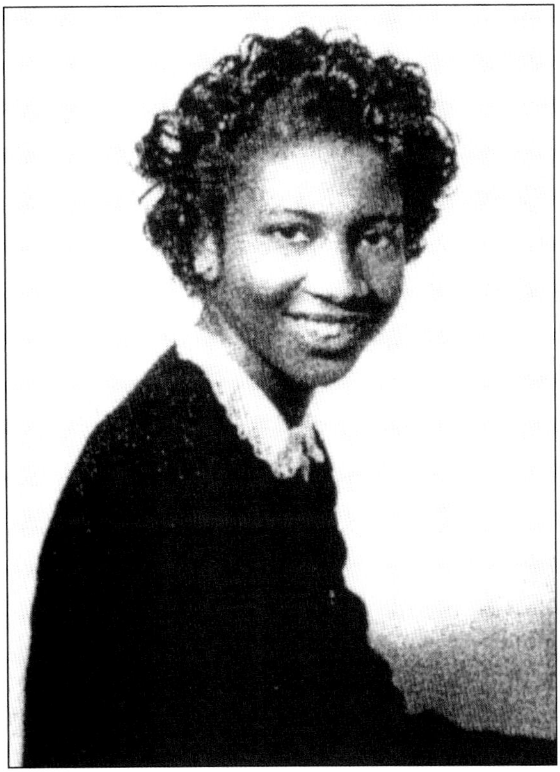

Naomi Gaines-Winchester, seen here in a 1960s photograph, was a Sunday school teacher and Methodist Youth Fellowship leader. She was a mentor to many of the youths in the church. Mrs. Gaines-Winchester later became a lay speaker. She developed many ministry programs at Coleman Memorial Methodist Church. She also saw to it that the Methodist youth studied the structure of the local church.

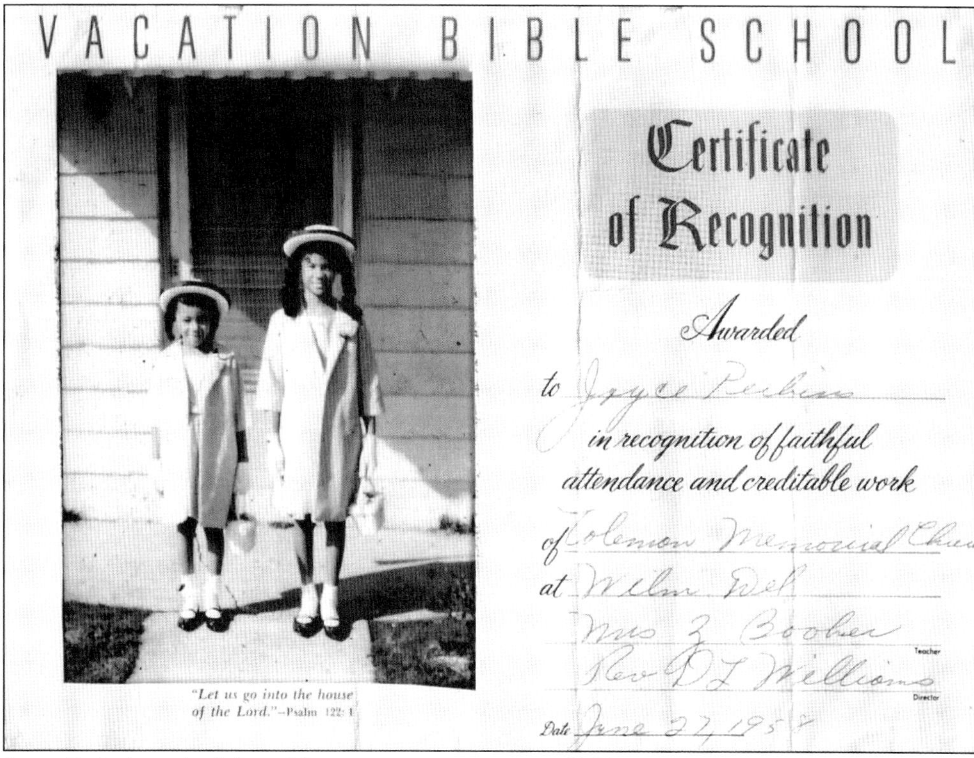

Joyce E. Perkins (right) and her younger sister, Lynn (left), were participants in the Vacation Bible School at Coleman Memorial Methodist Church in 1958. A ceremony was conducted at the end of the biblical study. Participants also received a certificate to recognize their accomplishments and their attendance. Many of the children who were regular Sunday school students attended the summer Bible session.

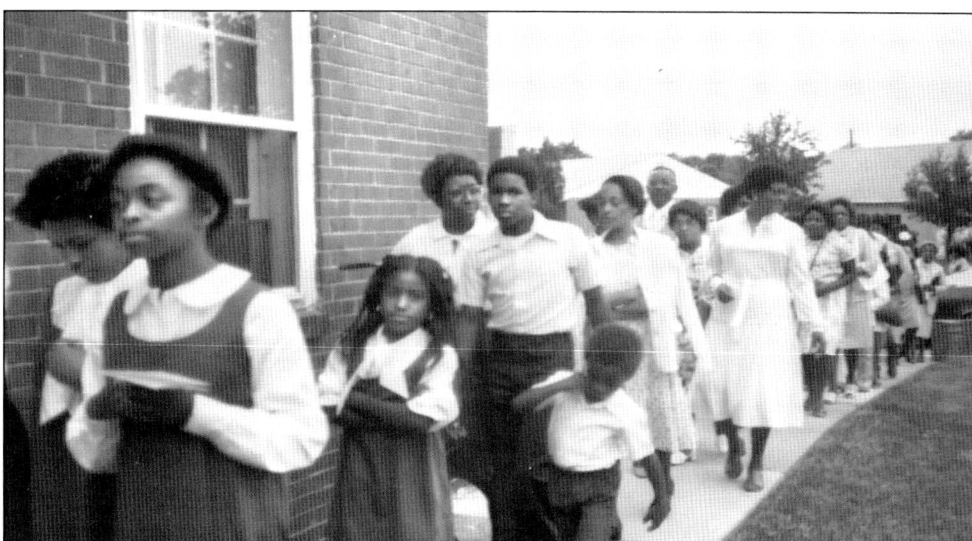

Here, the children's choir prepares to enter the church to sing in the late 1970s. The children were taught at an early age to participate in church functions. These children are preparing to sing during a part of the Sunday service.

Betty Horsey attended the Coleman Memorial Methodist Church Sunday school. She was also in classes that were taught by Hazel Quarles. She is seen in the 1950s. (Hazel Quarles collection.)

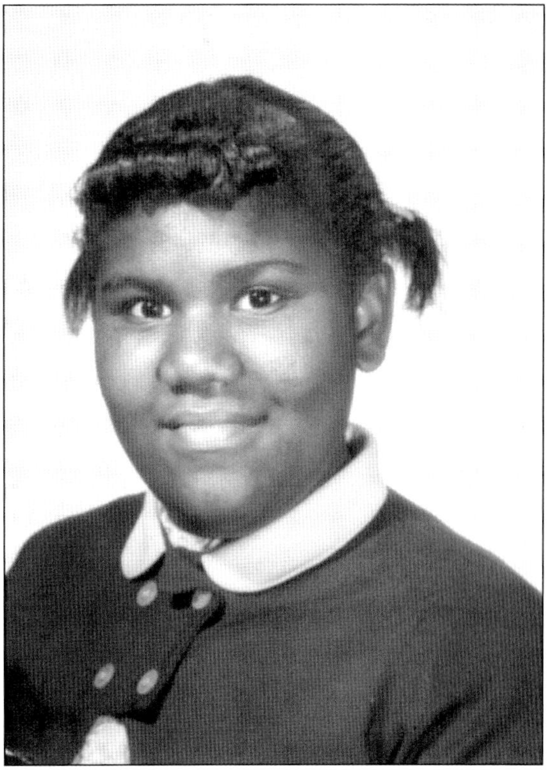

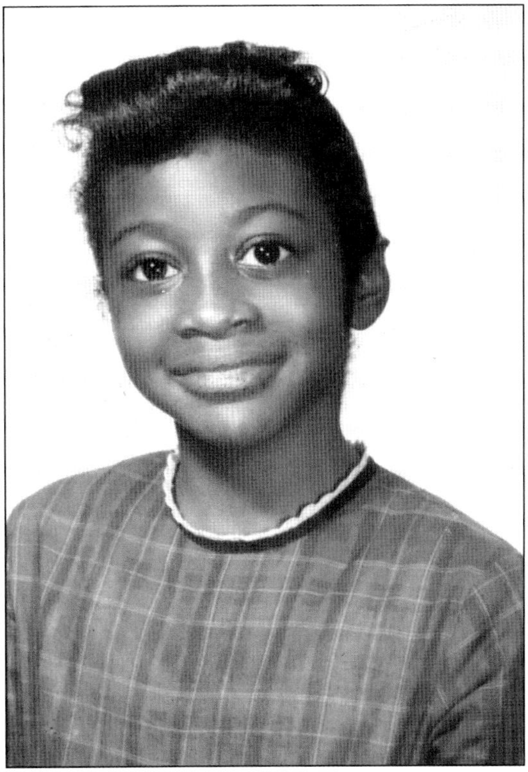

Norma Gaines was a Bible school student at Coleman Memorial Methodist Church. She was taught and mentored by Hazel Quarles. Norma received a scholarship to attend the University of Delaware in 1970. This picture shows her in the 1960s. (Hazel Quarles collection.)

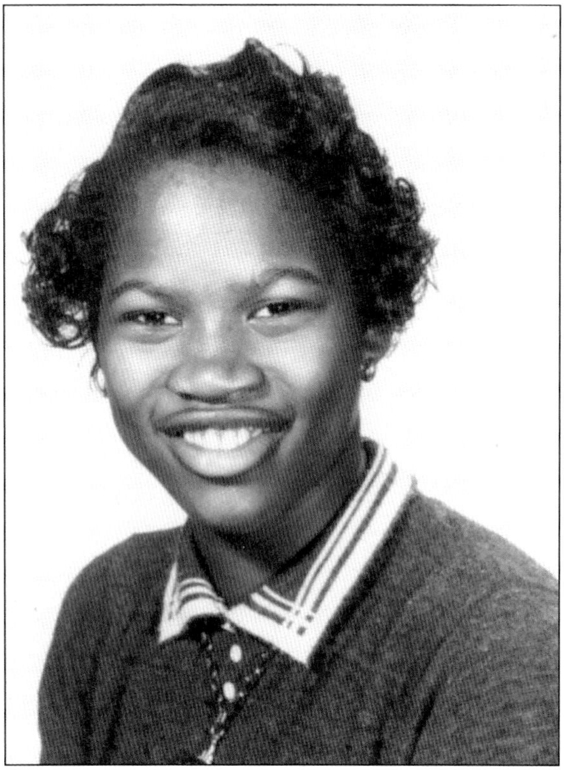

Barbara Britt was an enthusiastic student. Britt had great loyalty and interest in the church. She became a teacher of the Bible at Coleman Memorial Methodist Church in the 1950s and 1960s. She is pictured in the 1950s. (Hazel Quarles collection.)

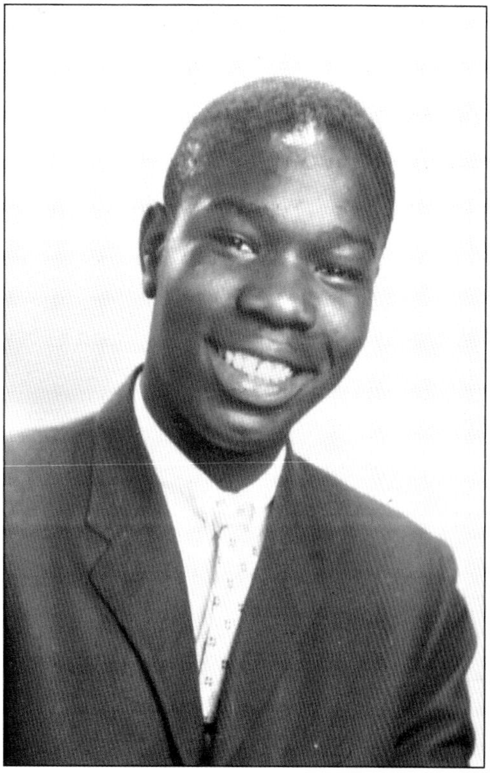

Alan Tatman attended Bible classes at Coleman Memorial Methodist Church. He was a student in the Methodist Youth Fellowship group in the 1960s, when this photograph was taken. (Hazel Quarles collection.)

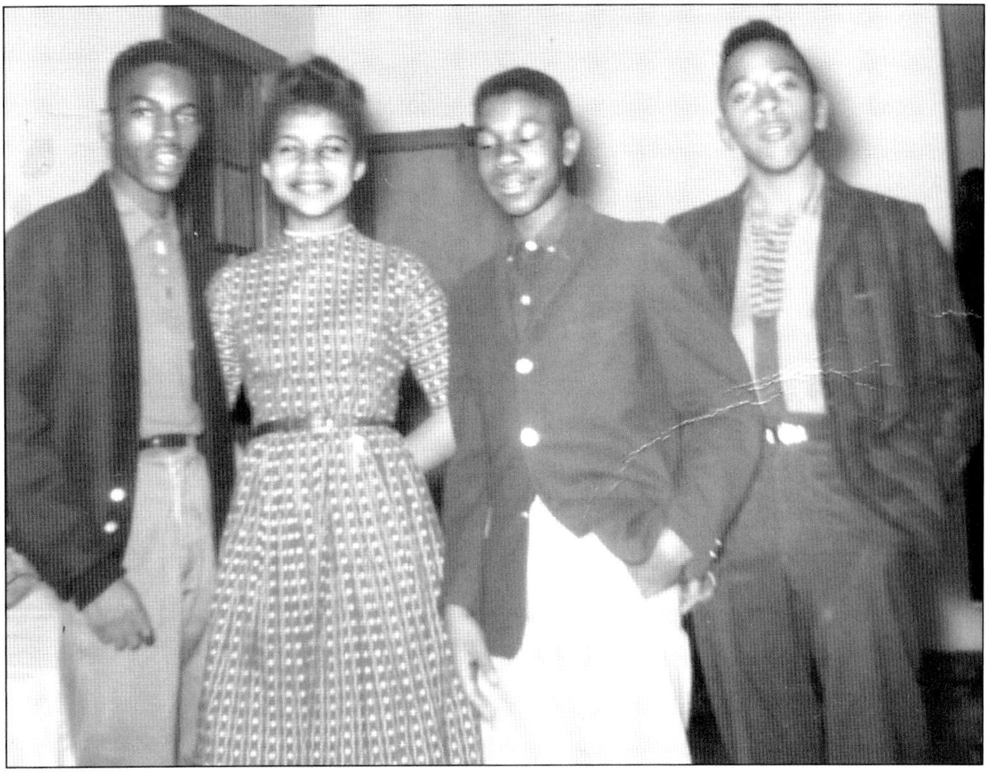

The youths who attended Sunday school at Coleman Memorial Methodist Church participated in a variety of church functions. From left to right in this 1960s photograph are Bernard Orr, Rita Barnhart, Woody Ivy, and Daniel Ridgeway. (Hazel Quarles collection.)

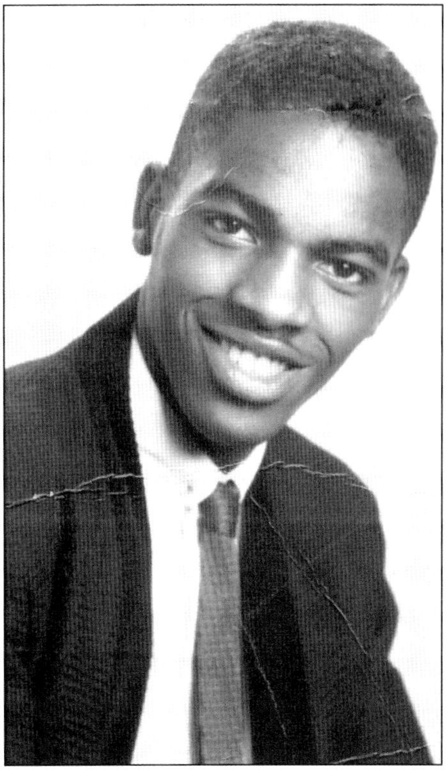

Bernard Orr was a member of the Methodist Youth Fellowship group. He was an active Bible school student in the 1960s, when he was photographed for this portrait. (Hazel Quarles collection.)

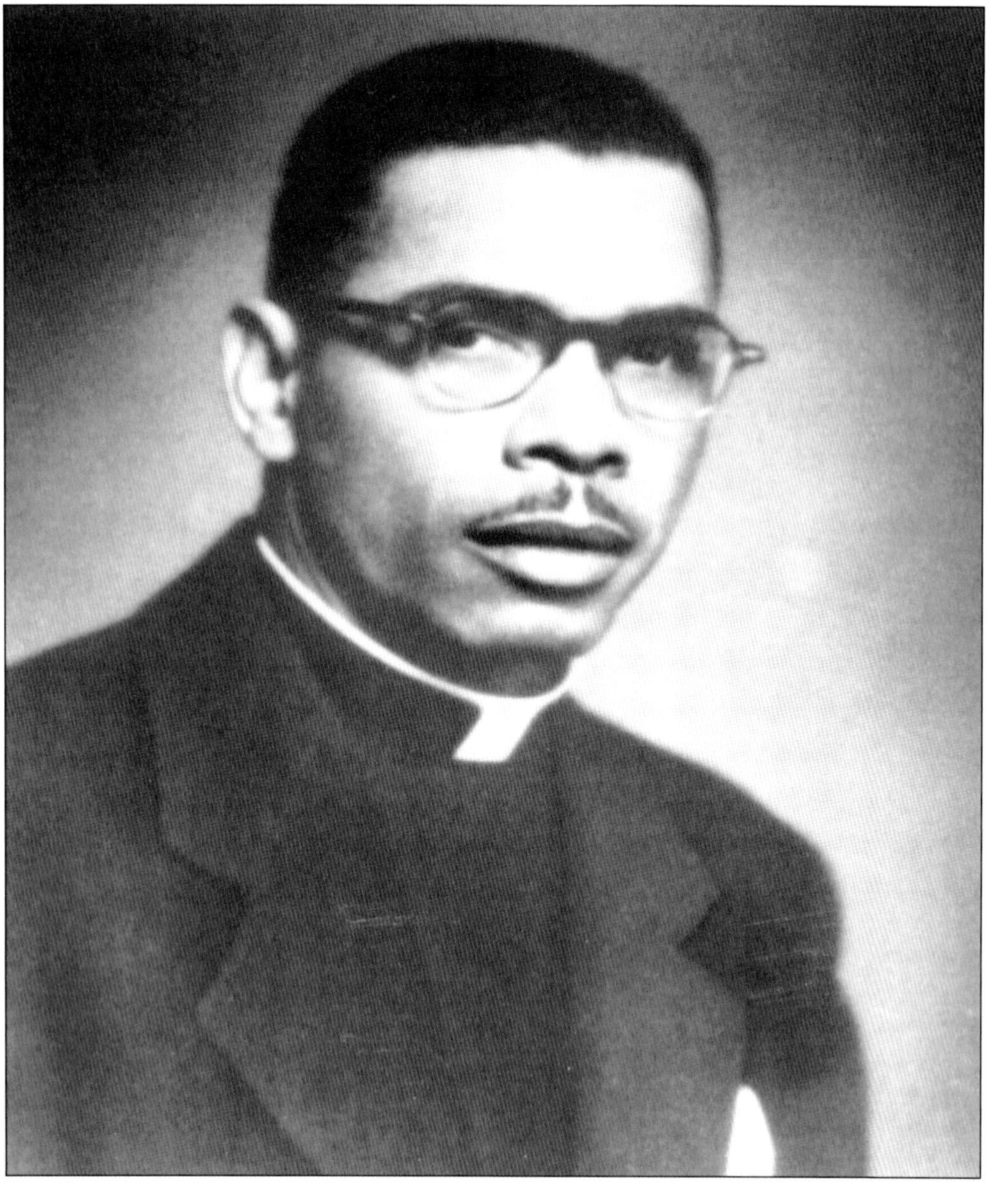

Rev. Harry R. Snead, seen here in the 1950s, joined the Delaware Conference in 1948. Reverend Snead was appointed pastor of Coleman Memorial Methodist Church in 1961. He comes from a family of ministers. Reverend Snead was known in the Delaware Conference as one of the most successful pastors. He served the church with a record of great achievements. He may be remembered as a counselor who was dedicated to his calling. He was pastor at Coleman Memorial Methodist Church from 1961 to 1969.

Catherine Snead was a dedicated wife alongside her husband, the Reverend Harry R. Snead, during his tenure at Coleman Memorial Methodist Church. Mrs. Snead was chairperson of the Annual Woman's Day in 1963. This photograph was taken in the 1960s.

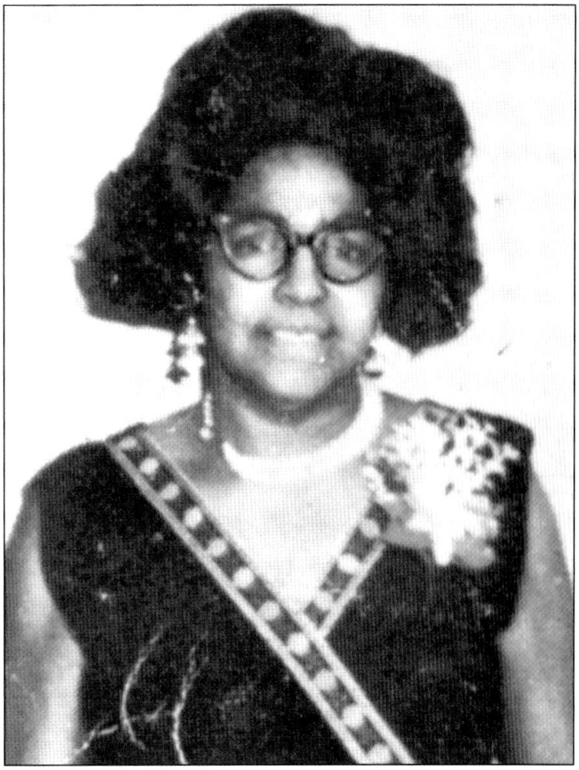

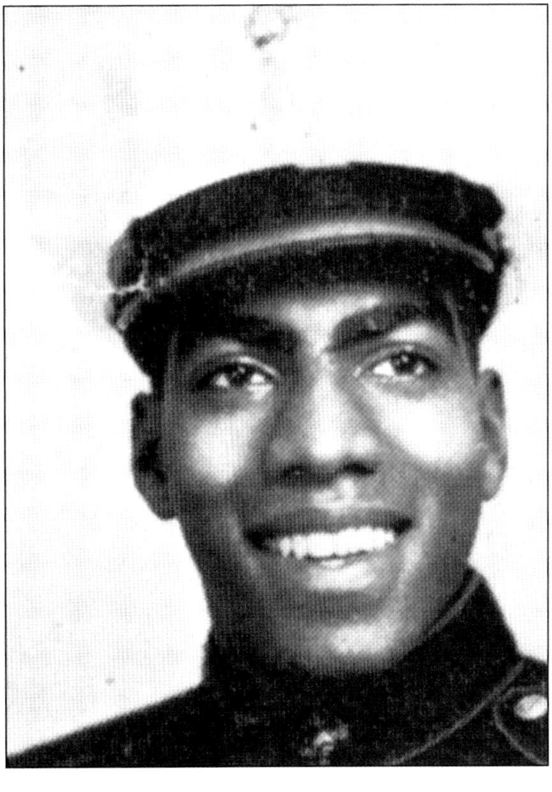

This is a picture of Ronald Snead, taken while he was in the Marines in the 1960s. His parents were Rev. Harry and Mrs. Catherine Snead.

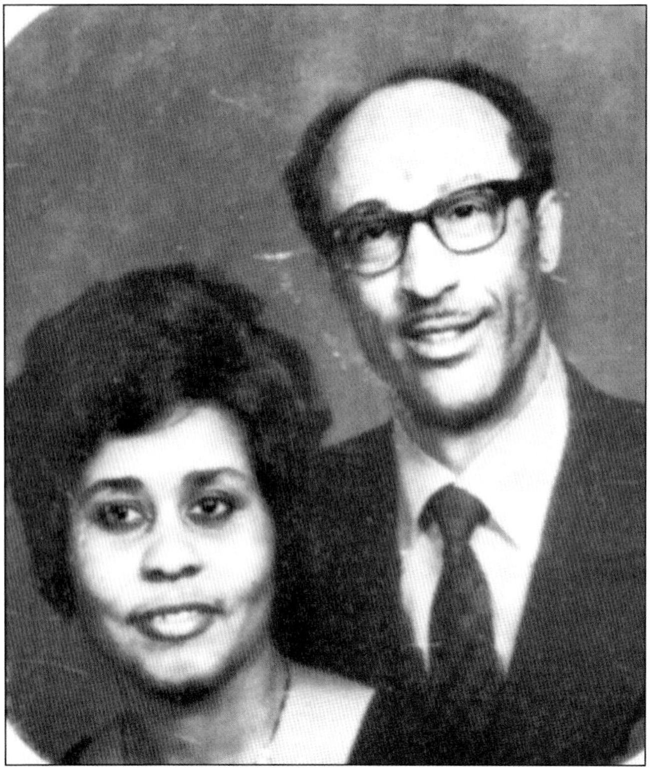

Henry and Mary Lou Spencer were active members of Coleman Memorial Methodist Church starting in the 1950s, when this picture was taken.

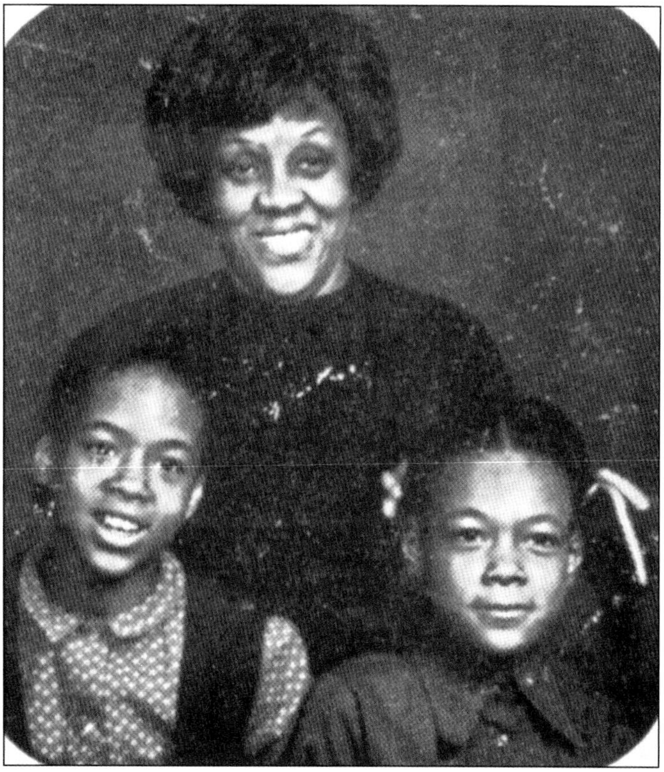

Alice Price, pictured here with her children in the 1960s, has been active at Coleman Memorial Methodist Church for more than four decades.

Nancy Gaines was a member of Coleman Memorial Methodist Church. Mrs. Gaines was on various committees and was chairperson of the Extravaganza Tea in the 1950s. This picture was taken in the 1960s.

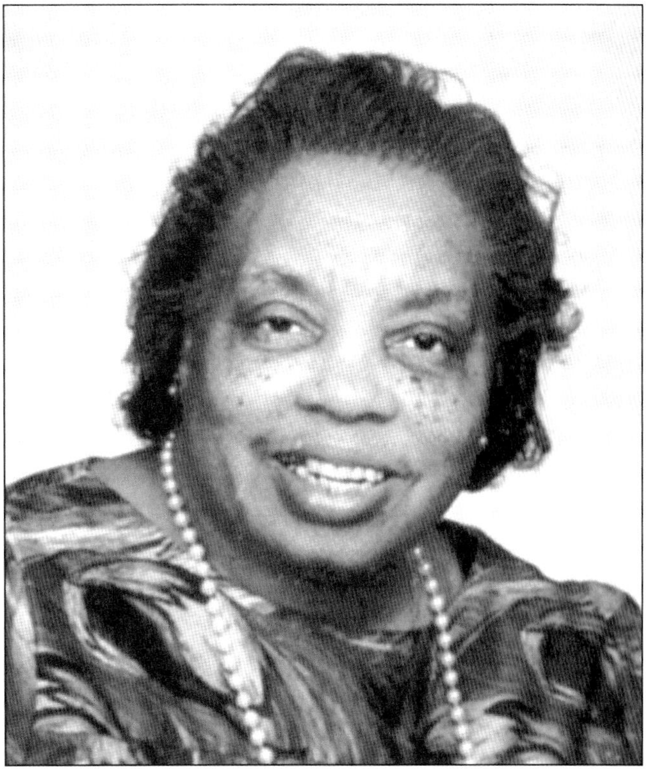

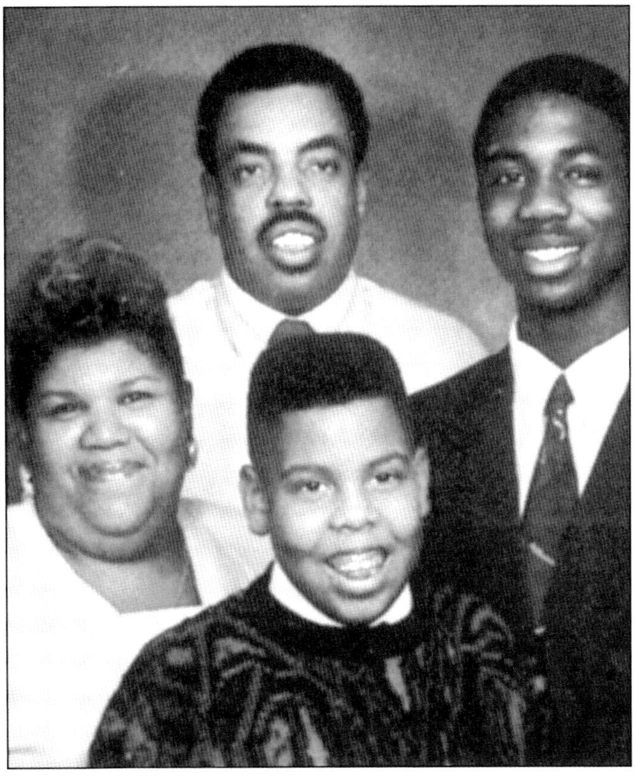

The Gaines family has been attending Coleman Memorial Methodist Church and providing church services since the 1950s. Shown here in the 1970s are Betty (left), William Sr. (top), William Jr. (right), and Lee (bottom).

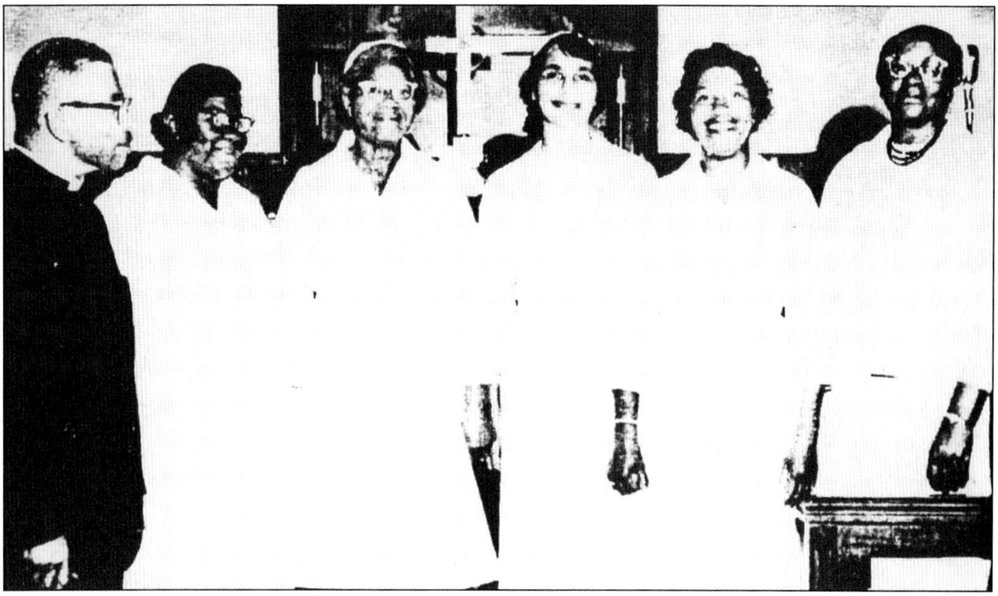

Rev. Harry Snead stands with the communion stewards. They were responsible for preparing the communion on the first Sunday of each month. Communion wafers and grape juice have been traditionally used to represent the body and the blood of the Lord Jesus Christ, who was sacrificed on the cross for the sins of all of mankind. From left to right are Rev. H. R. Snead, Irene DeShields, Velma Willis, Sarah Manlove, Marian Tilghman, and Sula Wilmore in the 1960s.

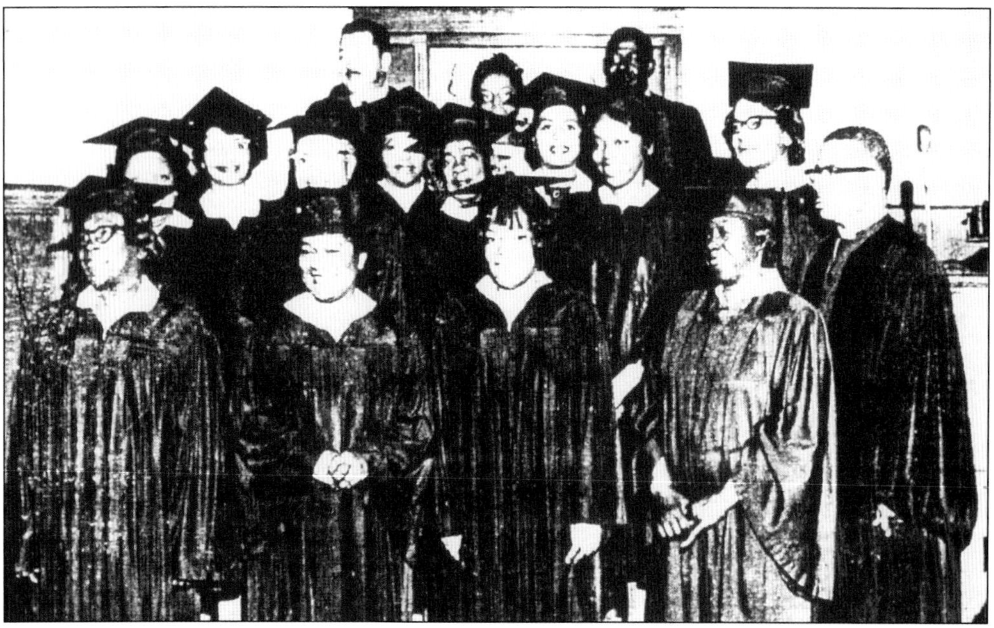

This is a 1960s picture of the Coleman Memorial Methodist Church Senior Choir. From left to right are (first row) Pearl Horsey (chairman), Violet Jenkins, Patricia Price, Margaret Black, and Rev. H. R. Snead; (second row) Alice Price, Sarah Manlove, Daisy Clark, Catherine Snead, Daisy Harrison, Lucy Wiggins, Gloria Faulkner, and Clara Jackson; (third row) Nathan Jackson, Margie Faulkner (organist), and A. O. Miller.

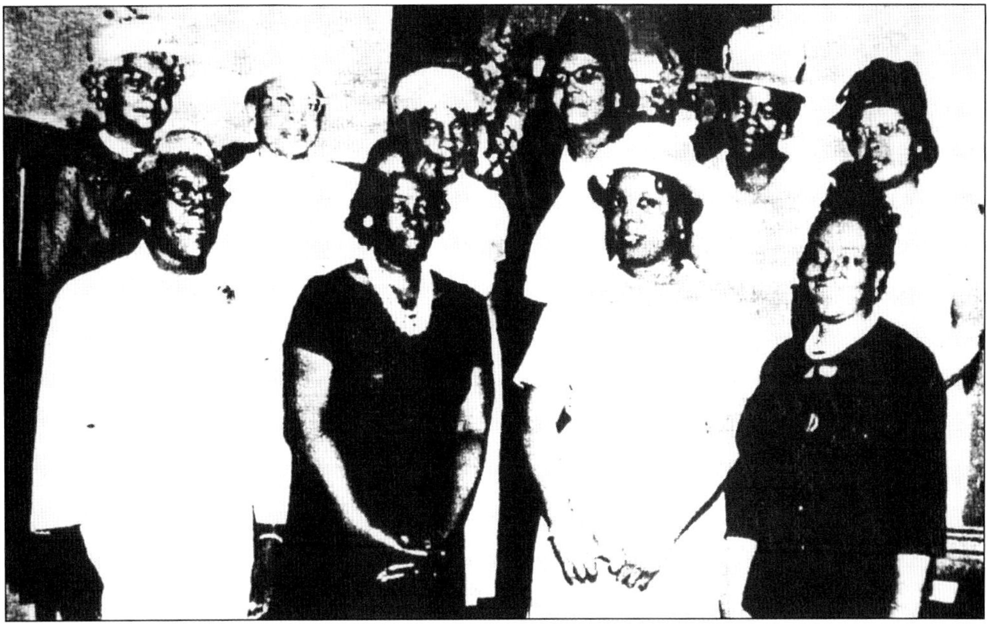

Pictured here in the 1960s are the lovely mothers who served on the commission on missions board. Mission offerings were used to help victims of Hurricane Camille. From left to right they are as follows: (front row) Pearl Horsey, Margaret Black, Nancy Gaines (chairman), and Margie Faulkner; (second row) Daisy Brown, Daisy Clark, Daisy Harrison, Clara Jackson, Rosetta Price, Florence Blackston, Joyce Seals, and Virginia Moaney.

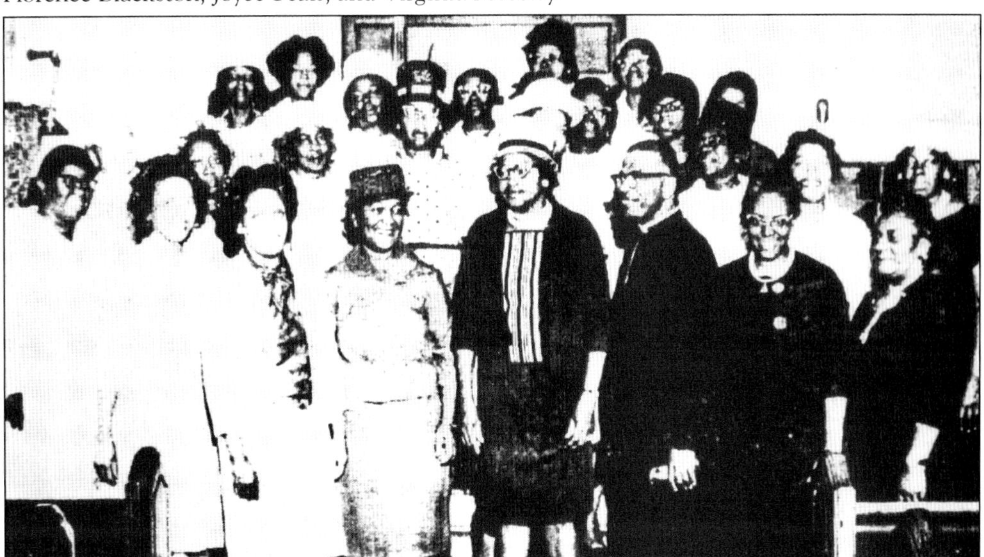

Shown here in the 1960s are women who participated in the Women's Society of Christian Service. From left to right are (front row) Irene DeShields, Delaney Butts, Alice Price, Violet Jenkins, Catherine Snead, Rev. H. R. Snead, Margie Faulkner, and Myrtle Tiller; (second row) Daisy Clark, Roberta Palmer, Daisy Harrison, Nancy Gaines, Anna Brooks, Pearl Horsey, Marian Tilghman, and Margaret Black (chairman); (third row) Lula Bunting, Patricia Price, Mamie Wilkinson, Mary Chandler, Sula Wilmore, and Joyce Seals; (fourth row) Florence Blackston, Velma Willis, and Virginia Moaney.

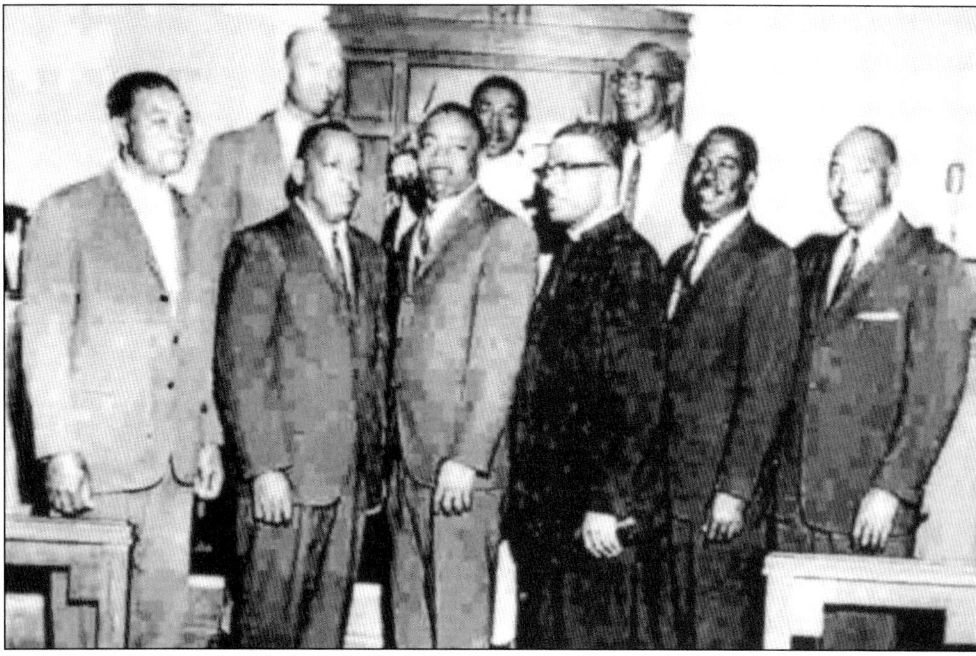

Rev. Harry R. Snead and the board of trustees were responsible for receiving and holding in trust all donations and bequests in accordance with the directions of the donor and in the interest of the church. The trustees also purchased insurance for the parsonage, the church, and the church furnishings. This picture is from the mid-1960s.

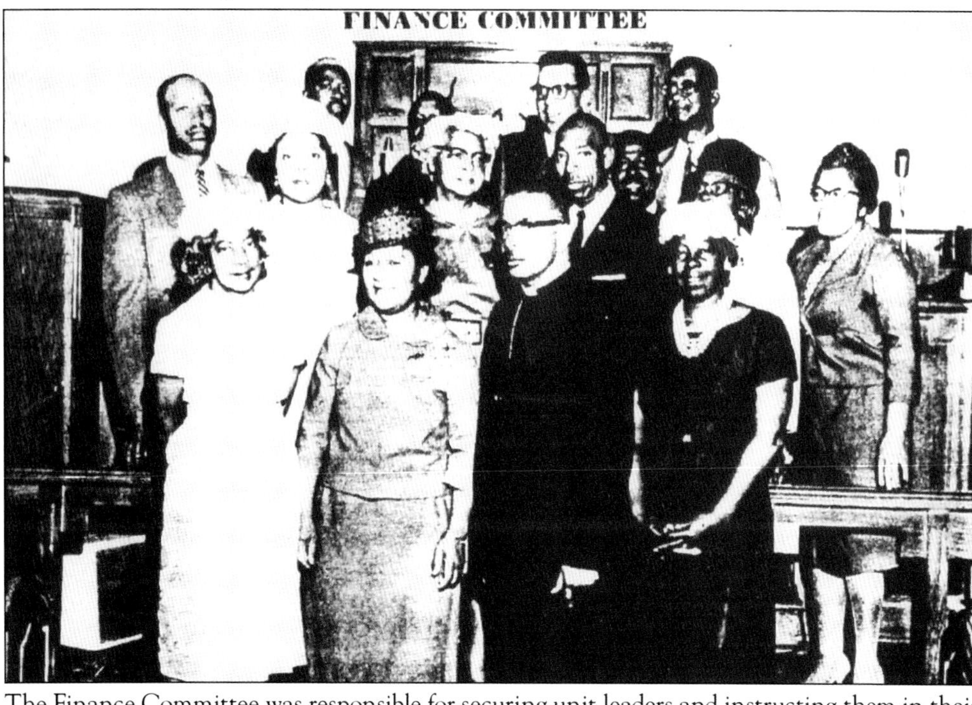

The Finance Committee was responsible for securing unit leaders and instructing them in their duties. They also kept records of all monies. Qualified persons in the area of bookkeeping and accounting were a vital part of the finance committee in the 1960s.

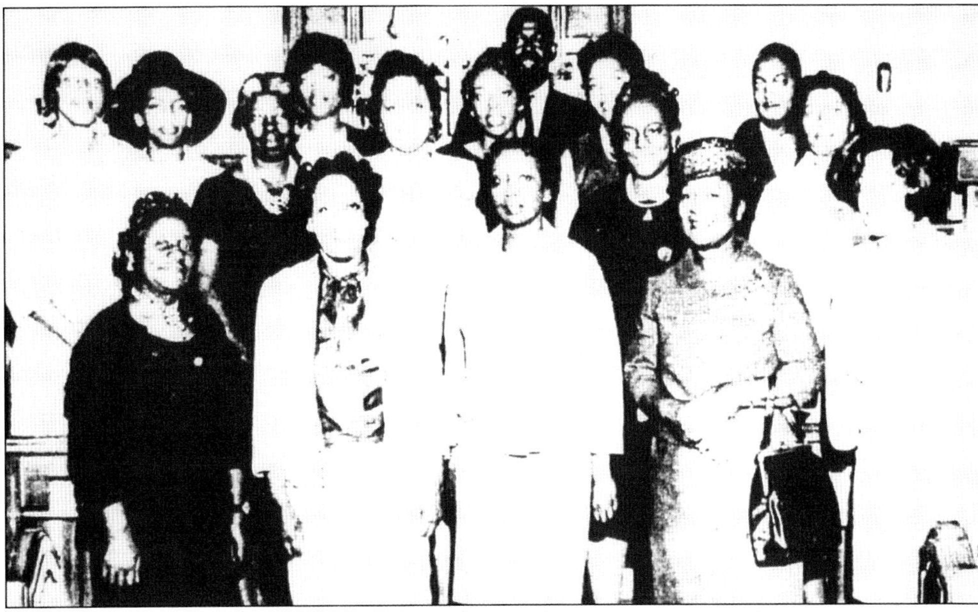

Pictured here are people who had a role to play on the commission on education committee in the 1960s. The scholarship committee of Coleman Memorial Methodist Church was organized under the direction of the commission on education and the pastoral guidance of Rev. Harry R. Snead. The idea of establishing a scholarship fund was brought to the members of the commission by Mrs. Roberta Palmer. She realized the problems that many of the students and their parents had in acquiring funds. She thought that it should be part of the church's mission to assist students financially.

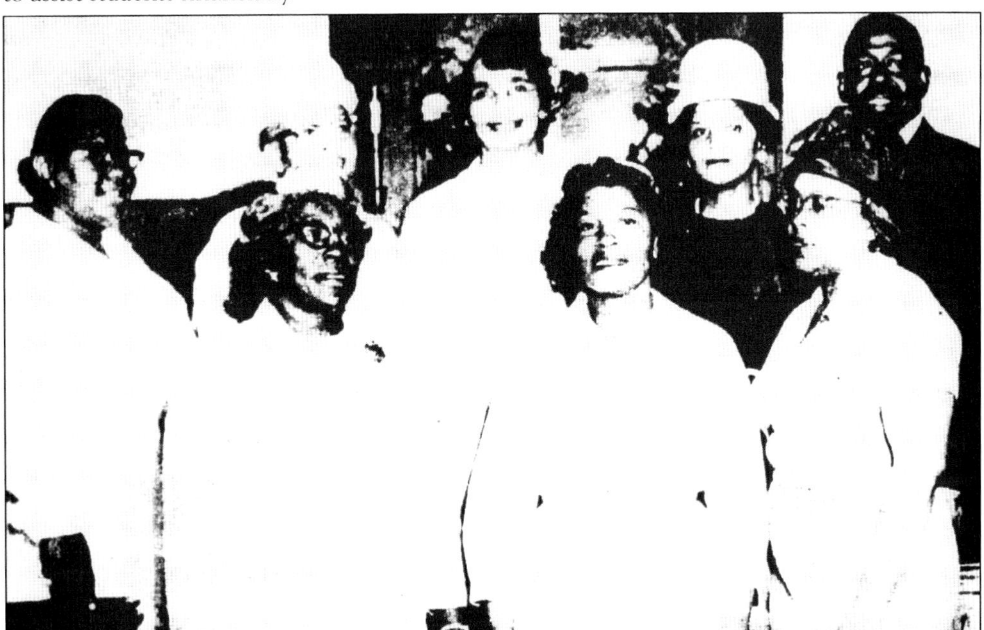

These dedicated soldiers, pictured in the 1960s, represented the commission on membership and evangelism. Their duty was to seek out, visit, and solicit new members for the church. Each new family moving into the community was to be visited and invited to the church.

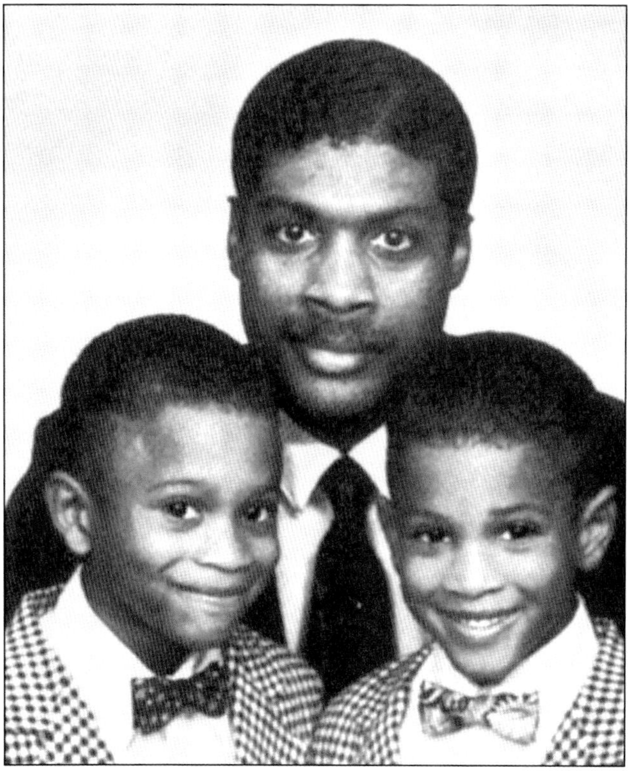

Frederick Gaines, pictured here in the 1960s with his sons, Brent (left) and Bryce, was a scholarship recipient attending Delaware State College in the 1970s. The Scholarship Committee of Coleman Memorial Methodist Church presented the award.

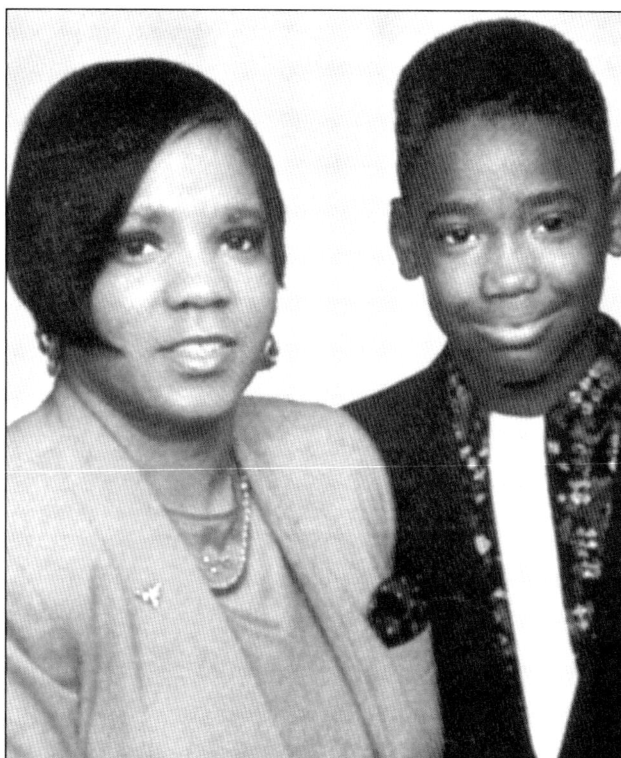

Janice Davis, shown here with her son, Donte, has attended Coleman Memorial Methodist Church since the 1960s, when this picture was taken.

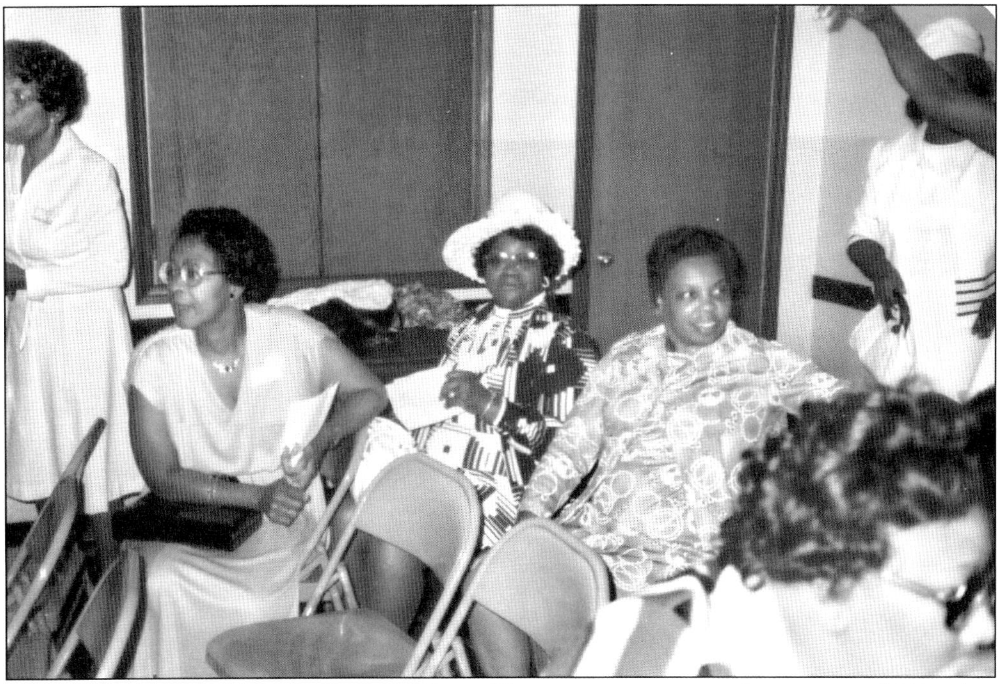

This is a picture of Coleman Sisters in Christ. They were enjoying a relaxing time of fellowship following a Sunday service. All of these women served faithfully at Coleman Memorial Methodist Church. From left to right are Iris Crosse, Sula Wilmore, and Nancy Gaines in the 1960s.

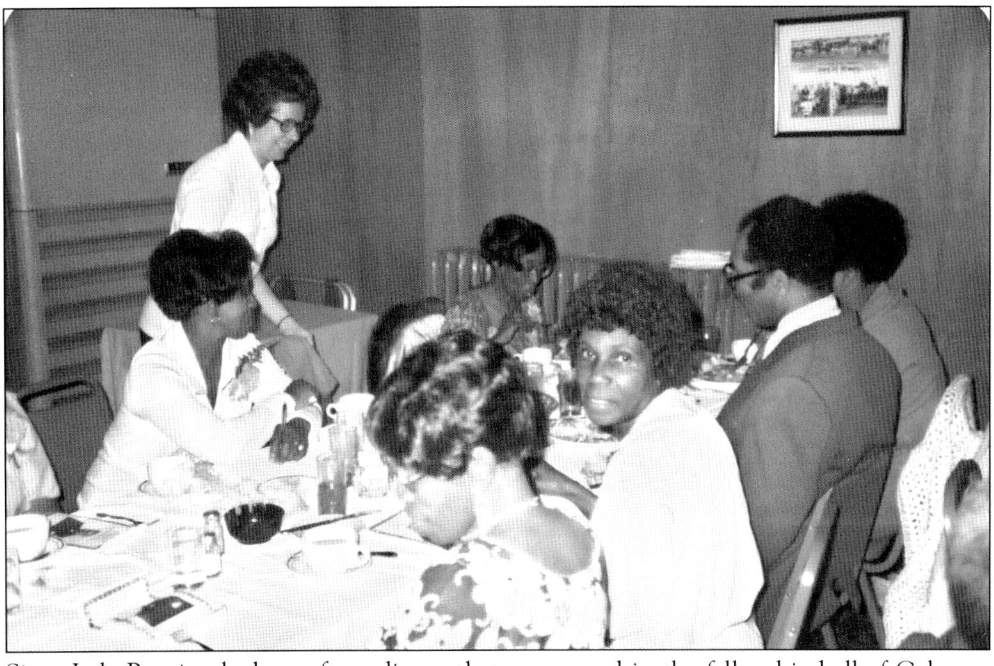

Sister Lula Bunting looks up from dinner that was served in the fellowship hall of Coleman Memorial Methodist Church in the 1960s. Sister Bunting was a prayer warrior and a worshipper who loved the Lord. As the stewardship chairperson, she was concerned about congregational care and outreach to the community. She served in the church with sincere dedication.

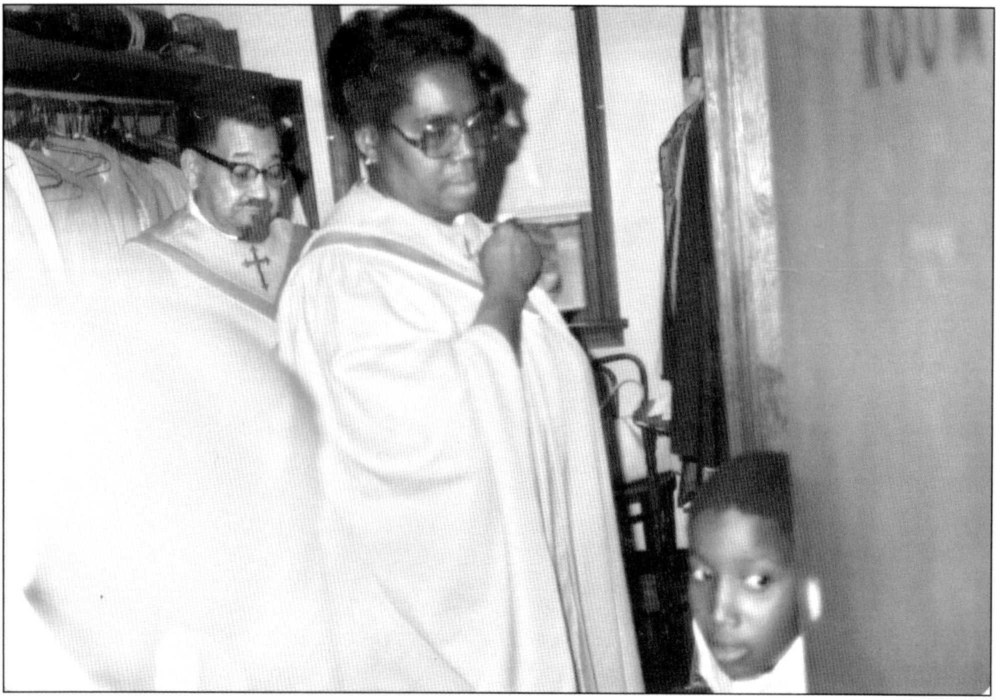

This is a picture of choir singers preparing to sing in the 1970s. The Coleman Memorial Methodist singers are Mr. Jackson, Becky Taylor, and an unidentified boy.

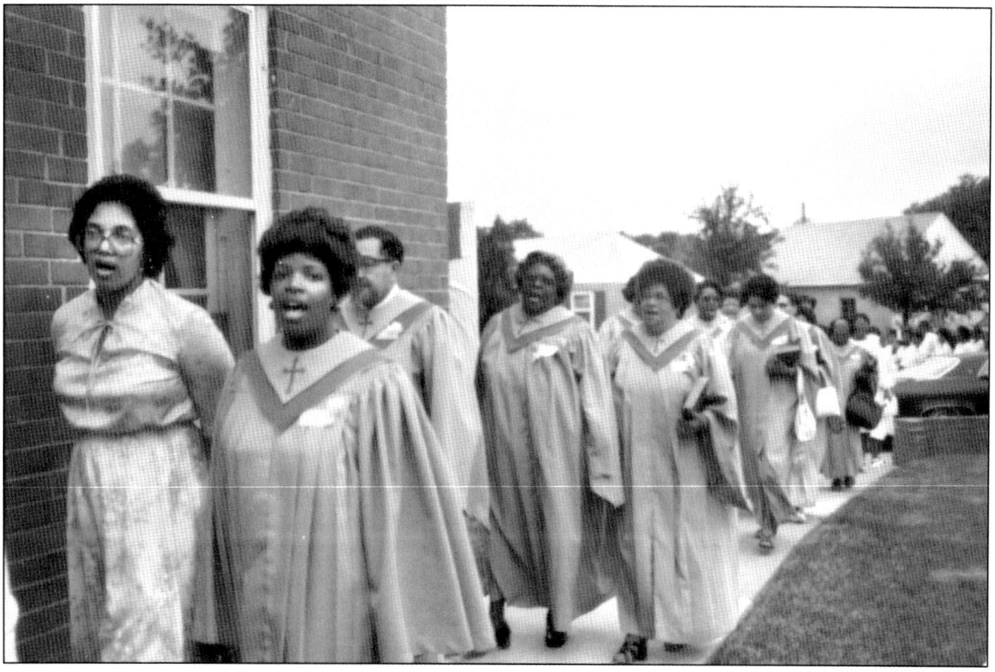

The senior choir sings as they enter the church for Sunday morning service in the late 1970s. The first president of the senior choir was Ruth Turpin, who served for four months. Sister Pearl Horsey served for the remainder of the year. The first organist and director was Celestine Lyght. The choir was organized in 1953 in the church parsonage on Bethune Drive.

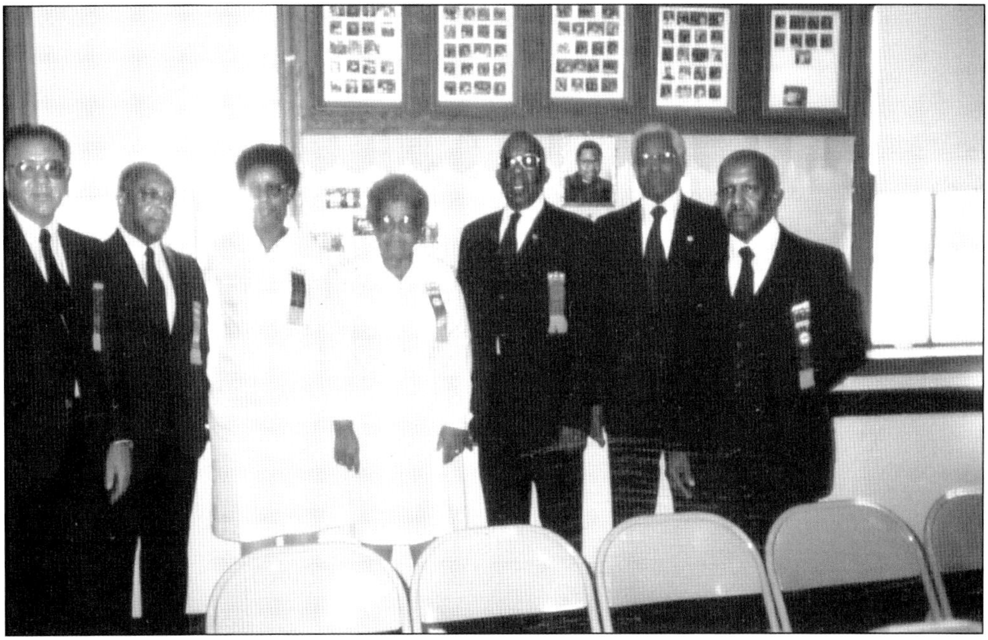

The senior ushers prepared to escort the congregation to their seats in the 1970s. The commencement of the prelude signaled the beginning of worship, and the ushers saw that all persons were in their pews and that the atmosphere of reverence was maintained. Pictured from left to right are Mr. Dillard, Mr. Wiggins, Mrs. Demby, Mrs. Moaney, Mr. Dickerson, Mr. Wilmore, and Mr. Congo. The ushers were expected to be at church prior to the beginning of the worship hour so that they could be ready to serve the people.

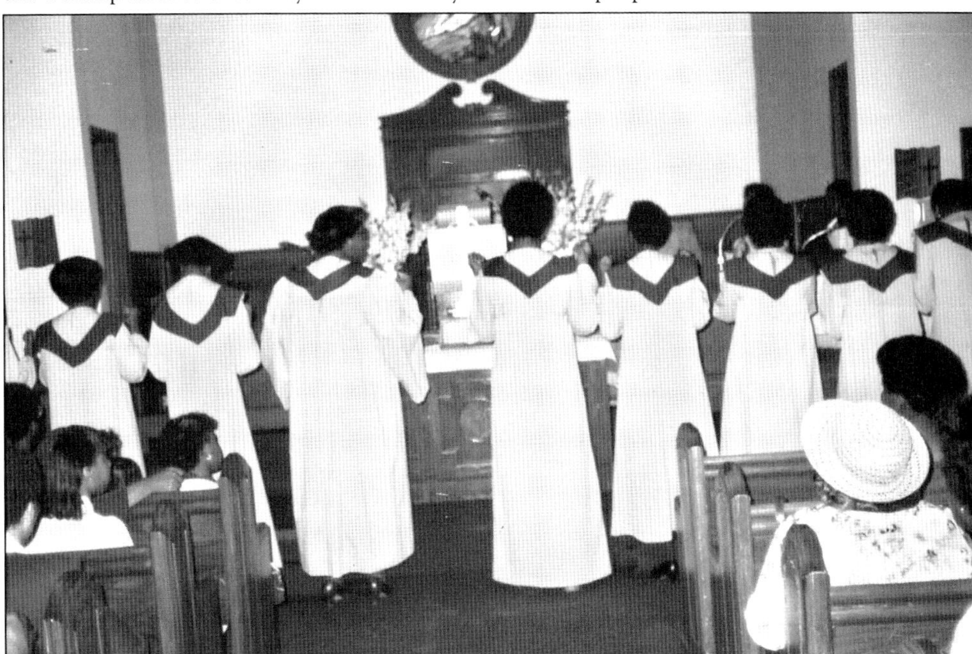

This is a picture of the Coleman Memorial Methodist choir members gathered at the altar for prayer in the late 1970s.

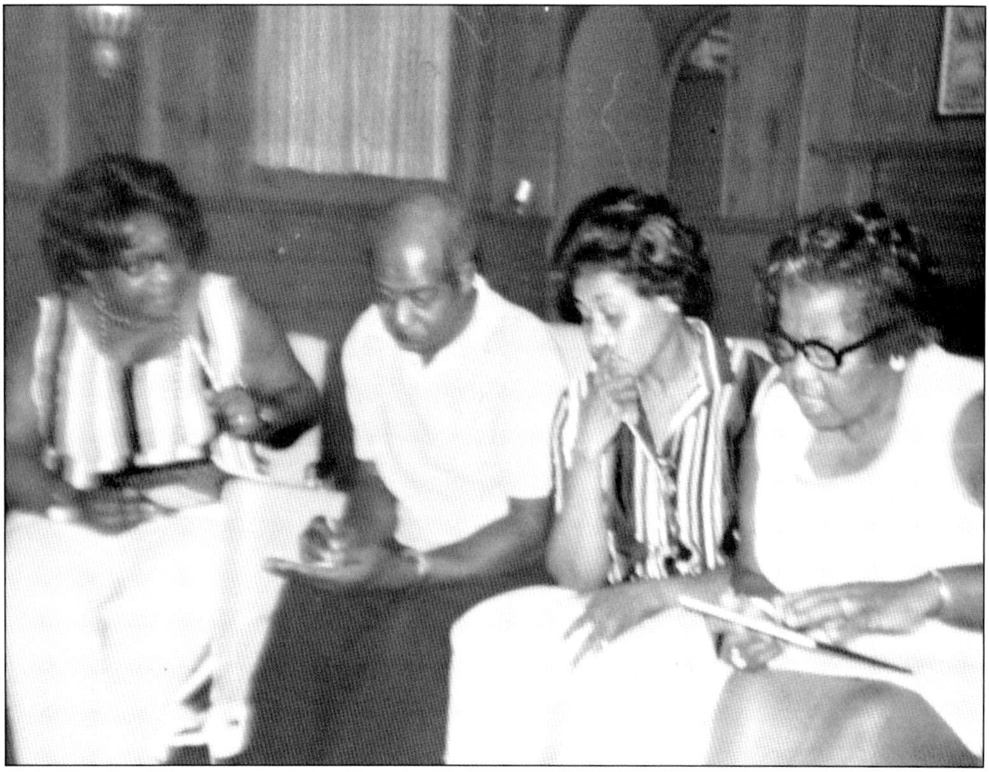

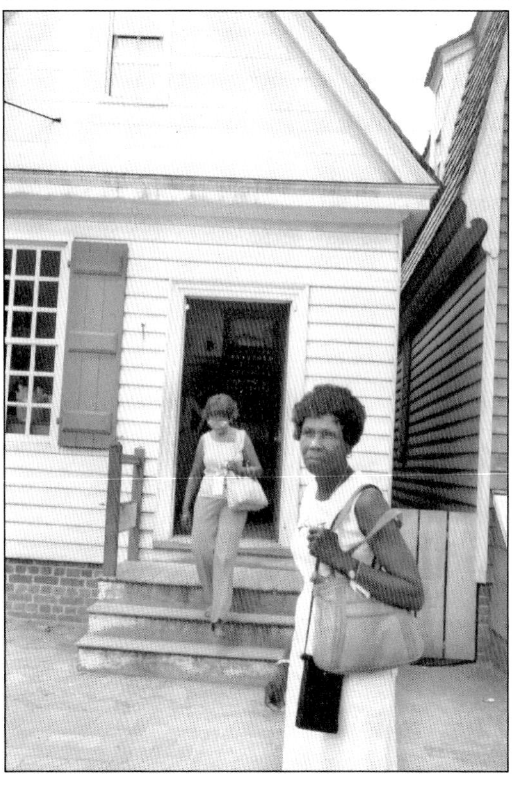

This church meeting in session at Coleman Memorial Methodist Church in the 1970s included, from left to right, Rebecca Taylor, A. O. Miller, Mary L. Spencer, and Virginia Moaney.

Lula Bunting joined the Coleman Memorial Methodist Church in the 1950s. This picture of her was taken in the 1970s, while on a trip to Williamsburg, Virginia. The woman in the background is unidentified.

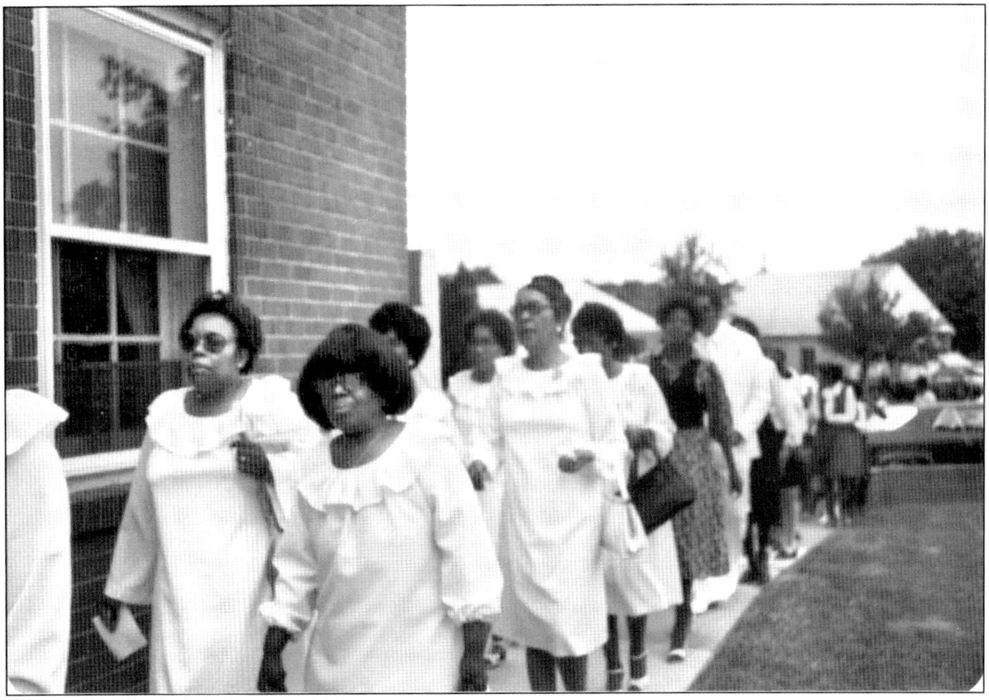

The gospel chorus marches while singing in this 1970s photograph.

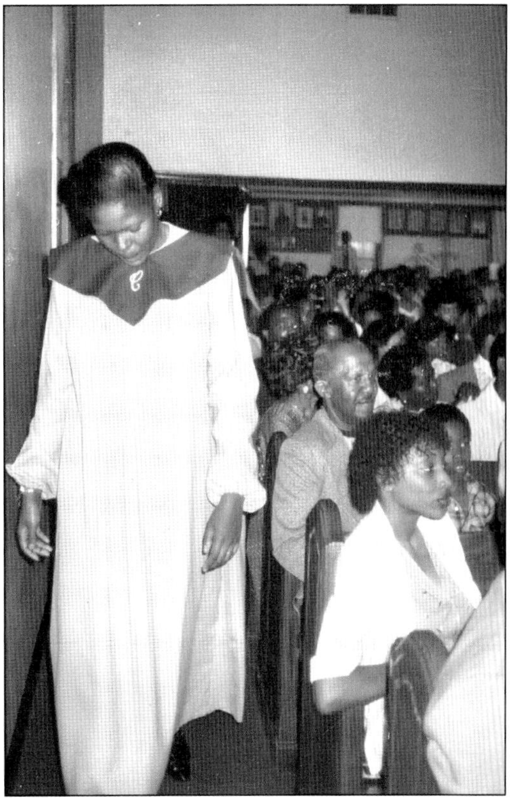

This is a picture of an unidentified junior choir member preparing to sing. The photograph was taken in the late 1970s.

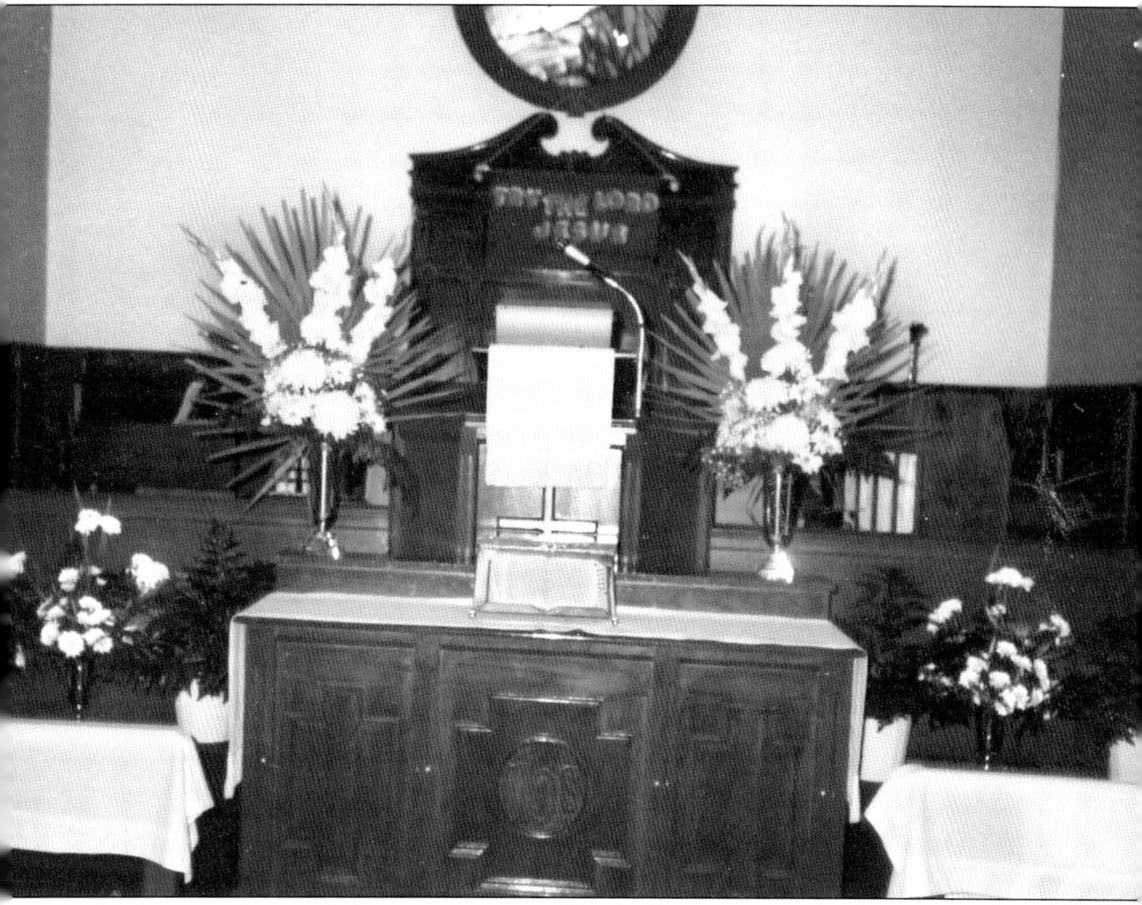

The beautiful Coleman Memorial Methodist Church altar is prepared for communion Sunday. The altar has been the same since construction in 1955.

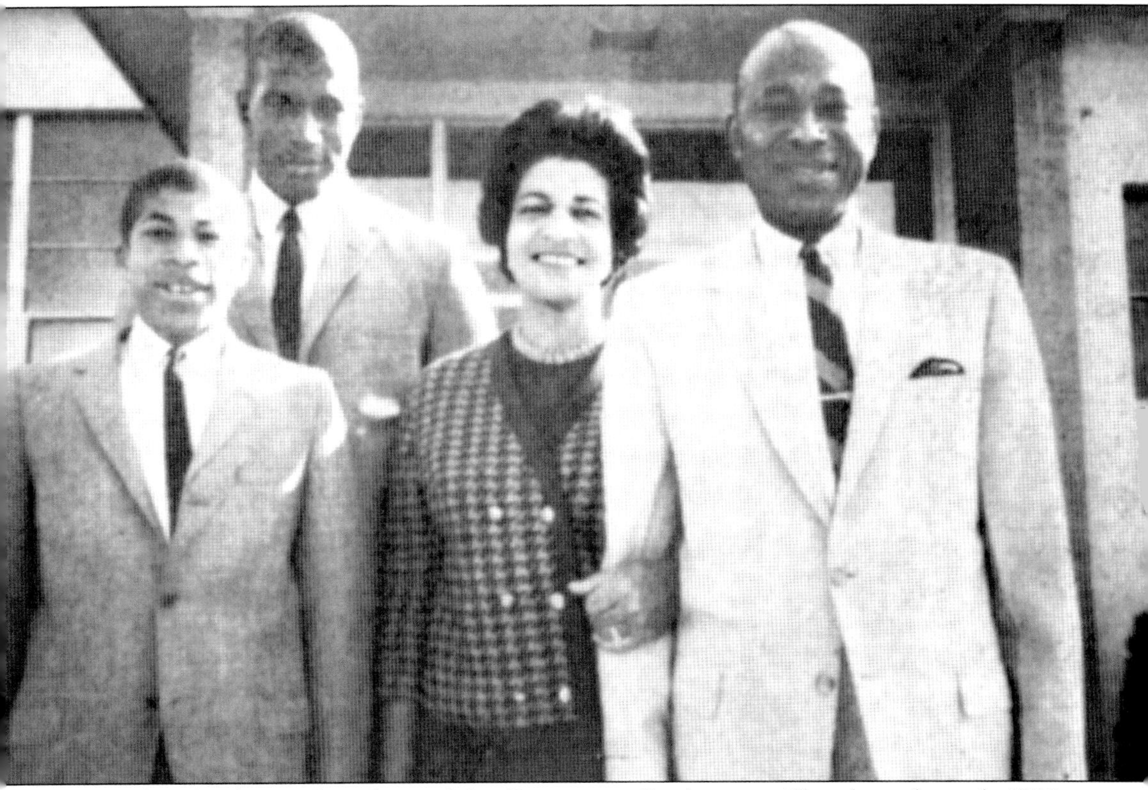

The first family stands in front of the Community Presbyterian Church in the early 1960s. From left to right are Norman, Thomas, First Lady Vivian C. Moyer, and the Reverend Maurice Moyer.

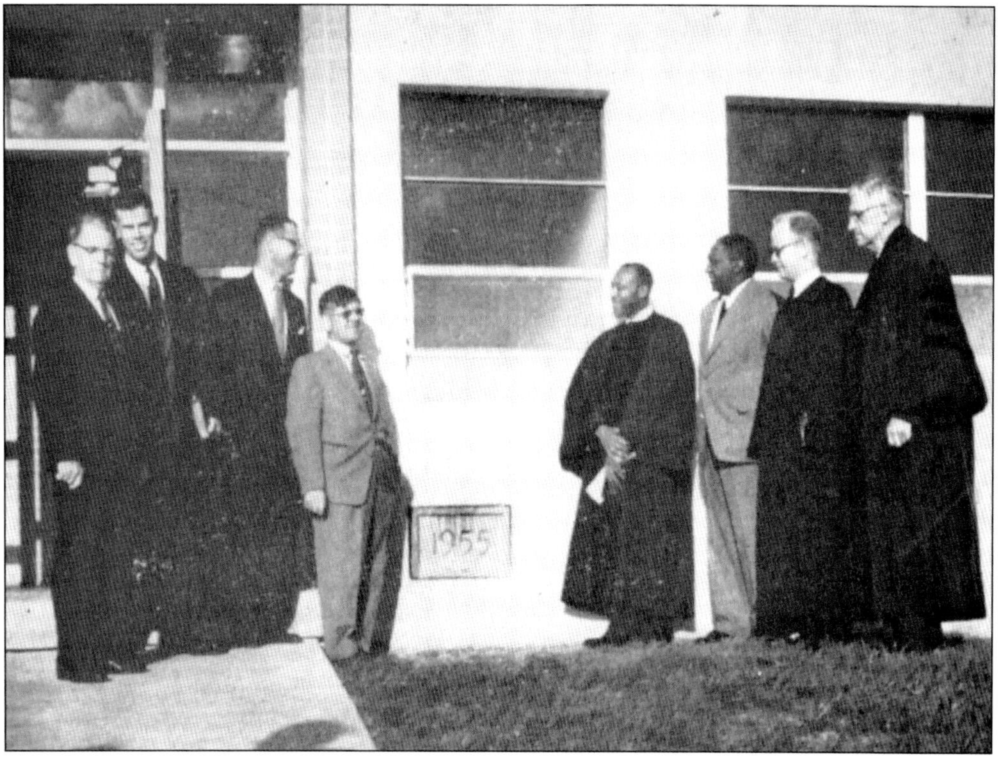

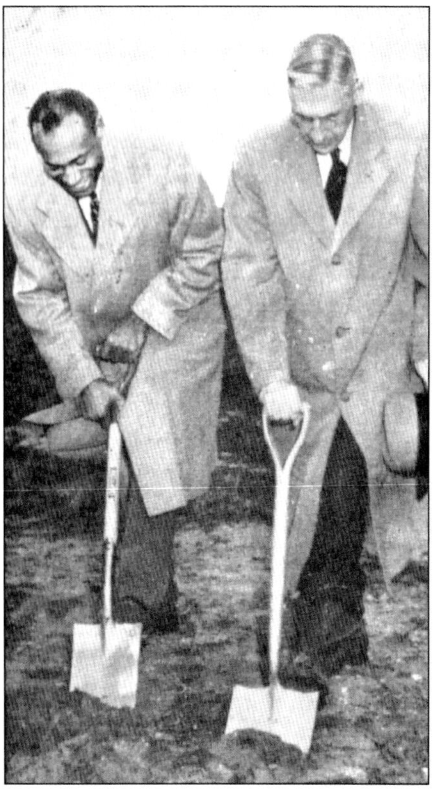

In this 1955 picture of the cornerstone-laying ceremony of the Community Presbyterian Church, Rev. Maurice Moyer is fourth from the right. The other participants are unidentified.

This is a picture of the groundbreaking ceremony for the Community Presbyterian Church, including the Reverend Maurice Moyer and the then-general presbyter, Dr. Sydney J. Venable. Reverend Moyer was ordained in 1953.

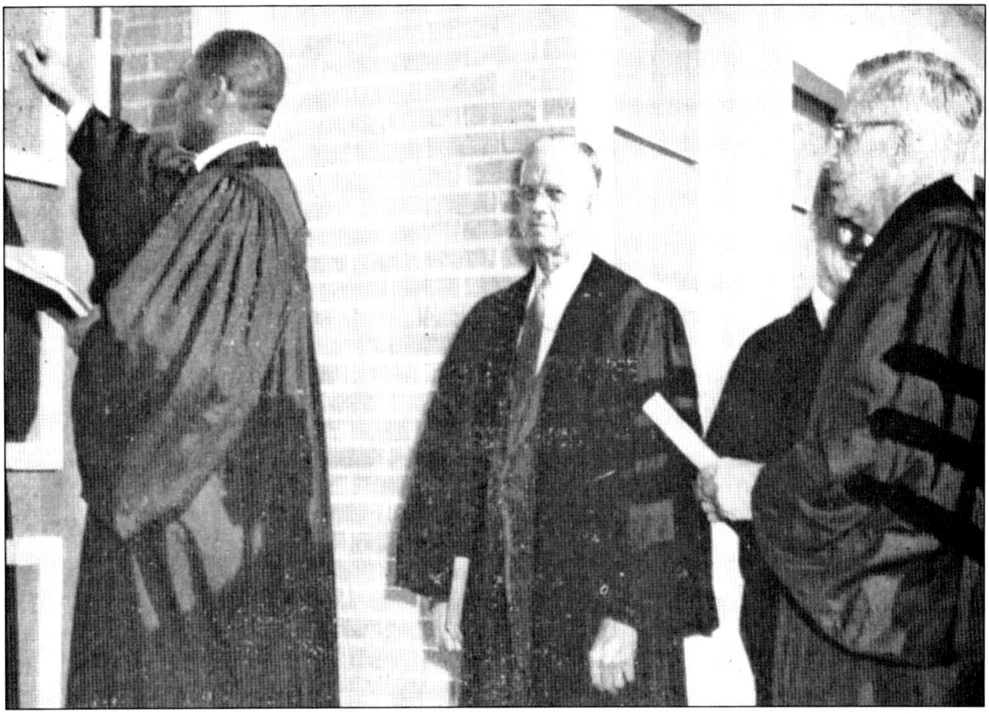

At Rev. Maurice Moyer's dedication service in 1955, he makes the traditional knock on the door before entering the Community Presbyterian Church. From left to right are Reverend Moyer (at the door); Dr. Harold Baldwin, secretary of the Board of National Missions of the Presbyterian Church (USA); Dr. Donald Douds, Hanover Presbyterian Church; and Dr. Sydney J. Venable, general presbyter of New Castle.

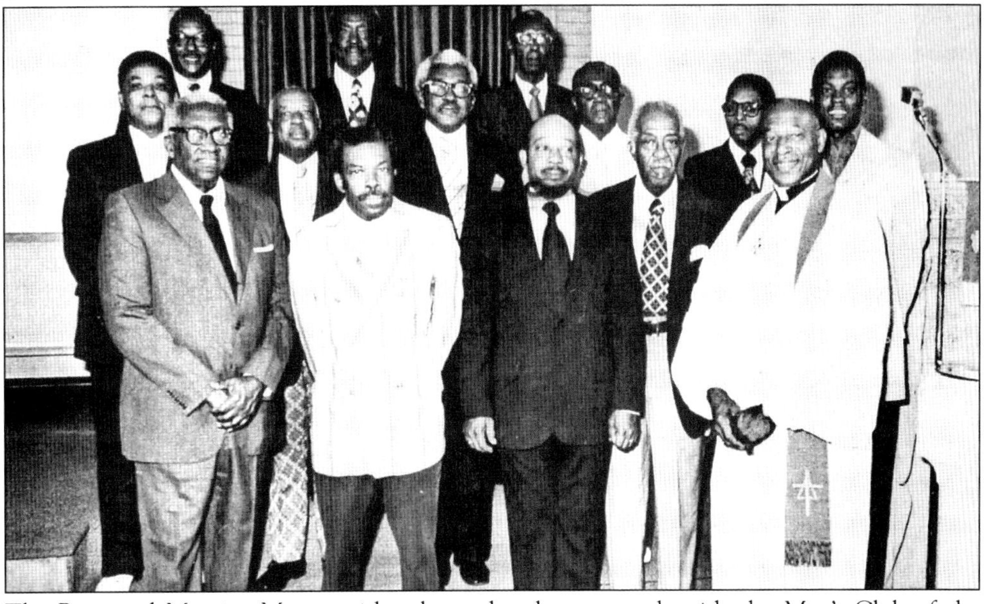

The Reverend Maurice Moyer, with robe and stole on, stands with the Men's Club of the Community Presbyterian Church. Included in this picture are church officers Pres. David Clark, Vice Pres. LeRoy Gaines, secretary Marion Mathis, and treasurer Roger Hawkins.

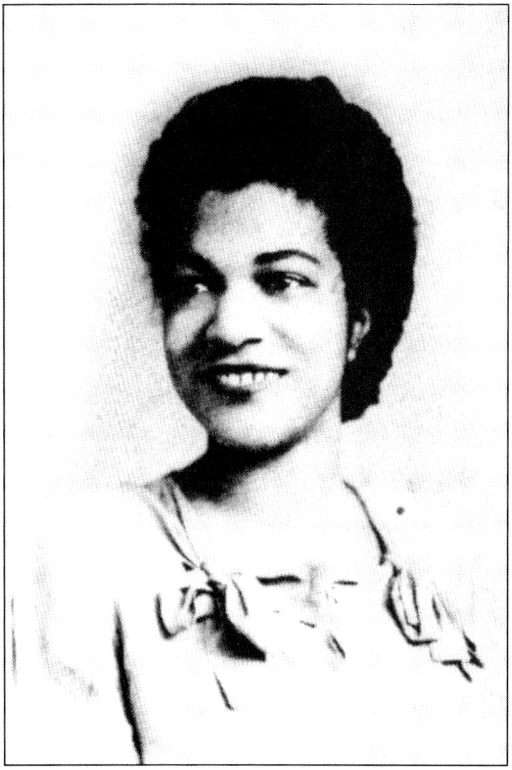

The beautiful Vivian C. Moyer is the wife of the Community Presbyterian Church minister Rev. Maurice Moyer. She is pictured in the 1940s.

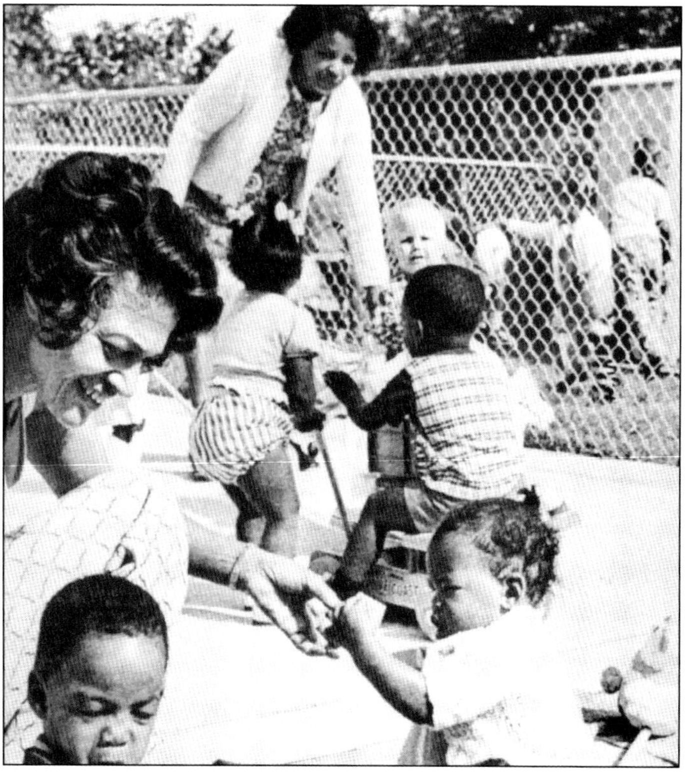

Vivian C. Moyer and an unidentified staff member are pictured here with the children in the day care center at the Community Presbyterian Church in the 1960s. Mrs. Moyer was in charge of the school. Many families depended on the nursery school to help keep the household costs low. The day care center was open six days for $6 a week. They were open from 7:00 a.m. to 6:00 p.m. The nursery took children from four months to five years old. The program was half supported by the Presbyterian Board of National Missions in 1956.

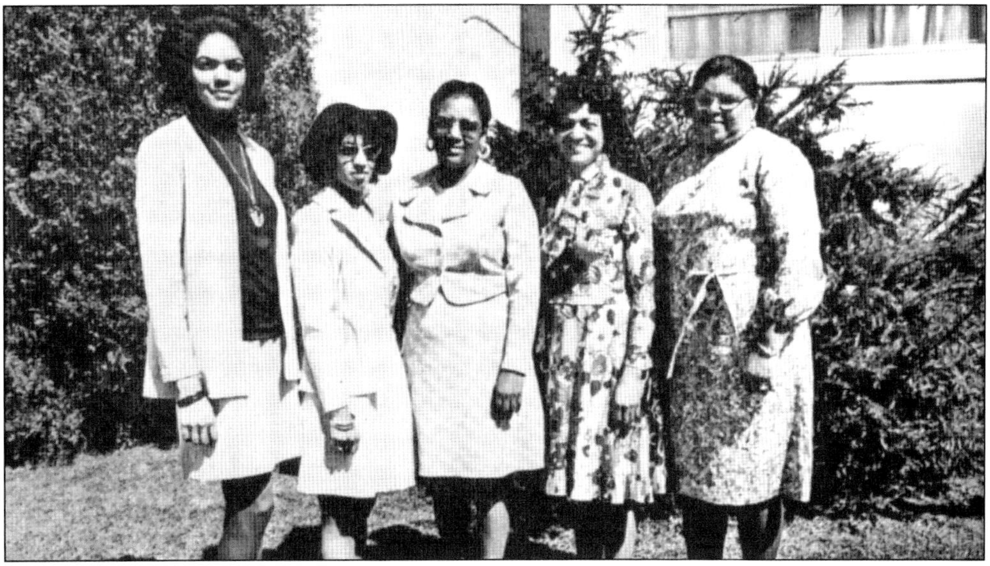

The Community Presbyterian Church Hour Nursery staff are, from left to right, Janice Robinson, A. LaDon Terry, Sydella Boone, Vivian C. Moyer, and Maizie Roy (chairman). They are pictured in the 1970s.

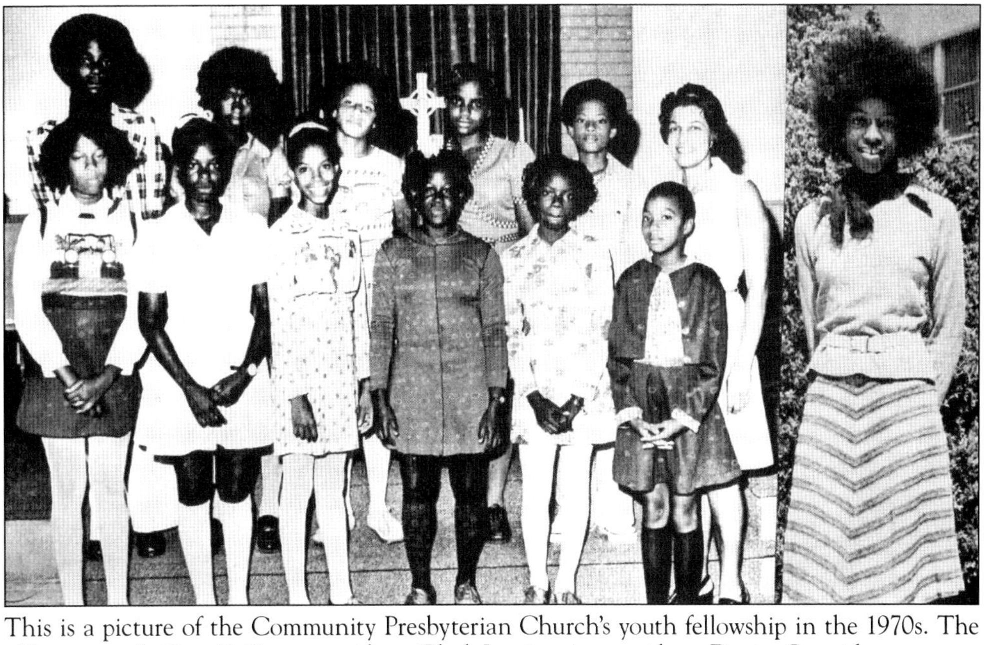

This is a picture of the Community Presbyterian Church's youth fellowship in the 1970s. The officers were LaDon R. Terry, president; Clark Lewis, vice president; Denise Spanish, secretary; Paula Jenkins, assistant secretary; Sharon Benson, treasurer; and Willie Mae Collins, chaplain.

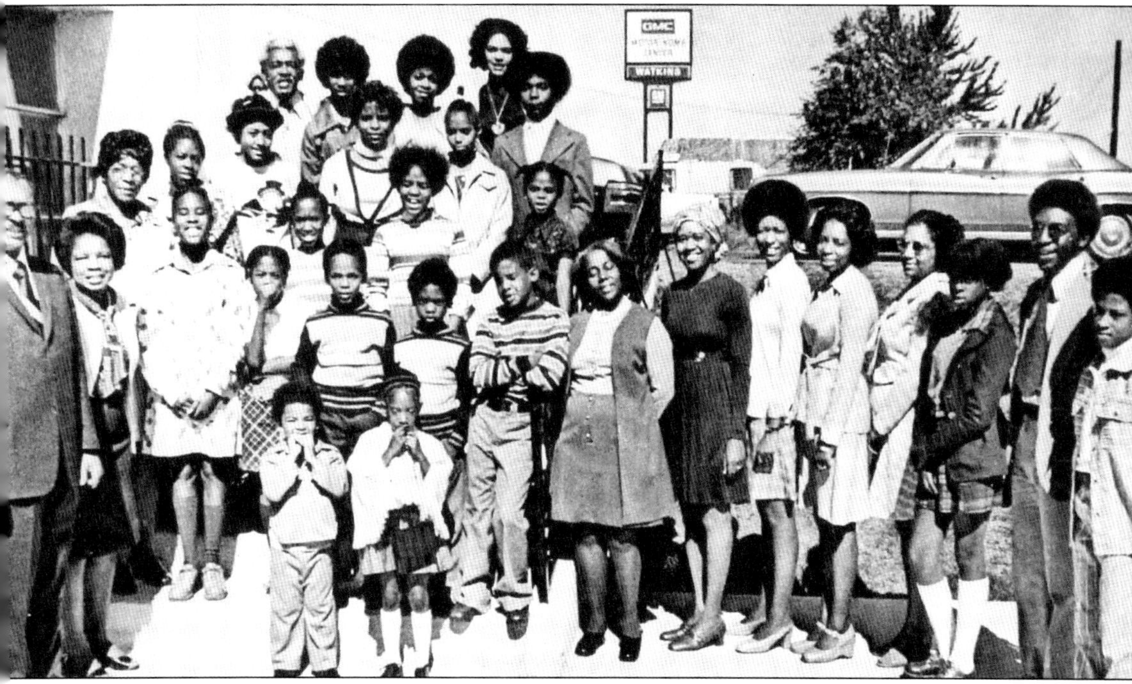

This is a picture of the Community Presbyterian Church Sunday school in the 1970s.

Six

School Days

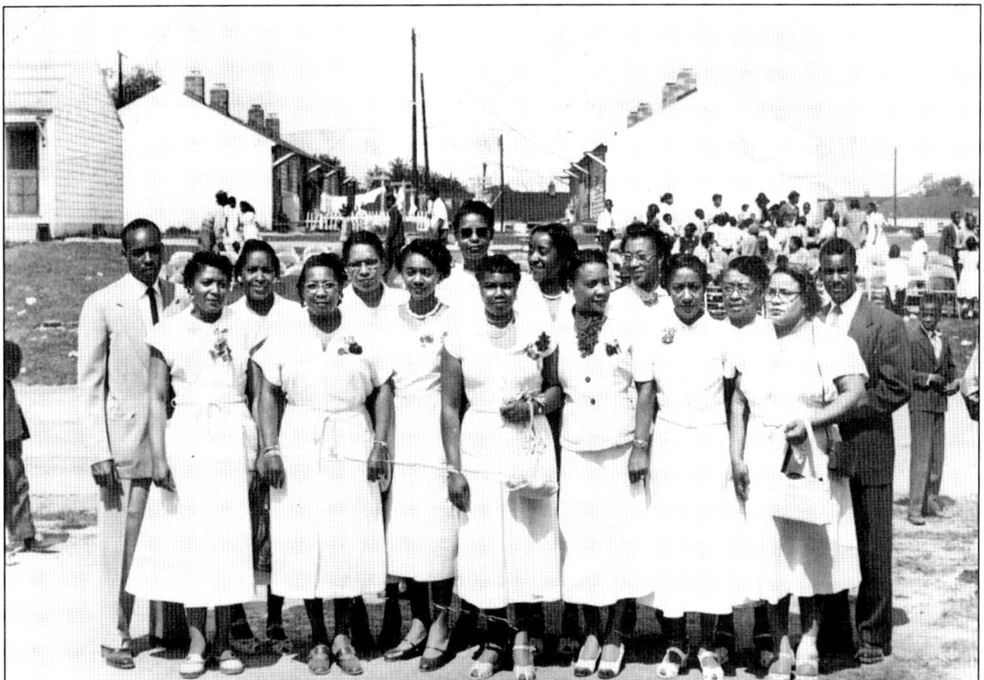

The old Millside School faculty celebrates their 1955 May Day festivities. They later became the Dunleith Community School faculty. From left to right are Victor Smith, Menthal Brewington, Reba DeShields, Ethel Lynn Chambers, Edythe Pridgen, Gloria Holland, Doris Rile, Maude Evans, Margaret C. West, Eleanor B. Tiggs, Marjorie Mulligan-Priest, Hannah S. Johnson, Ethel C. Jackson, Marian Beaujon, and Raymond Woodward. (Margaret C. West collection.)

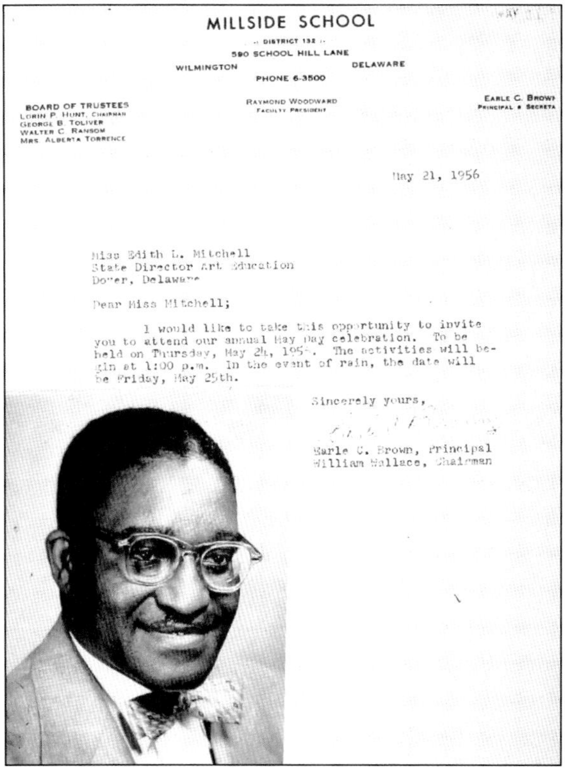

MILLSIDE SCHOOL

DISTRICT 132

590 SCHOOL HILL LANE

WILMINGTON DELAWARE

PHONE 6-3500

BOARD OF TRUSTEES
LORIN P. HUNT, CHAIRMAN
GEORGE B. TOLIVER
WALTER C. RANSOM
MRS. ALBERTA TORRENCE

RAYMOND WOODWARD
FACULTY PRESIDENT

EARLE C. BROWN
PRINCIPAL & SECRETA

May 21, 1956

Miss Edith L. Mitchell
State Director Art Education
Dover, Delaware

Dear Miss Mitchell;

I would like to take this opportunity to invite you to attend our annual May Day celebration. To be held on Thursday, May 24, 1956. The activities will begin at 1:00 p.m. In the event of rain, the date will be Friday, May 25th.

Sincerely yours,

Earle C. Brown, Principal
William Wallace, Chairman

This picture of Mr. Earle C. Brown, principal of the Millside School, is on a letter of invitation inviting the state director of art to the school's annual May Day festivities in 1956. (Margaret C. West collection.)

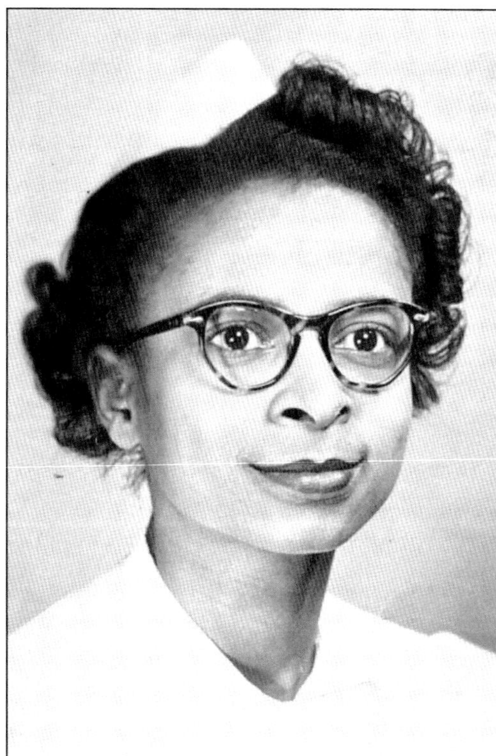

Mrs. Mary Q. Brown, the school nurse at the Dunleith Community School, was said to have been caring and compassionate towards the students. She administered mandatory vaccinations to students for diseases such as polio in the 1950s. This picture of Mrs. Brown is from the 1960s.

William Ellis Preston was the building architect for the school that was eventually named the Dunleith Community School. Preston was a prominent architect in Delaware. He was a past president of the Delaware Institute of Architects. He was a member of the old Advisory Council for Mental Retardation Facilities and Mental Health Centers. Preston practiced architecture in the state of Delaware from May 1938 to January 1972.

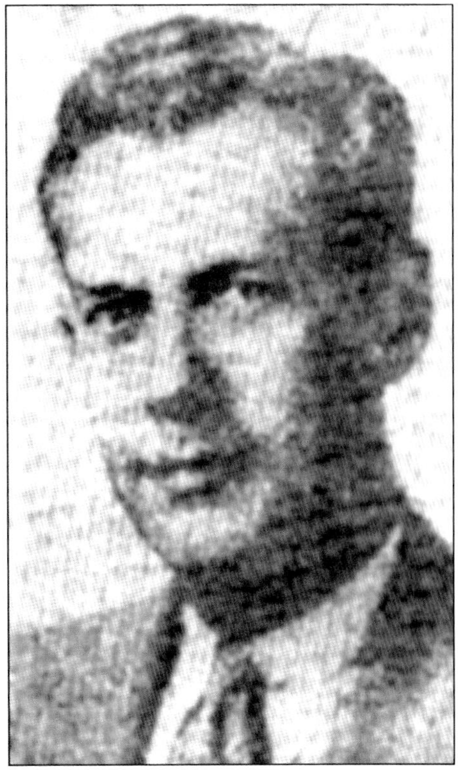

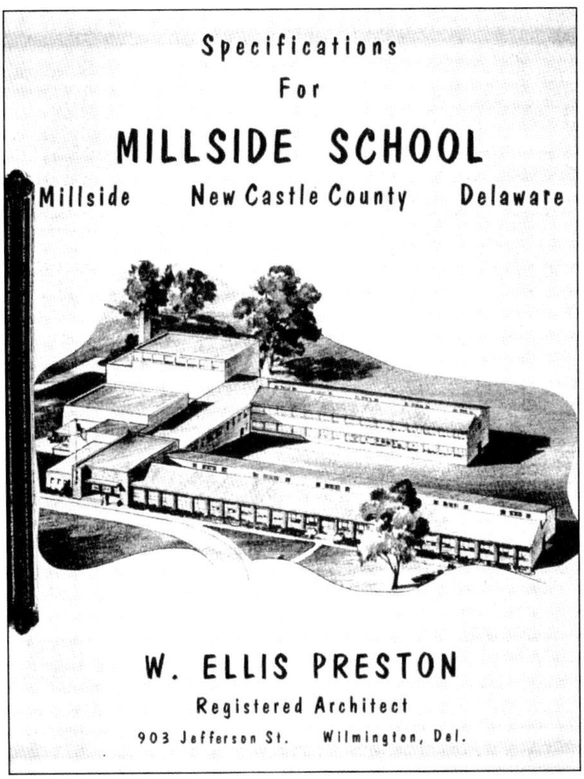

This is a picture of the new Dunleith Community School, which replaced the old Millside School in 1956. The drawing and specifications for the school were done by W. Ellis Preston.

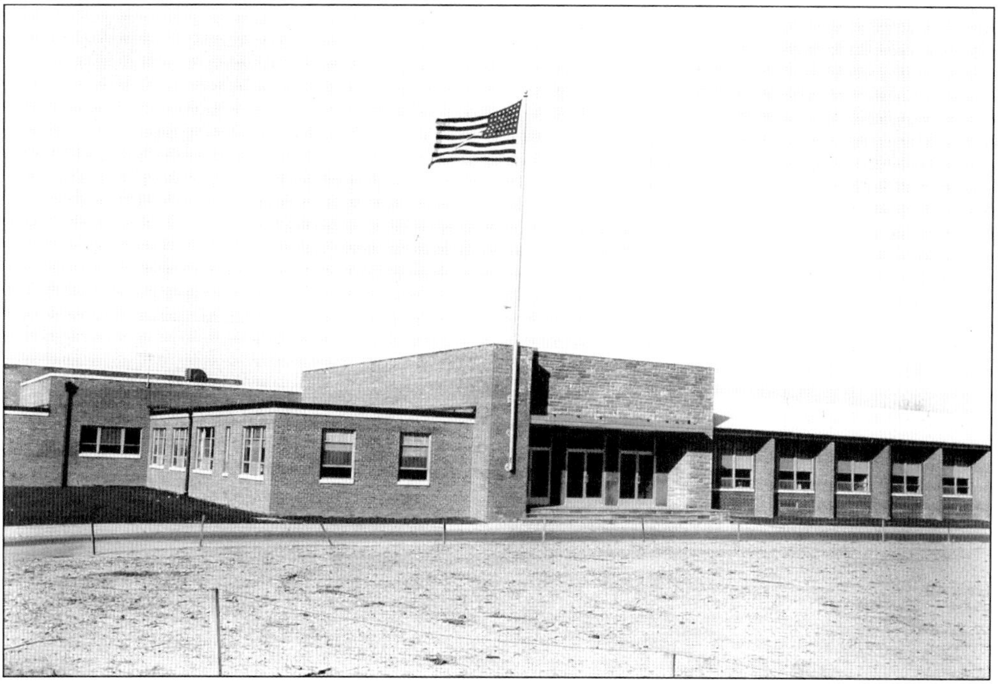

The new Dunleith Community School was located at Talladega and Hastie Drives. This is a picture of the school taken in 1956, before the grass grew in.

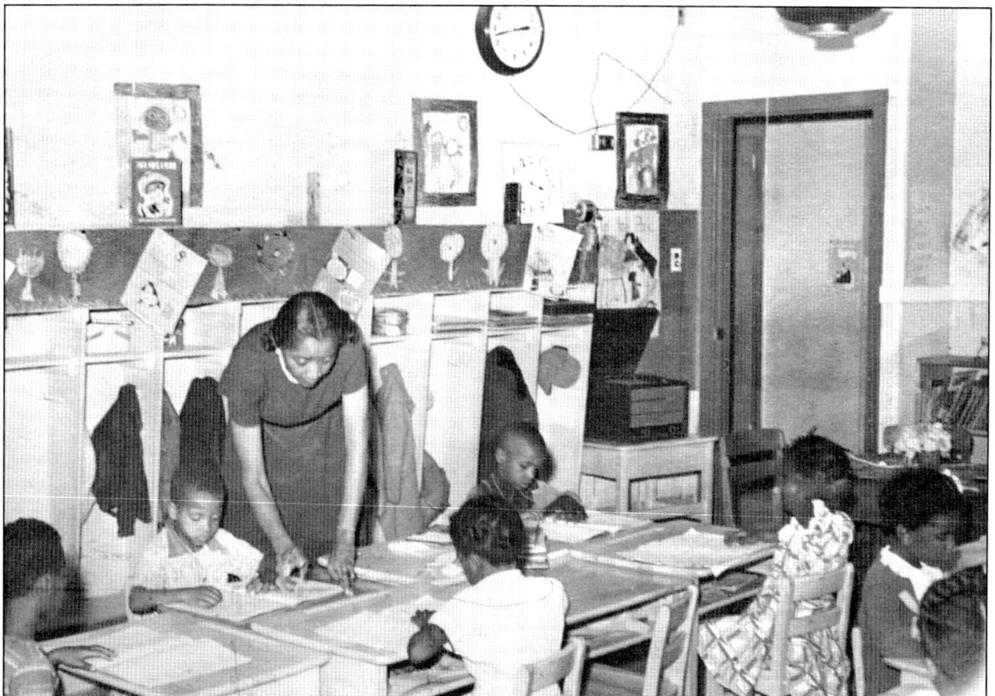

Margaret C. West teaches first-grade students in her Millside classroom in 1954. Mrs. West was also responsible for training student teachers. The children sat together in groups. (Margaret C. West collection.)

This is a picture of Margaret C. West during her career as a schoolteacher. Mrs. West was often called on to say a prayer before meals in the school cafeteria. This picture was taken in the 1950s.

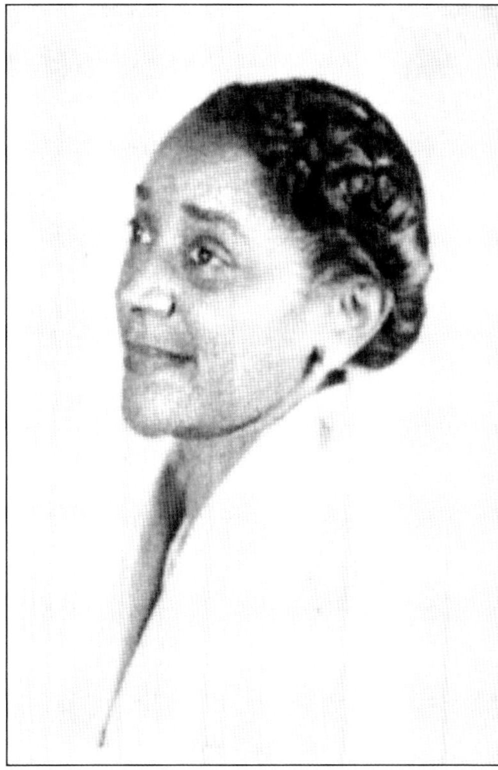

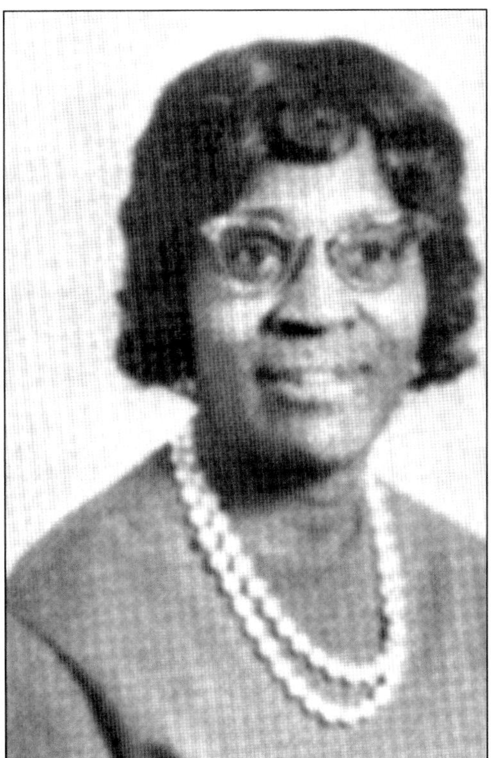

Dunleith Community School's home economics teacher, Florence Foddrell, commuted from Philadelphia to Wilmington daily to teach. Mrs. Foddrell was the home economics teacher for the junior high school students. She was said to have been an excellent instructor for both genders. Students were taught home skills such as cooking and sewing. Independent living and personal hygiene were also taught. She is pictured here in the late 1960s.

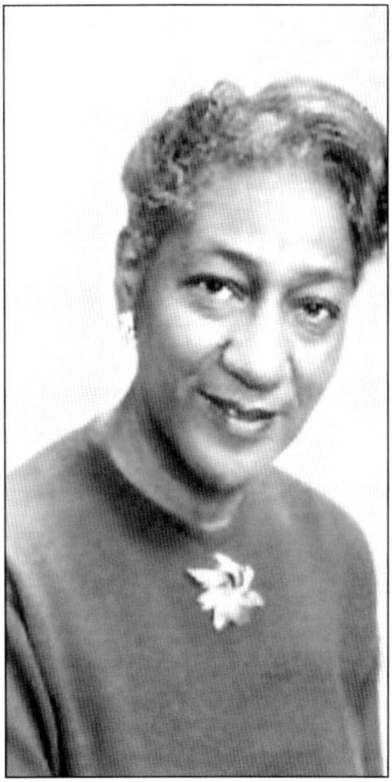

Hannah S. Johnson was a second-grade teacher in the 1950s and 1960s.

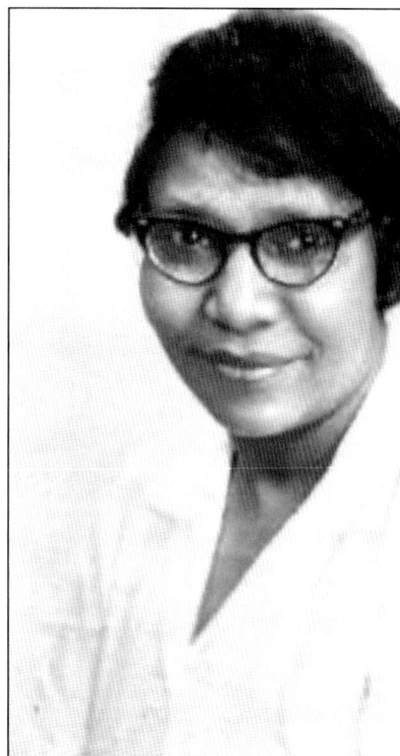

Pictured here is Margaret Laws, who was a teacher in the 1950s.

This is a picture of Menthal Watkins Brewington, a second-grade teacher in the 1950s.

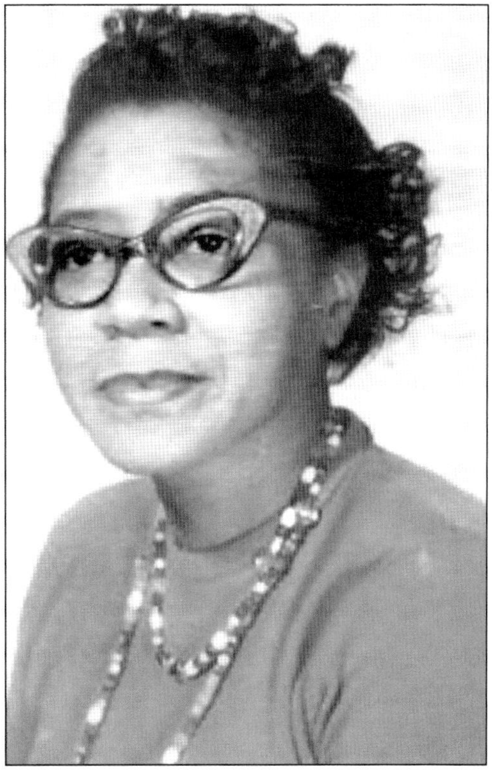

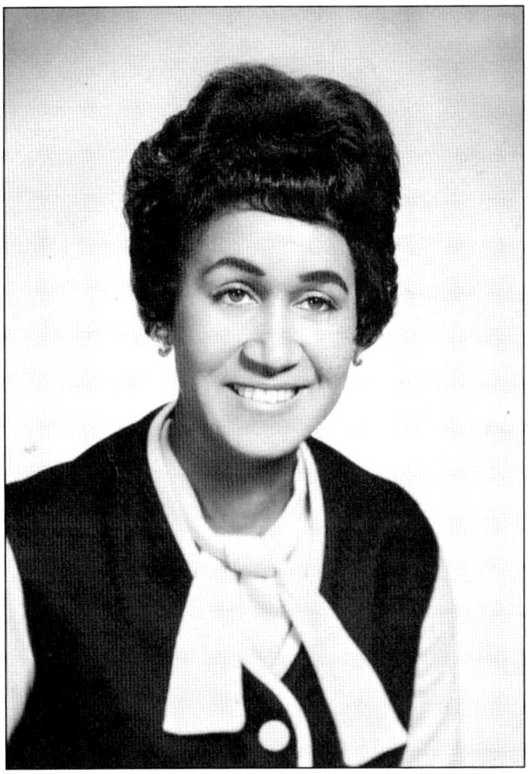

Mme Cherron P. Miller taught French to the junior high school students at Dunleith Community School. The female students especially admired her. She was noted for dressing in the latest fashions. Madame Miller was a teacher who was disciplined and also a mentor to students. She is pictured in the mid-1960s.

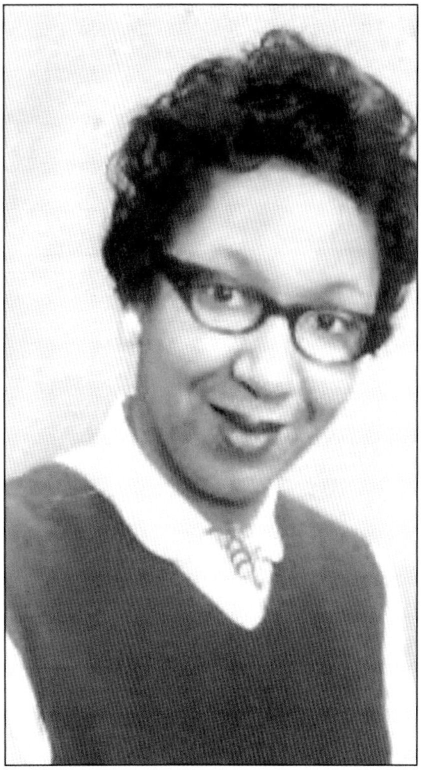

Erma Boyer taught science to the junior-high students at Dunleith Community School. She was known as a no-nonsense teacher. Her classroom resembled a miniature science lab. She is pictured here in the early 1960s.

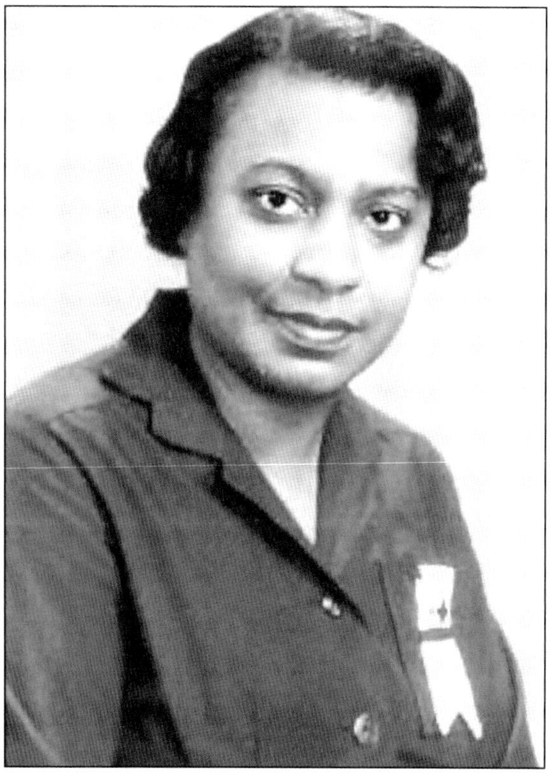

Dorothy Morgan was a school nurse at the Dunleith Community School. She is pictured in the mid-1960s.

This is a picture of Ruth Neal Dixon, who was a first-grade teacher during the 1950s and 1960s.

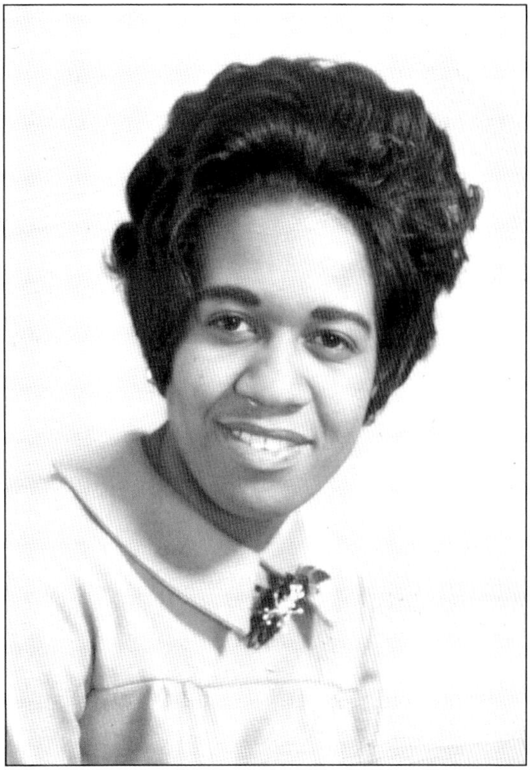

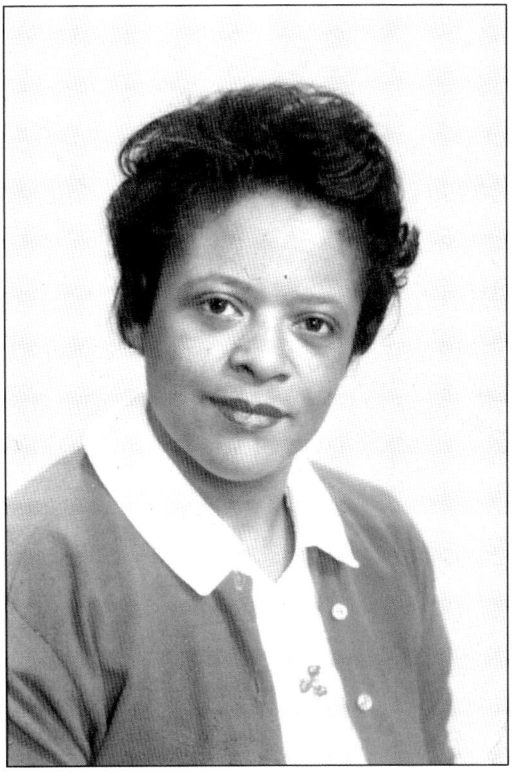

Delores Jerry, pictured here in the early 1960s, was the cafeteria supervisor. Ms. Jerry was known for her delicious, homemade baked goods. Many students purchased weekly meal tickets that were punched after they went through the lunch line. Children who could not afford the $1.25 tickets ate free lunches.

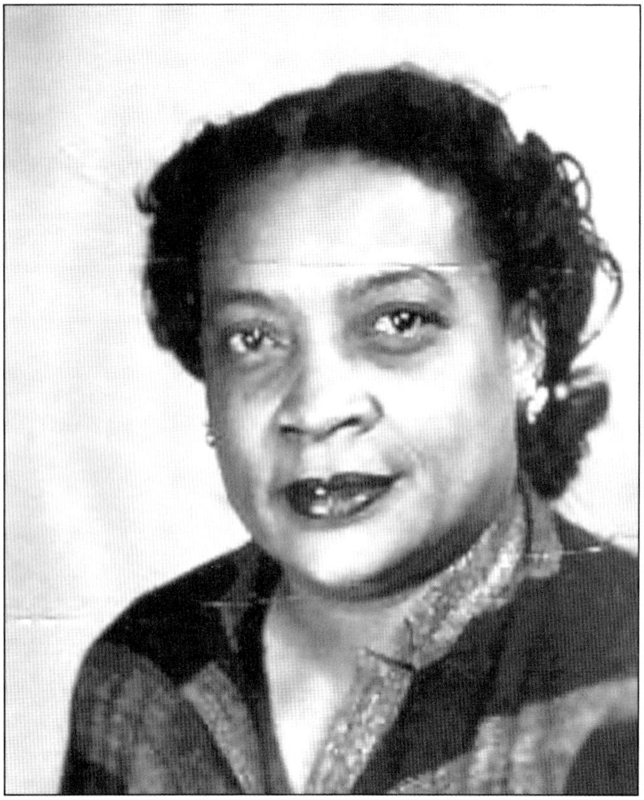

Eleanor B. Tiggs taught the third grade and instructed students how to write in cursive. Students were placed in groups according to their writing abilities. This picture of Ms. Tiggs dates from the 1950s.

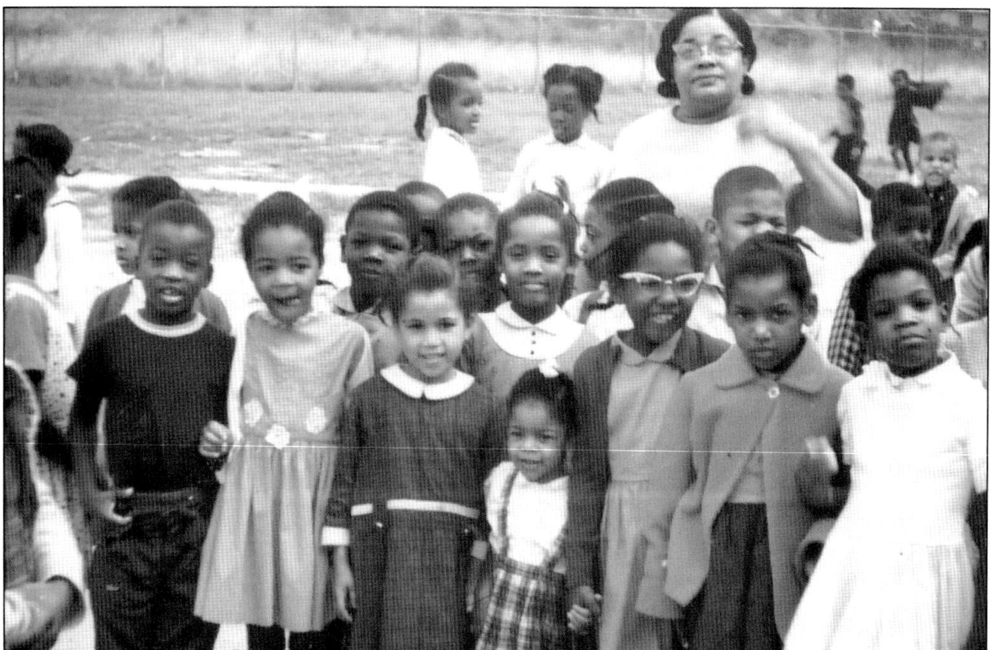

This is a picture of Marian Beaujon with her first-grade students in the 1960s. She was like a mother hen with all of her baby chicks gathered around her. Beaujon nurtured her students.

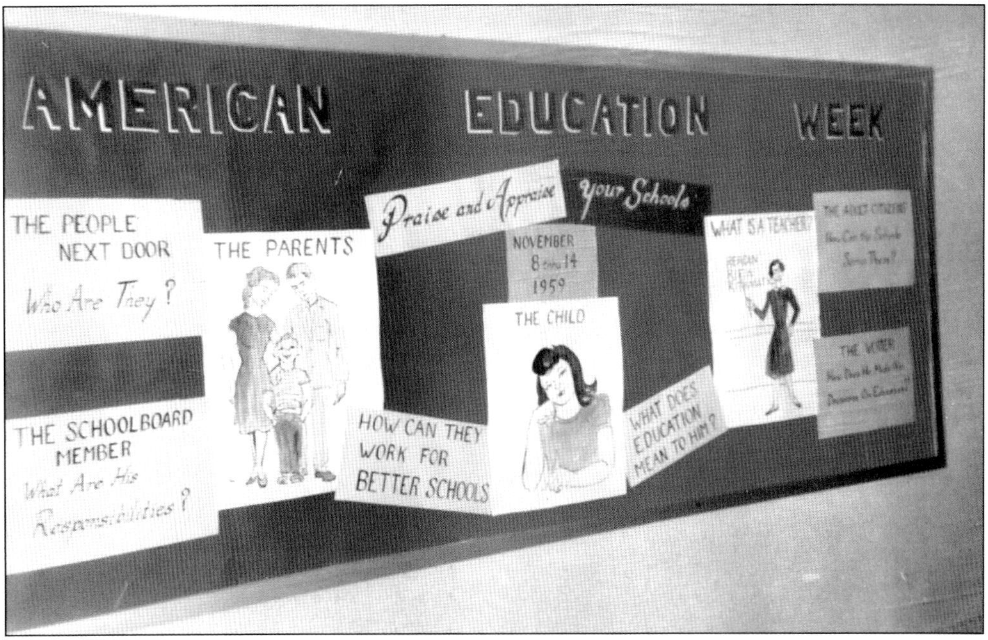

Here is Florence Foddrell's home economics class during American Education Week in the 1960s. Her class was larger than the average classroom in the school. The room had space for a dozen sewing machines, irons, ironing boards, and fabric cutting tables. The room had a sitting room that resembled a home living room for students to relax in. The other half of the room contained an over-sized kitchen with cooking equipment, sinks, and refrigerators. (Florence Foddrell collection.)

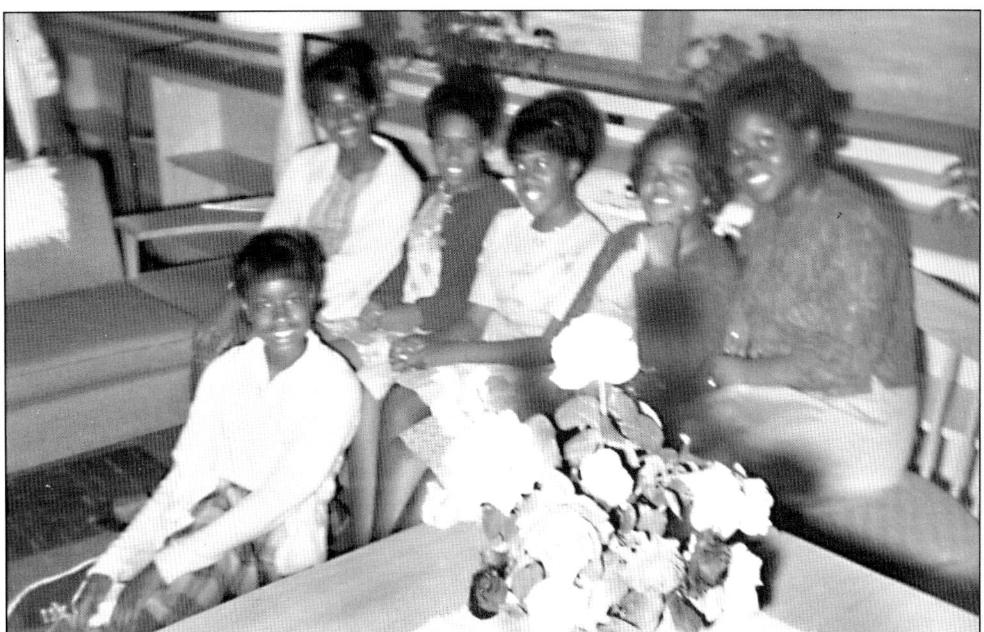

Mrs. Foddrell's home economics students are shown here in the 1960s in an area of the room that resembled a home living room. (Florence Foddrell collection.)

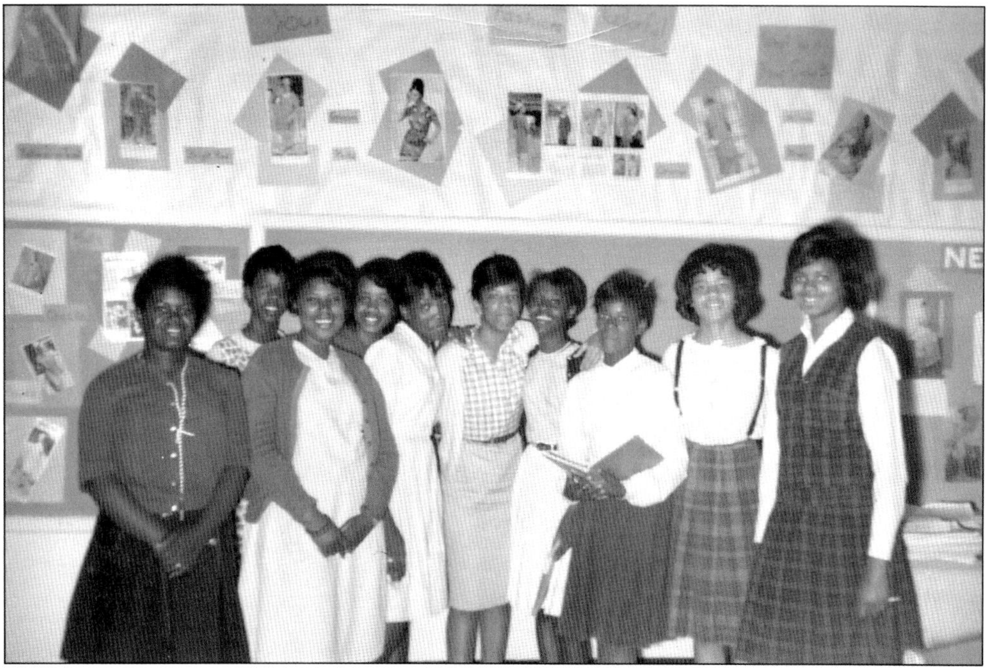

Students in a seventh-grade sewing class in the early 1960s are (from left to right) unidentified, Darlene Congo, Patricia Butler, Hariett Davis, Barbara Kilgoe, Betty Roberts, Mary Harley, Sara Cottman, Vicky Perkins, and Cenobia Stokes. (Florence Foddrell collection.)

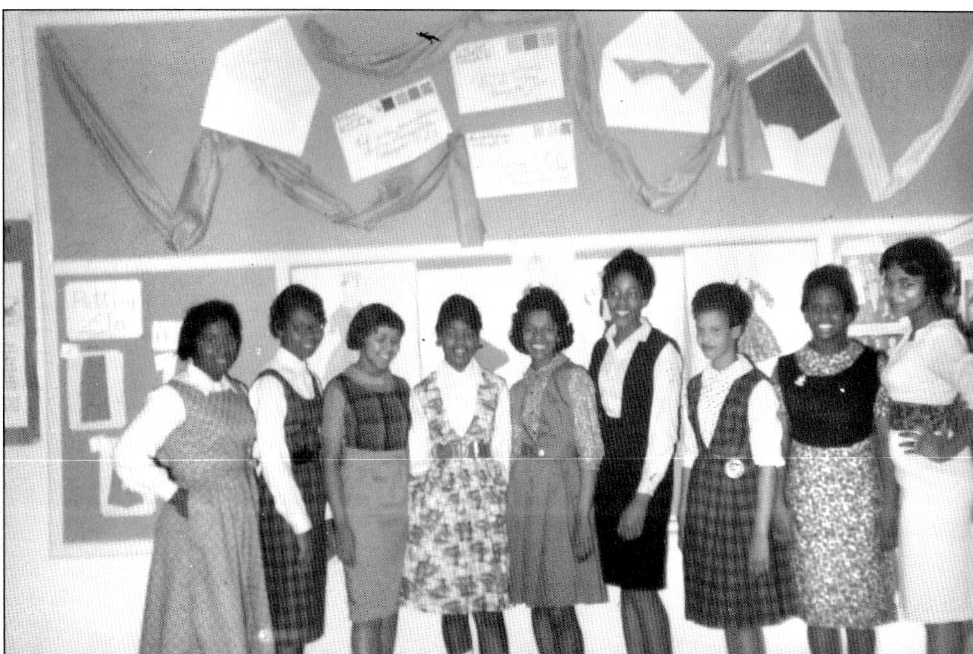

This is a picture of a 1960s upper-class sewing class showing off their dresses. From left to right are Tanya Torrence, Beverly Holland, Emma Barnes, Clara Thomas, Maureen Sims, Loretta Young, Joanne Butler, Arlene Wilson, and Kathleen Bractor. (Florence Foddrell collection.)

Emma Barnes (left) and Shirley Corbin show off their new, handmade suits in the early 1960s. (Florence Foddrell collection.)

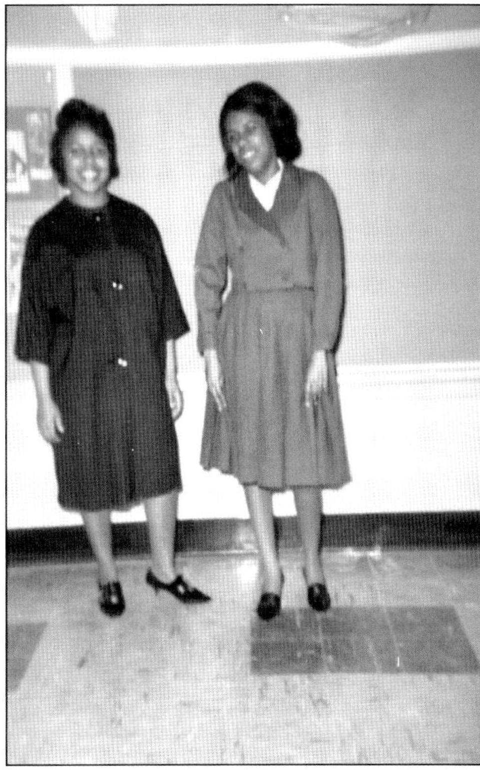

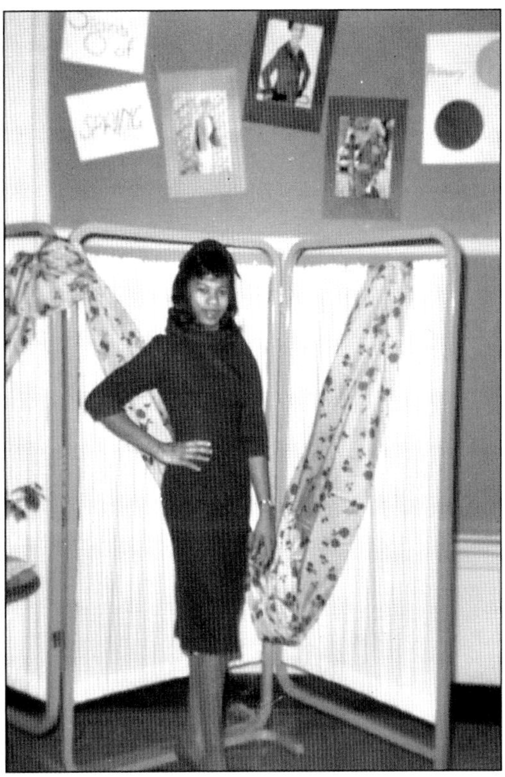

Margarite Quinn was a first-class 1960s teenage model. (Florence Foddrell collection.)

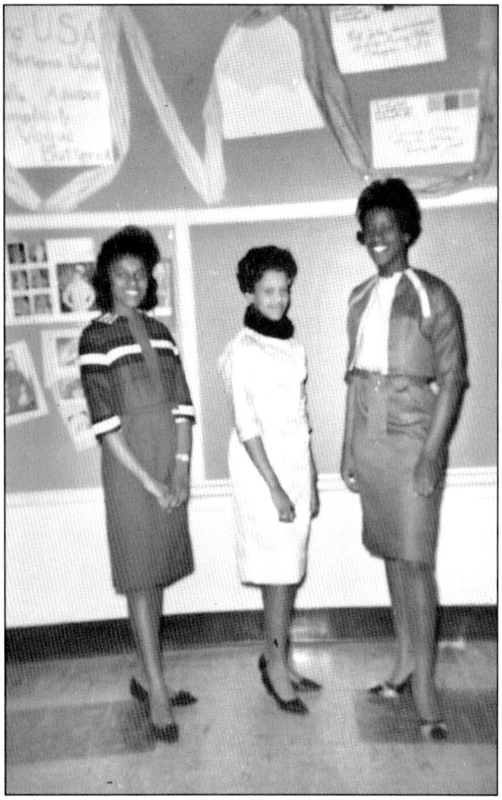

Maureen Sims (left), JoAnn Butler (center), and Brenda Brown were the talk of the fashion show in their outfits. They are pictured in the early 1960s. (Florence Foddrell collection.)

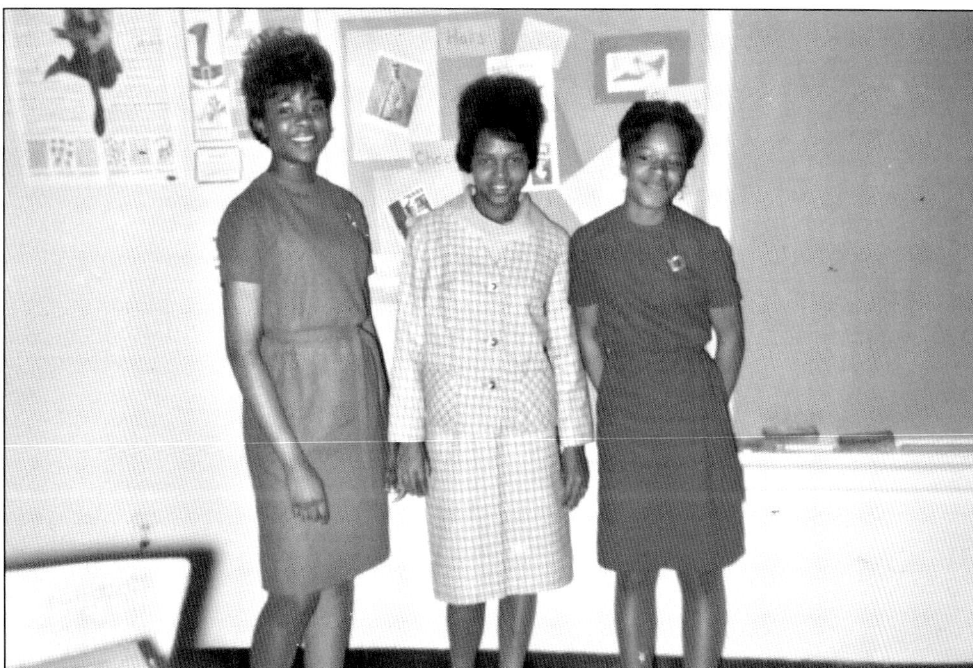

Ernestine Banks (left), Mary Barnes (center), and Joan Thompson sewed fantastic outfits in the early 1960s. (Florence Foddrell collection.)

This is a picture of neighbors and schoolmates Mark Howard (left), Rob Perkins (center), and Herb Everett on their way to school in the 1970s.

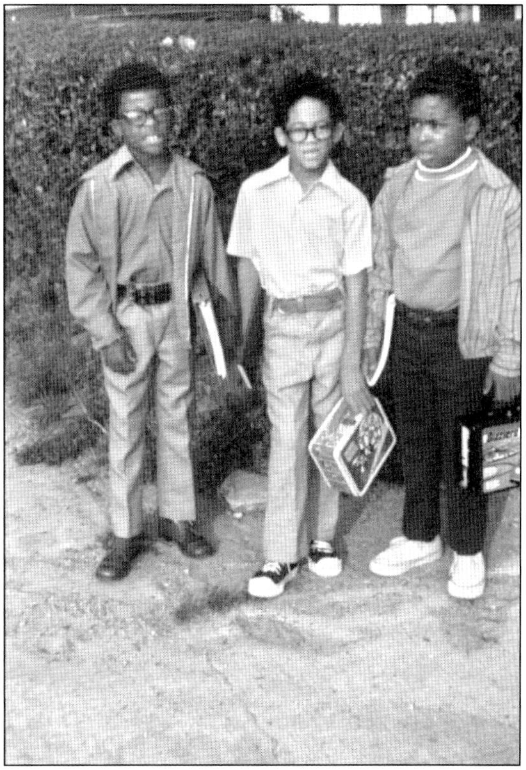

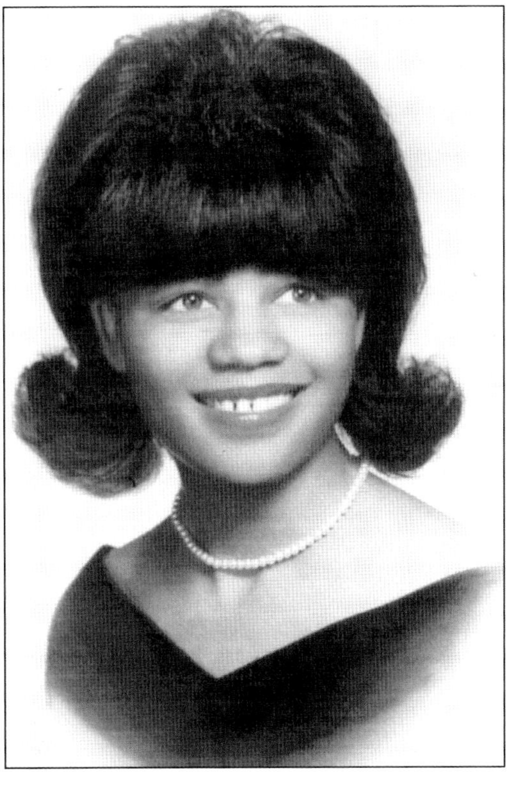

Pictured here is Vicky Perkins. She was the first African American nominated from the Dunleith community to run for homecoming queen in the DeLaWarr School District in 1967.

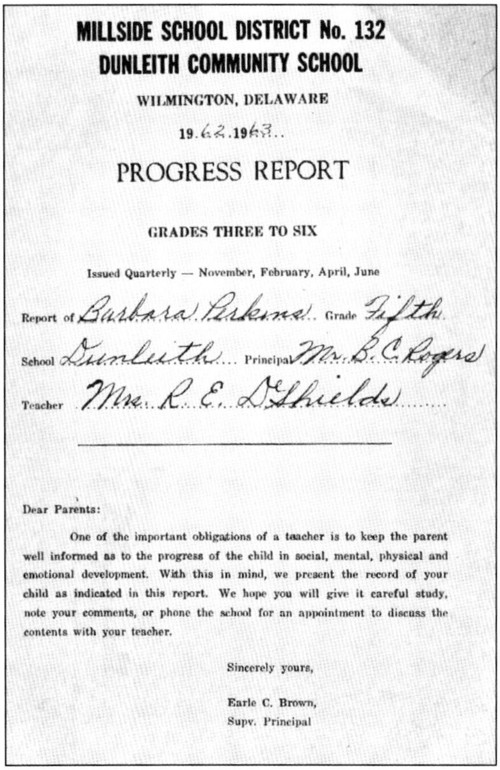

MILLSIDE SCHOOL DISTRICT No. 132
DUNLEITH COMMUNITY SCHOOL

WILMINGTON, DELAWARE

19.62.1963..

PROGRESS REPORT

GRADES THREE TO SIX

Issued Quarterly — November, February, April, June

Report of Barbara Perkins Grade Fifth

School Dunleith Principal Mr. B. C. Rogers

Teacher Mrs. R. E. DeShields

Dear Parents:

One of the important obligations of a teacher is to keep the parent well informed as to the progress of the child in social, mental, physical and emotional development. With this in mind, we present the record of your child as indicated in this report. We hope you will give it careful study, note your comments, or phone the school for an appointment to discuss the contents with your teacher.

Sincerely yours,

Earle C. Brown,
Supv. Principal

This is an original report card from the Dunleith Community School. The school districts were segregated in the 1960s.

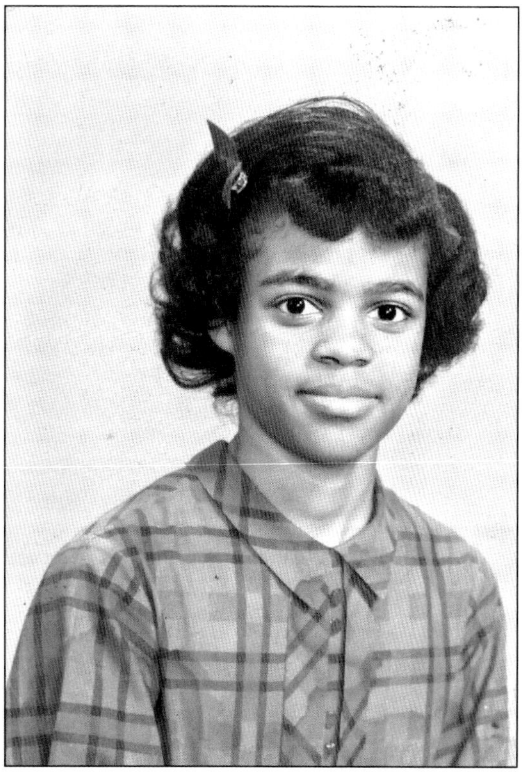

Barbara Perkins was a conscientious student when she was in the fifth grade in the early 1960s.

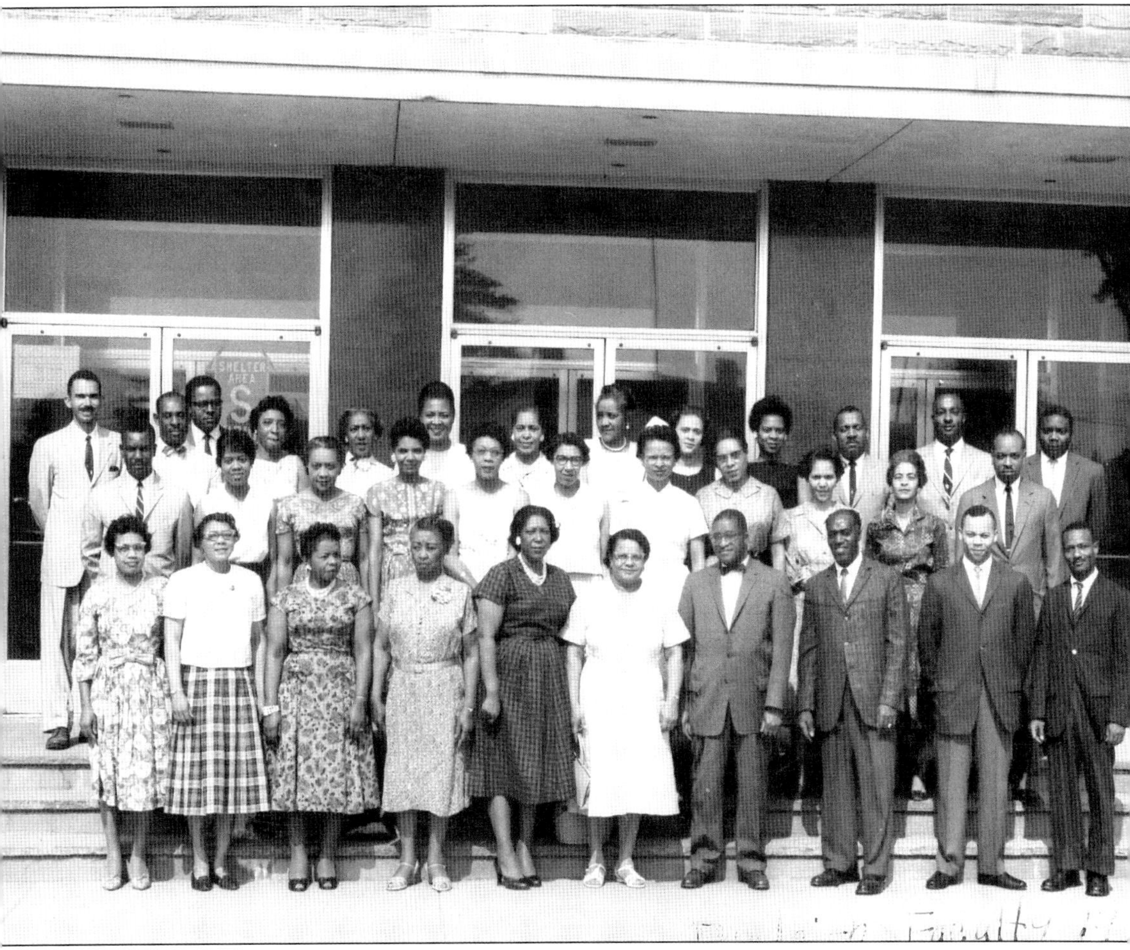

The Dunleith Community School faculty in the early 1960s was, from left to right, (first row) Ruth Brown, Menthal B. Watkins, Maude Evans, Ethel C. Jackson, Bernice Horner, Marian Beaujon, Earl C. Brown (principal), Benjamin Rogers (assistant principal), Frank Purnell, and William Shipley; (second row) Raymond Woodward, Ruth Neal Dixon, Eleanor B. Tiggs, Lillian Quarles, Marjorie Priest, Erma Boyer, Mary Q. Brown, Edith Pridgen, Harriett Seldon, Betty Hunt, and Victor Smith; (third row) Hilmar Jensen, Gilbert Jackson, Mr. Hayes, Gloria Wilson, Hannah Johnson, Doris Riley, Reba DeShields, Margaret C. West, unidentified, Litilia Braxton, Patrick Walker, Joseph Threadgill, and William Carr. (Margaret C. West collection.)

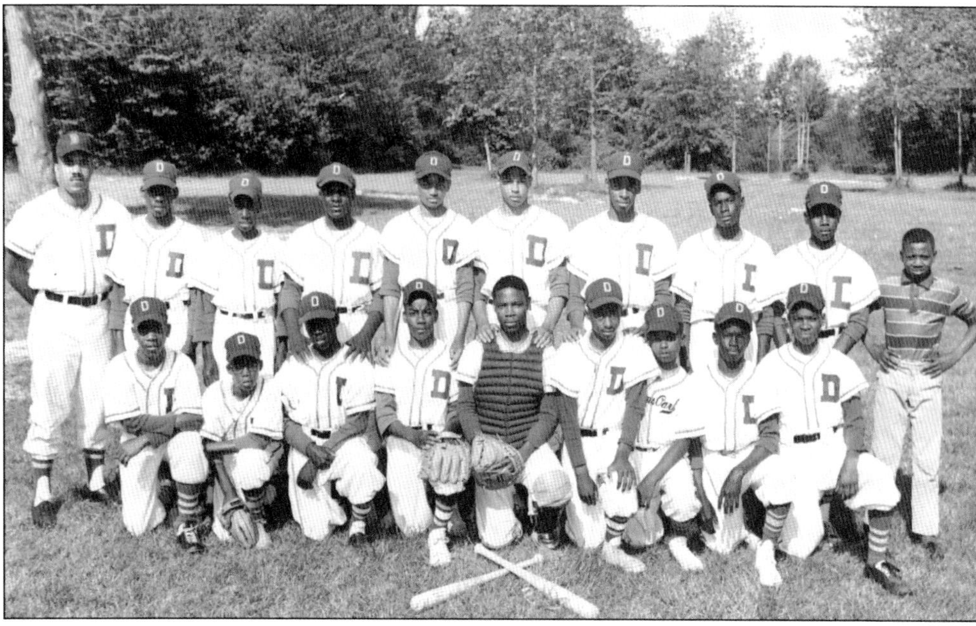

Mr. Wilbert "Bunny" Miller and his Dunleith Community School baseball team of the 1960s included, from left to right, (first row) Robert Thomas, Luther Carnes, Roland Conquest, Leo Parker, Donald Jones, Harry Jackson, Elbert Butler, Tyrone Wilson, and Charles Wilson; (second row) Bunny Miller, Charles Bowers, John Surratte, James DeShields, Otis Hightower, Lacy Jackson, Joe Rykard, Peter Carter, Norman Grinnage, and Marvin Prophet.

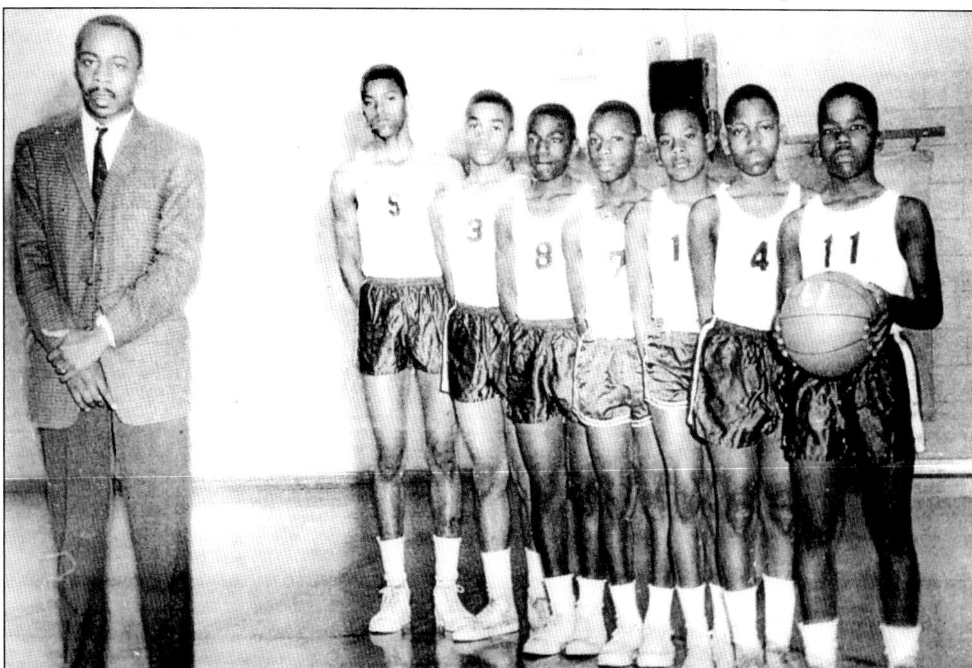

This is a picture of Mr. Eugene Stallings and the 1960s basketball team. From left to right are E. Stallings (coach), Joey Williams, D. Collins, Ernest Norman, B. Lee, Lester Dickerson, Wilbert Braxton, and Herman Thornton. The junior varsity record shows they won six and lost zero.

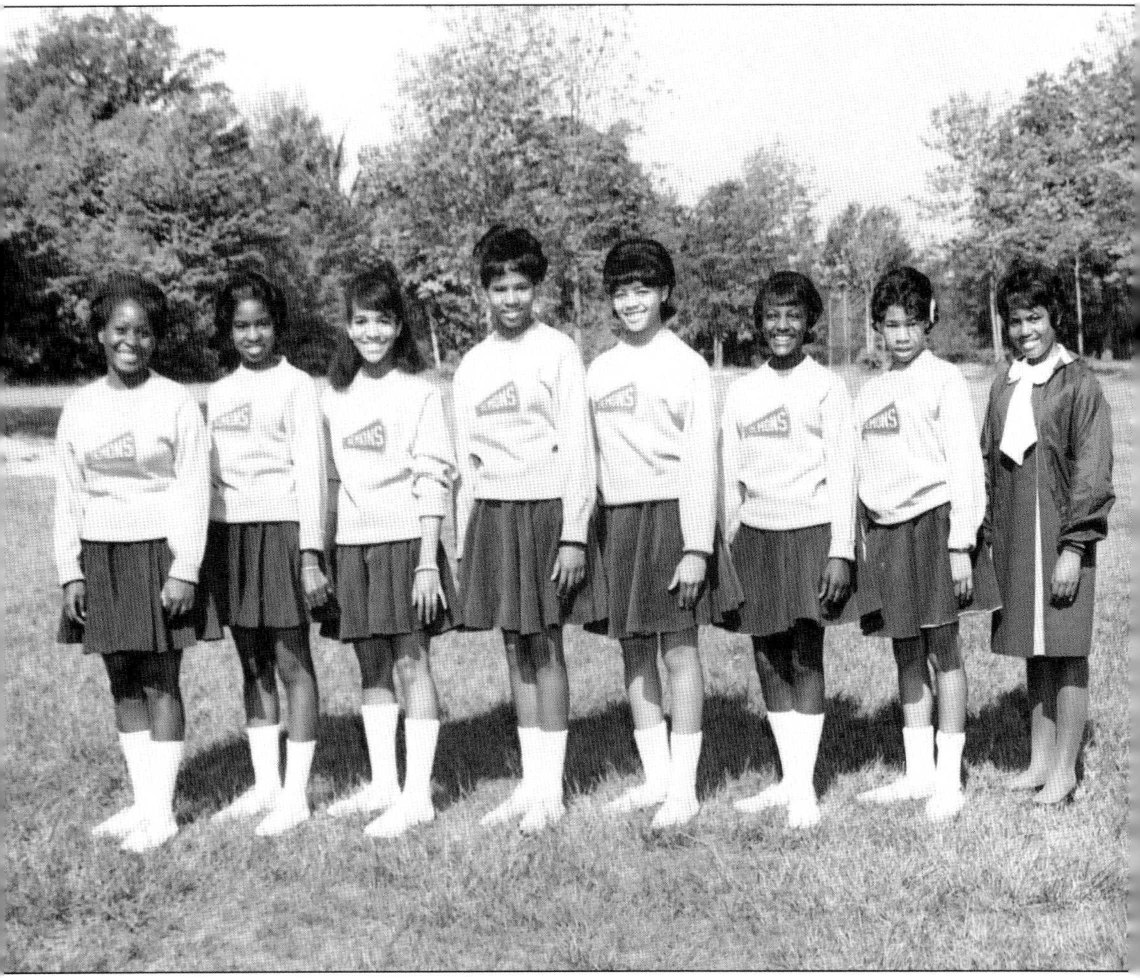

The Dunleith cheerleaders from the early 1960s are, from left to right, Claudette DeShields, Brenda Orr, Linda Holland, Sharon Johnson, Vicky Perkins, Brenda Emory, Cathy Quinn, and Linda Woodard.

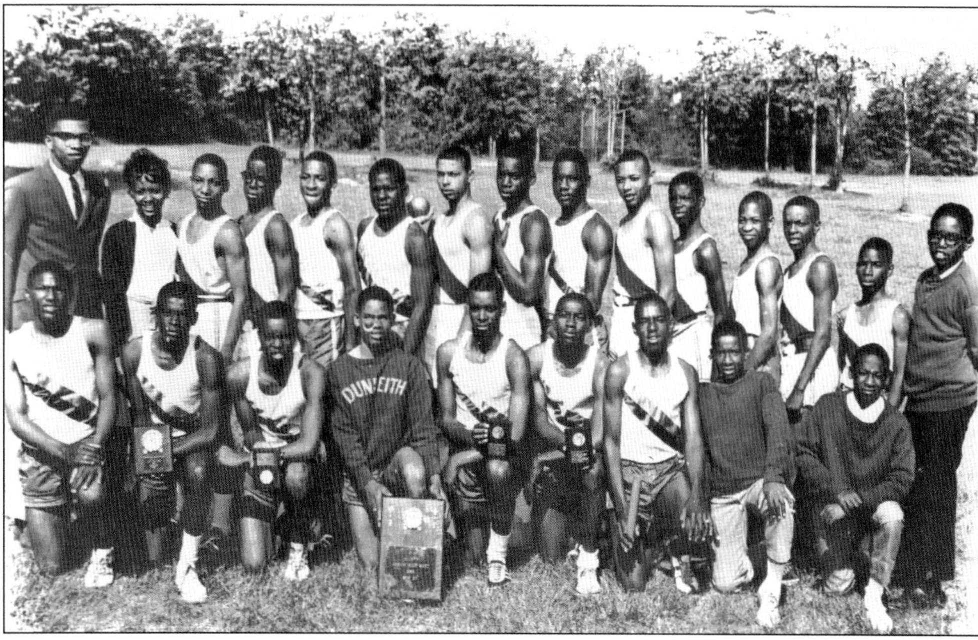

Members of this early 1960s Dunleith track team are, from left to right, (first row) Winfield Cunningham, Peter Carter, Sylvester Howard, Bill Jackson, Joe Rykard, Ben Prophet, Theodore Torrance, Alonzo Mosley, and Carl Lucas; (second row) Sy Williams, Mary Harley, Louis Laws, Ernest Moody, David Mosley, James DeShields, Lacy Jackson, Theodore Gregory, Cecil Williams, Norris Milburn, Millard Howard, Clarence Dickerson, Arnold Tucker, Rourke Moore, and Frank Spencer.

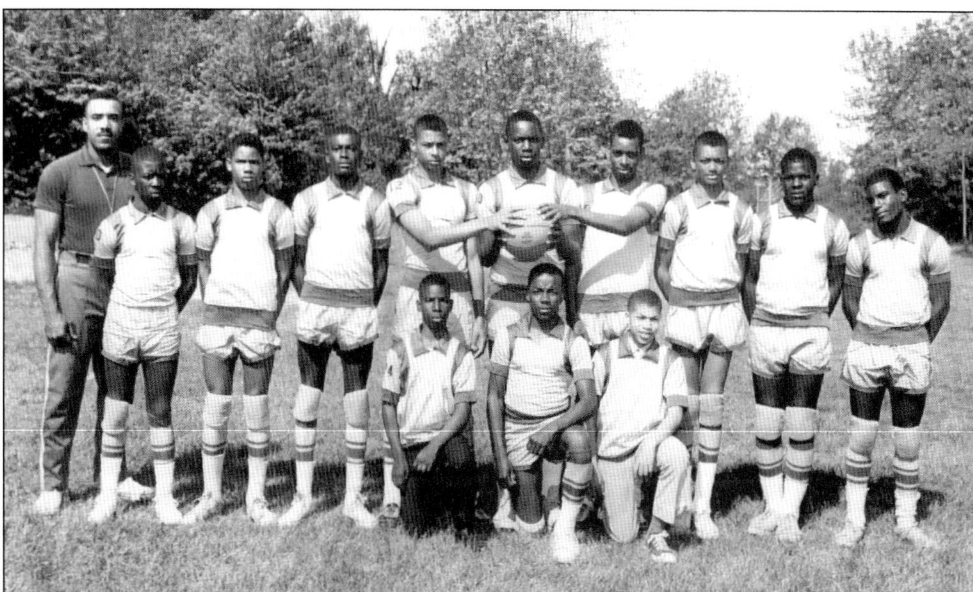

Coach Wilbert "Bunny" Miller poses here with his basketball team in the 1960s. From left to right are (first row) Rourke Moore, Leo Parker, and Norman Moyer; (second row) Roland Conquest, William Jackson, Peter Carter, Lacy Jackson, Theodore Gregory, Joe Rykard, Otis Hightower, James DeShields, Charles Bowers. (Henrietta Nelson collection.)

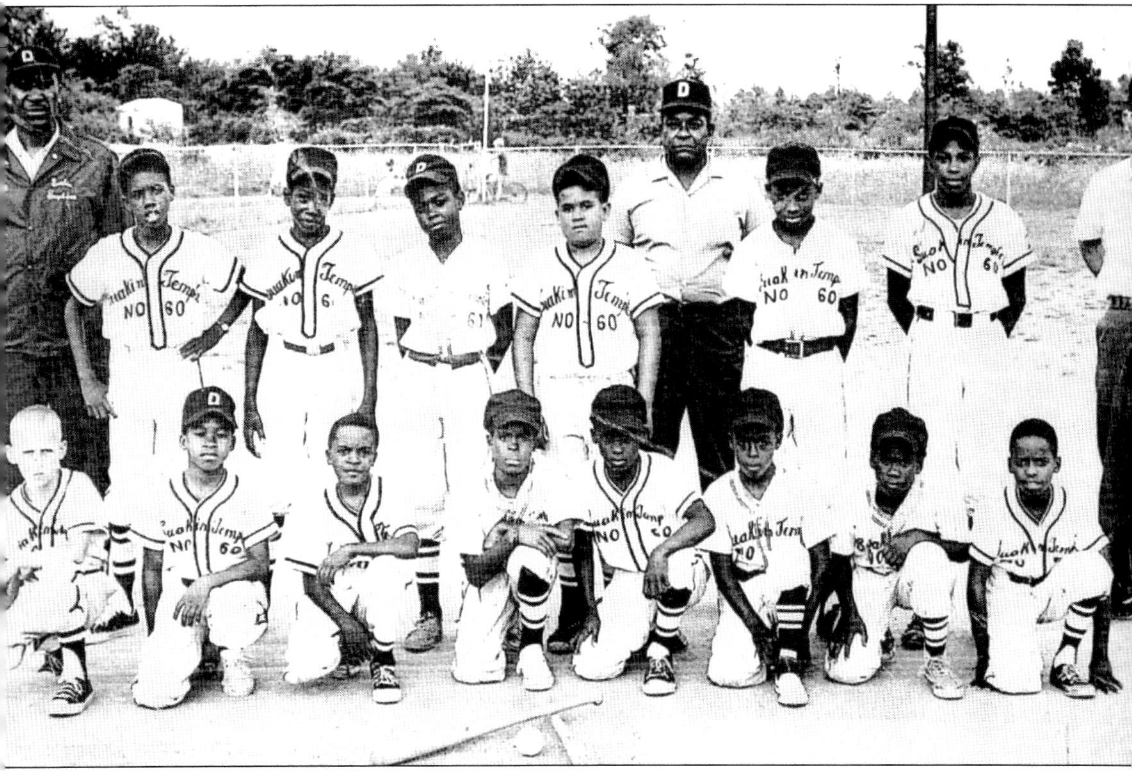

Pictured here is coach John Surratte (far left) and the Dunleith Community School baseball team of the early 1970s. In memory of Mr. Surratte, the Dunleith Community Park on Bethune Drive was named Surratte Park. The players are unidentified.

DUNLEITH COMMUNITY SCHOOL PERSONNEL

Administrative Staff

Supervising Principal .... Mr. Earle C. Brown
Vice Principal .... Mr. Benjamin C. Rogers

Junior High Faculty

Mrs. Erma K. Boyer	Hilmar L. Jensen
Wilbur R. Carr	Frank E. Purnell
Mrs. Florence J. Foddrell	Miss Cherron Pindell
James A. Hayes	Robert W. Shipley, Jr.
Gilbert H. Jackson, Jr.	Victor W. Smith
Mrs. Luetilla M. Lambert	Patrick H. Walker, Jr.
Miss Selene McIntyre	William L. Wallace

Elementary Faculty

Mrs. Rocelia Allen	Mrs. Edith H. Pridgen
Miss Marion Beaujon	Mrs. Marjorie M. Priest
Mrs. Annie R. Brown	Mrs. Harriett Seldon
Mrs. Reba DeShields	Mrs. Eleanor Tiggs
Mrs. Verdella R. Fason	Mrs. Menthal B. Watkins
Mrs. Bernice Horner	Mrs. Margaret C. West
Mrs. Elizabeth Hunt	Miss Gloria Wilson
Mrs. Hannah Johnson	Raymond Woodard
Miss Ruth Neal	Joseph T. Threadgill
Mrs. Maude Evans	

School Nurse

Mrs. Mary Q. Brown

Secretarial Staff

Mrs. Arlene B. Cooke — Mrs. Jacqueline E. Roberts
Mrs. Delores W. Edmonds

GRADUATION EXERCISES

OF THE

DUNLEITH COMMUNITY SCHOOL

MONDAY EVENING, JUNE 12, 1961

8:00 o'clock

This is a picture of the Dunleith Community School graduation program in 1961. The names listed are of the Dunleith Community School faculty.

PROGRAM

Processional* .... Class of 1961
Dunleith Community School Band
William Wallace, Director

Invocation .... Rev. Maurice Moyer
Community Presbyterian Church

Welcome Address .... Margaret Dixon

Selection .... Dunleith Chorus
Rocelia Allen, Director

Student Speaker .... Jacqueline Francis

Selection .... Chorus

Presentation of Class .... Victor Smith
Chairman, Junior High School

Presentation of Certificates .... Lorin P. Hunt
Chairman, Board of Trustees, Dunleith Community School

Farewell Address .... Patricia Dillard

Presentation of Class Gift .... Michael Doran
Class President

Remarks .... Earle C. Brown
Supervising Principal, Dunleith Community School

Selection .... Chorus

Benediction .... Rev. Maurice Moyer

Recessional* .... Class of 1961

*Audience will please remain seated

CLASS OF 1961

Alston, Nathan	Berry, Francis
Brooks, Curtis	Booker, Letitia
Brown, Ernest	Britt, Barbara
Brown, Willie	Burton, Theodora
Brunson, Moses	Carnes, Delores
Carter, Thomas	Butler, Lauretta
DeShields, George	Collins, Marion
Dixon, Lonnie	Corbin, Peggy
Doran, Michael	Conyer, Gwendolyn
Emory, Charles	Cunningham, Phyllis
Gillis, Chester	Davis, Vivian
Harley, Albert	Dillard, Patricia
Hyland, James	Dixon, Margaret
Kilgoe, Charles	Duckery, Linda
Kilgoe, Frank	Eubanks, Margaret
King, Eugene	*Francis, Jacqueline
Lanier, Daniel	Green, Alzetta
Mathis, Autry	Howard, Emma
Matthews, Clifton	Jones, Kathleen
McCurdy, Anthony	Johnson, Florence
Meredith, William	Palmer, Ruth
Orr, William	Phillips, Ramona
Roberts, Oliver	Ridgeway, Jacqueline
Roberts, Tyrone	Roy, Lois
Simmons, James	Smith, Doris
Shoffner, Waymond	Thomas, Barbara
Barnhart, Oretha	Torrence, Mary

*With highest honors

CLASS SPONSORS

Mrs. Luetilla Lambert — Patrick H. Walker, Jr.

CLASS MOTTO

Nothing Is Impossible To Him Who Will

This is a picture of the Dunleith graduation program for the class of 1961.

Seven

Family Life

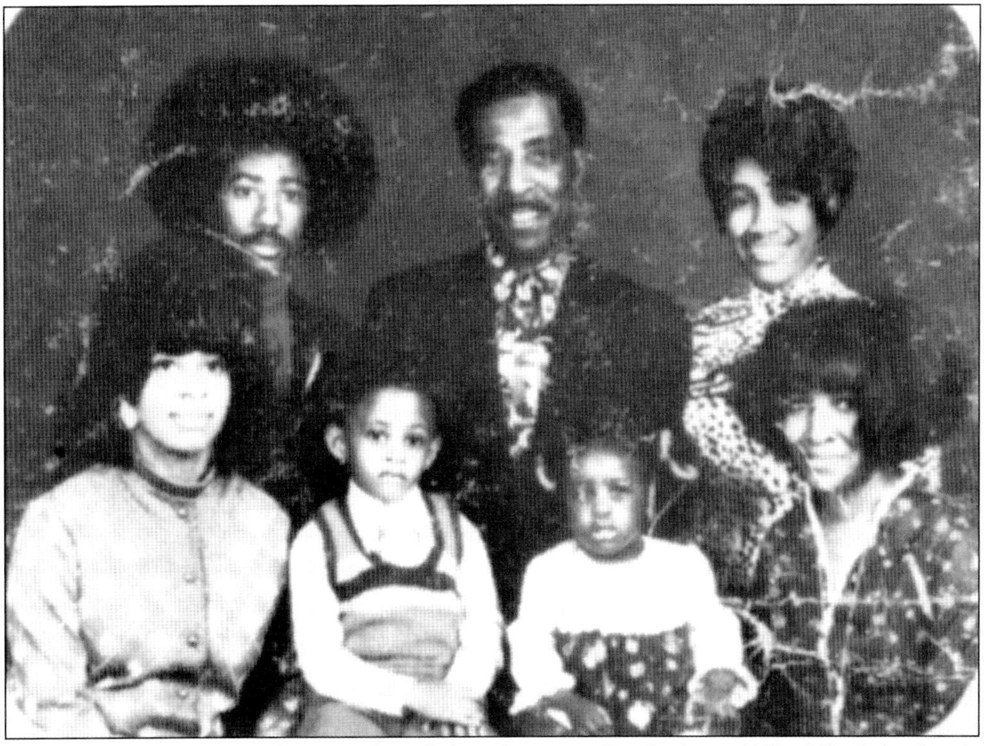

Ernest Sr. and Doris Lambert purchased their home in Dunleith in 1951. All of the family members are pictured from left to right as follows: (standing) Ernest Jr., Ernest Sr., and Doris; (seated) Adonica, Derek, Meiko, and Ruth.

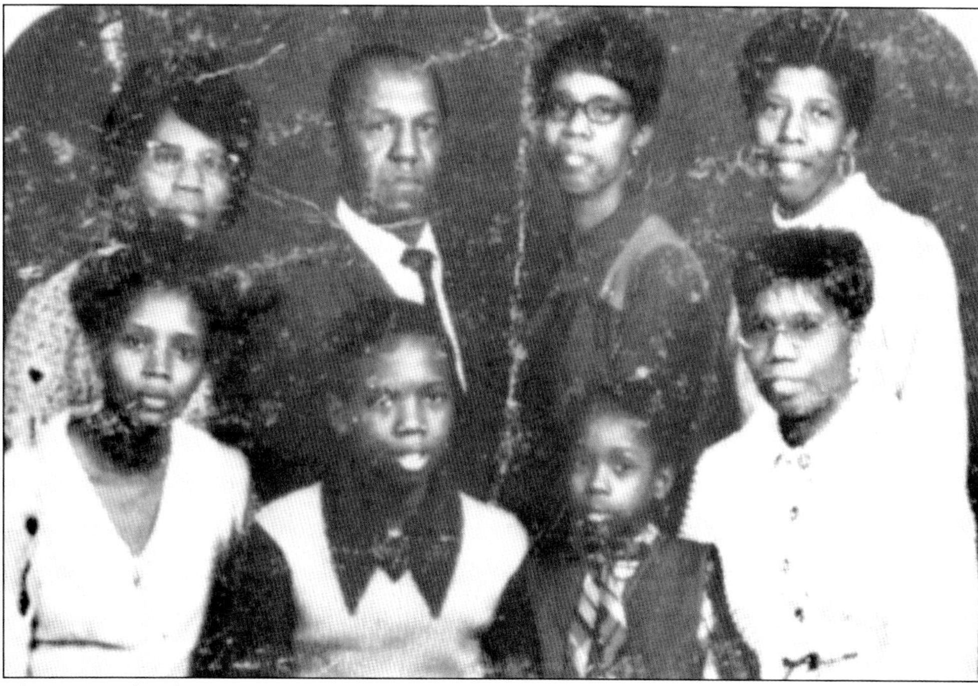

The Congo family, pictured here in the early 1960s, included, from left to right, (first row) Julie, Rudolph Jr., Wendy, and Barbara; (second row) Mrs. Hattie Congo, Rudolph Sr., Darlene, and Virginia. The Congo family lived on Talladega Drive in Dunleith.

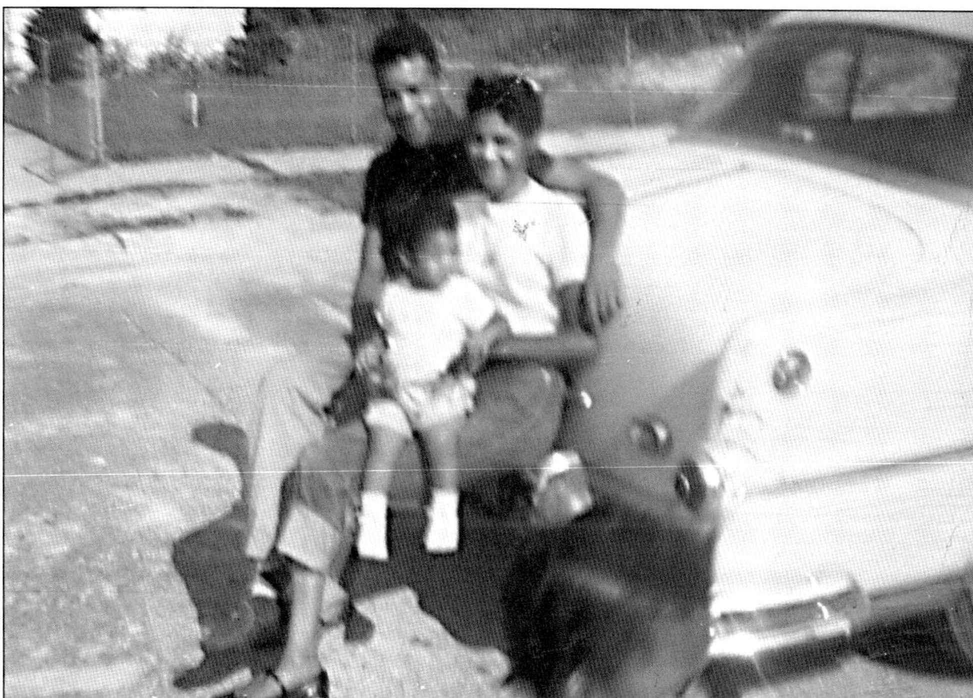

This is a picture of Matthew and Marion Perkins and their son, Timothy, in the early 1950s. The picture was taken on Talladega Drive in front of an unidentified neighbor's home.

Otis and Nettie Hightower moved to Wilmington from Alabama. Mr. Hightower worked for the Purina Company. His wife was a homemaker. Their Dunleith deed was recorded in 1950. This picture was taken in the 1960s.

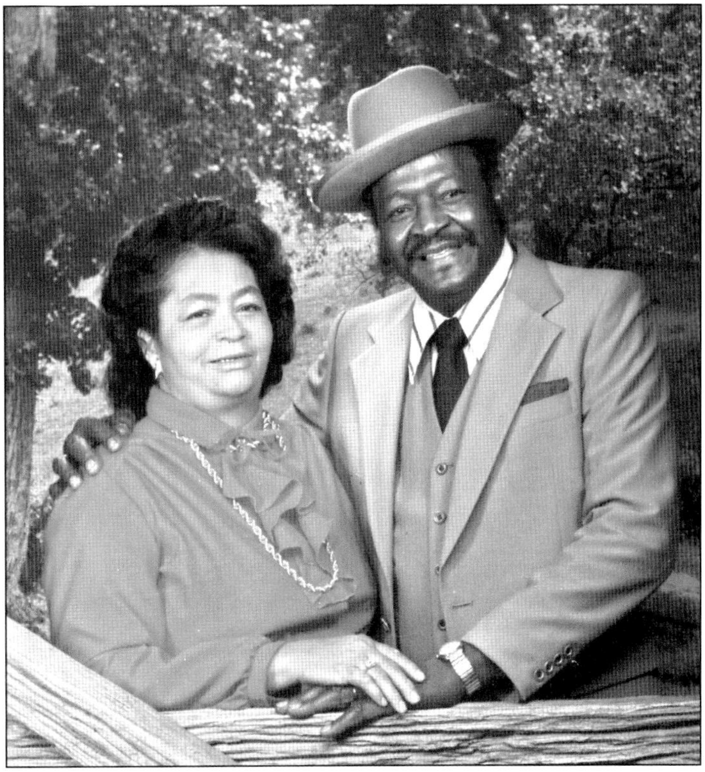

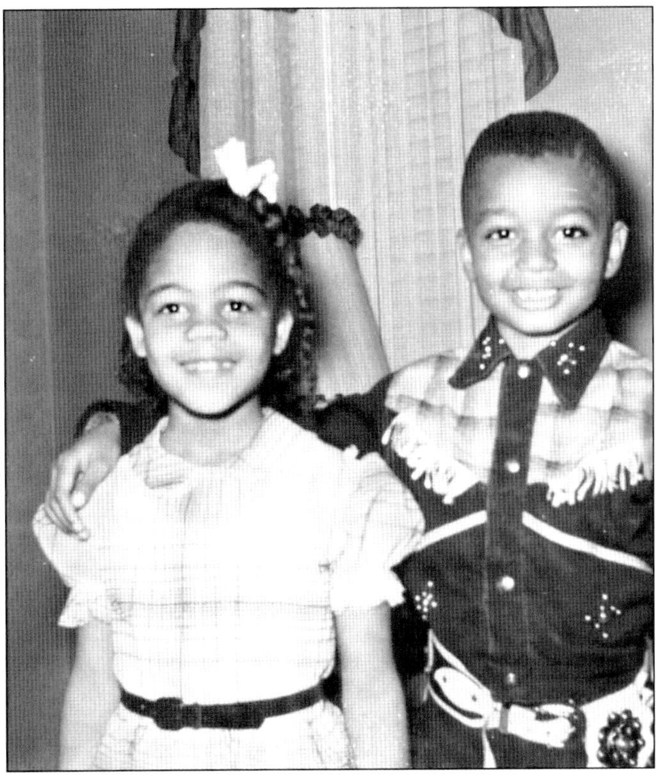

This is an early-1950s picture of Vicky Perkins and Otis Hightower Jr. Otis is dressed in his Hop-a-long Cassidy cowboy outfit. The children were neighbors who lived across the street from each other on Talladega Drive.

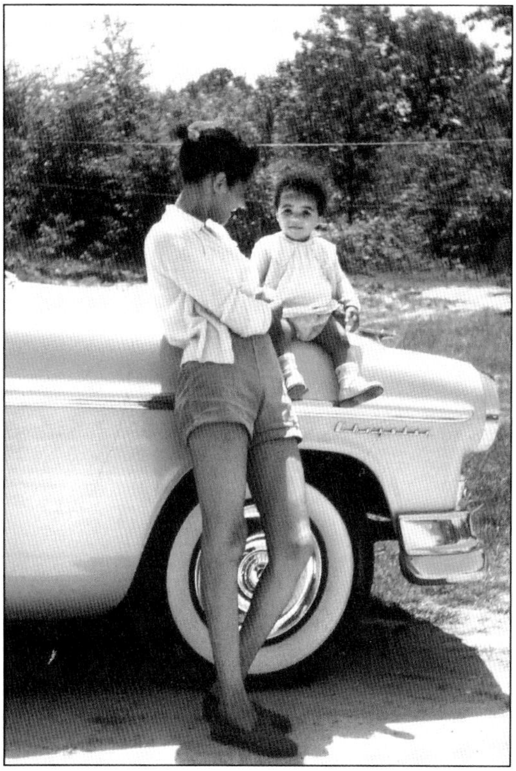

Marion Perkins holds her baby, Lynn, on the fender of their car in their back yard on Talladega Drive in the 1960s.

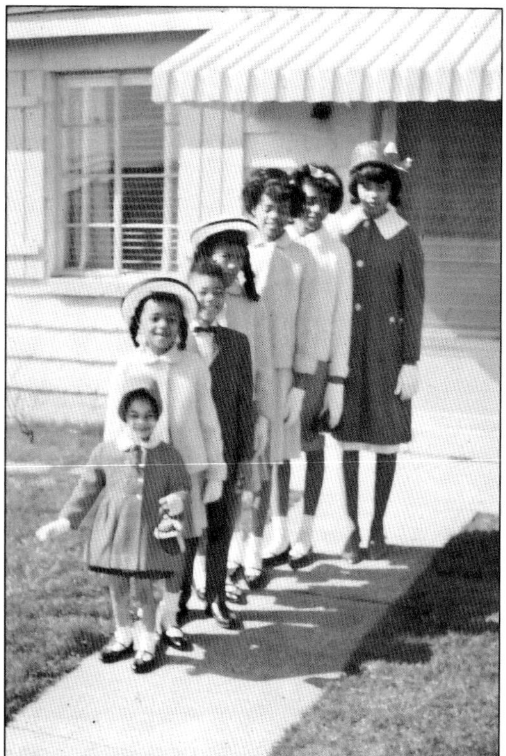

The Perkins children are, from left to right, Sandy, Lynn, Timothy, Joyce, Barbara, Penny, and Vicky. Mr. Perkins took this picture of his children in the early 1960s.

Older sister Lynn Perkins helps Sandra to take some first steps in the 1960s.

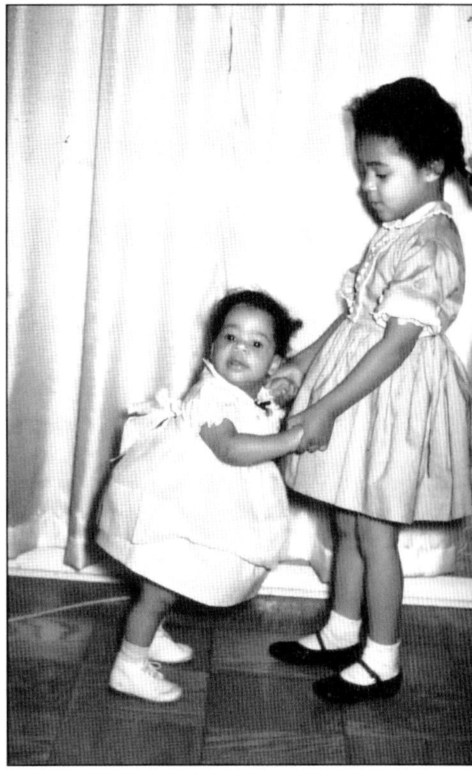

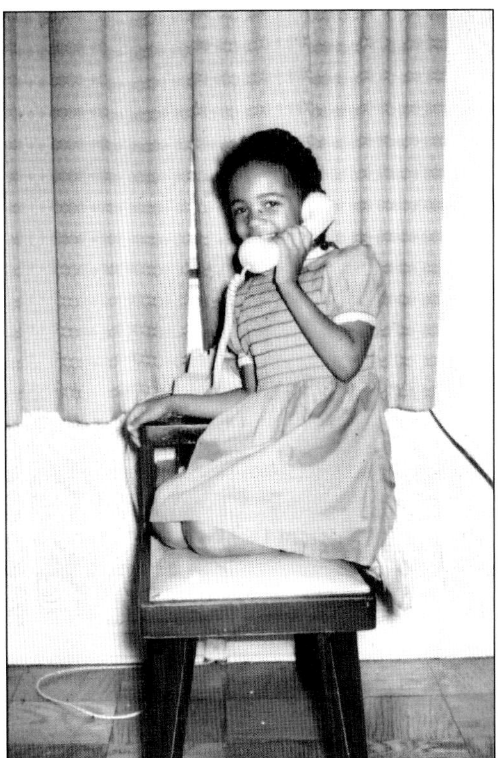

Lynn Perkins enjoys a conversation on her princess phone in the 1960s.

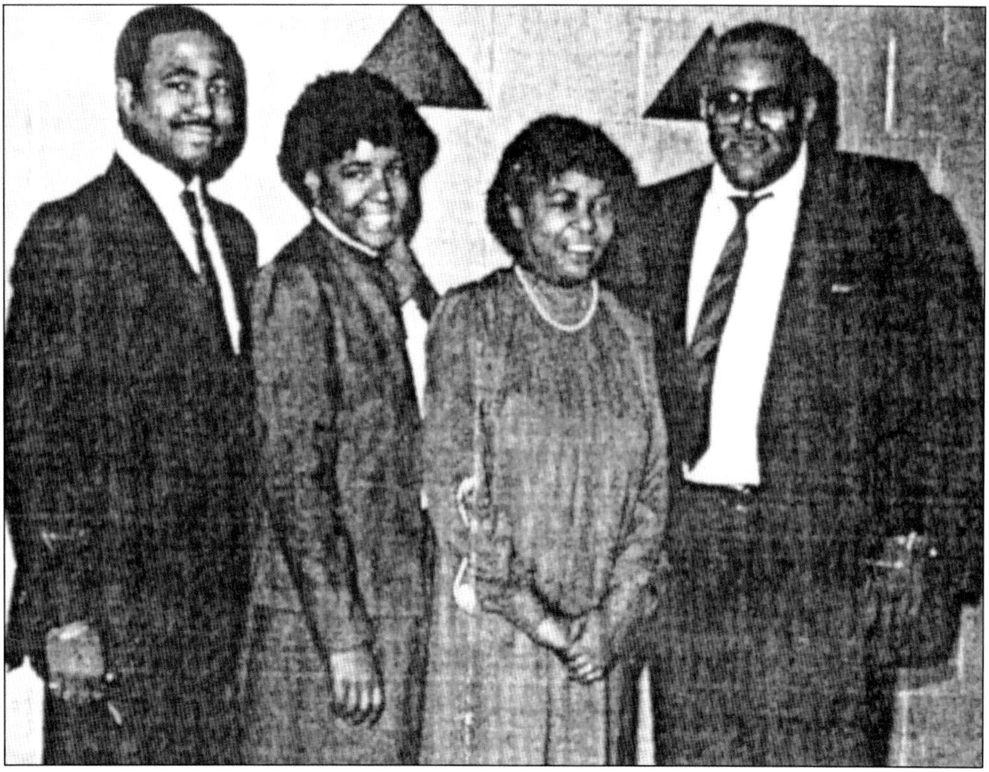

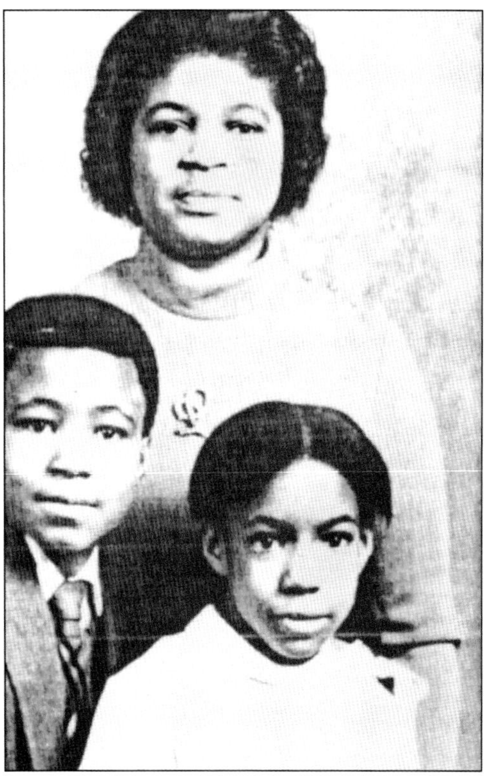

This is a picture of the Cooke family in the 1960s. From left to right are Frank Jr., Paula, Arlene, and Frank Sr. The Cooke family lived on Talladega Drive in Dunleith Estates. Mr. Cooke was employed as a dock worker in a Wilmington shipyard.

Pictured here is Mrs. Arlene Cooke with her children, Frank and Paula. Mrs. Cooke was an administrative secretary at the Dunleith Community School during the 1960s. This picture was taken early in that decade.

Pictured here in the 1950s is George Quarles. Mr. Quarles was a letter carrier for the U.S. Postal Service in Wilmington. George and Hazel Quarles signed the deed for their Dunleith home in 1951. (Hazel Quarles collection.)

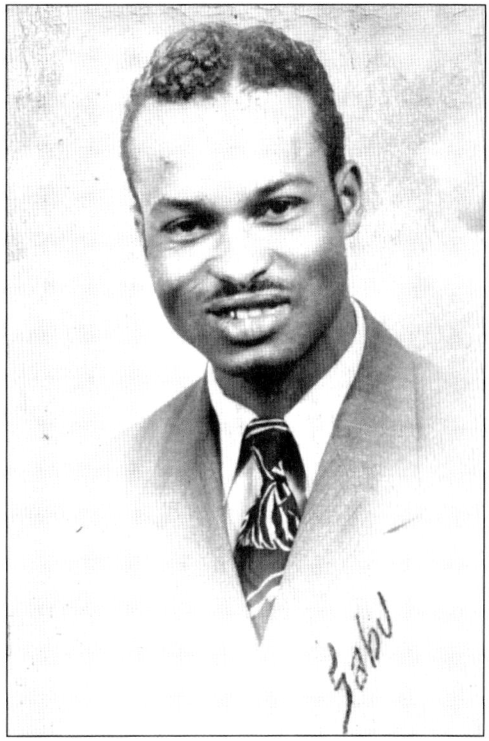

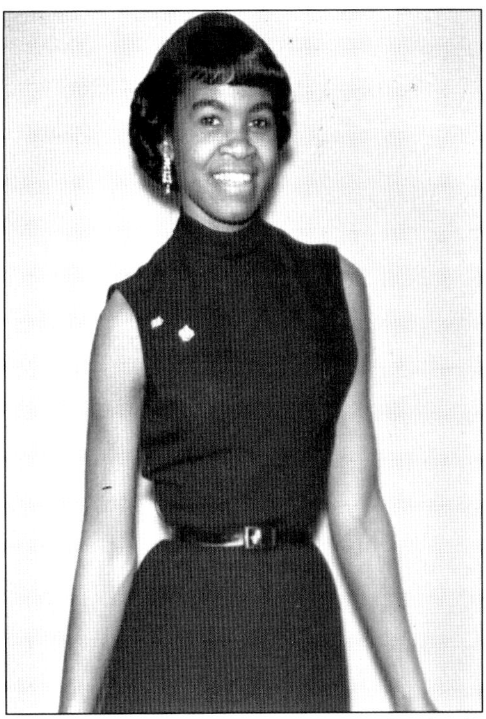

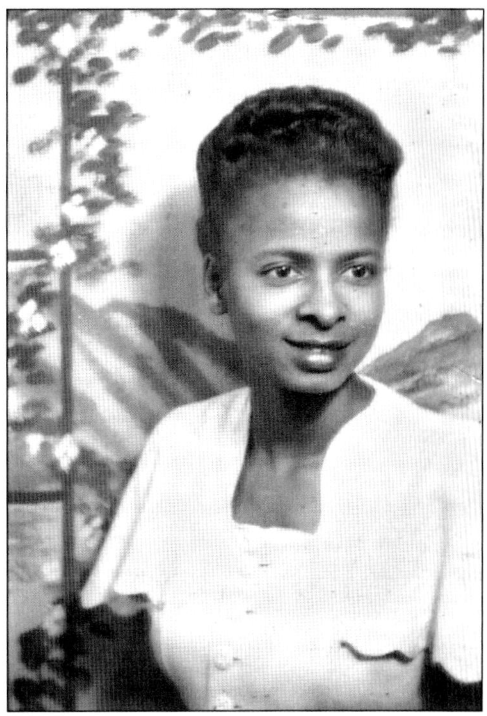

Above left: Pictured here is Mrs. Hazel Tyler-Quarles. (Hazel Quarles collection.)
Above right: Mrs. Mary Quarles Brown was the sister of George Quarles. Both of the above pictures date from the 1950s. (Hazel Quarles collection.)

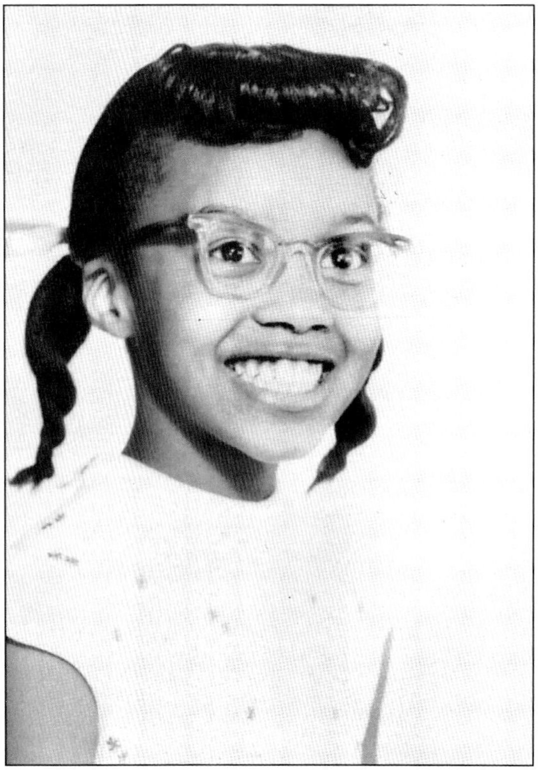

This is a picture of Sheena Quarles in the 1950s. (Hazel Quarles collection.)

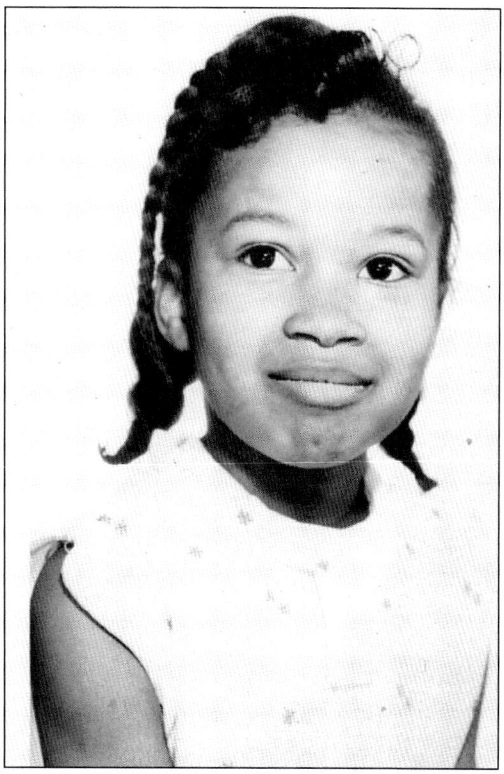

Zorveda Quarles is pictured here in the 1950s. (Hazel Quarles collection.)

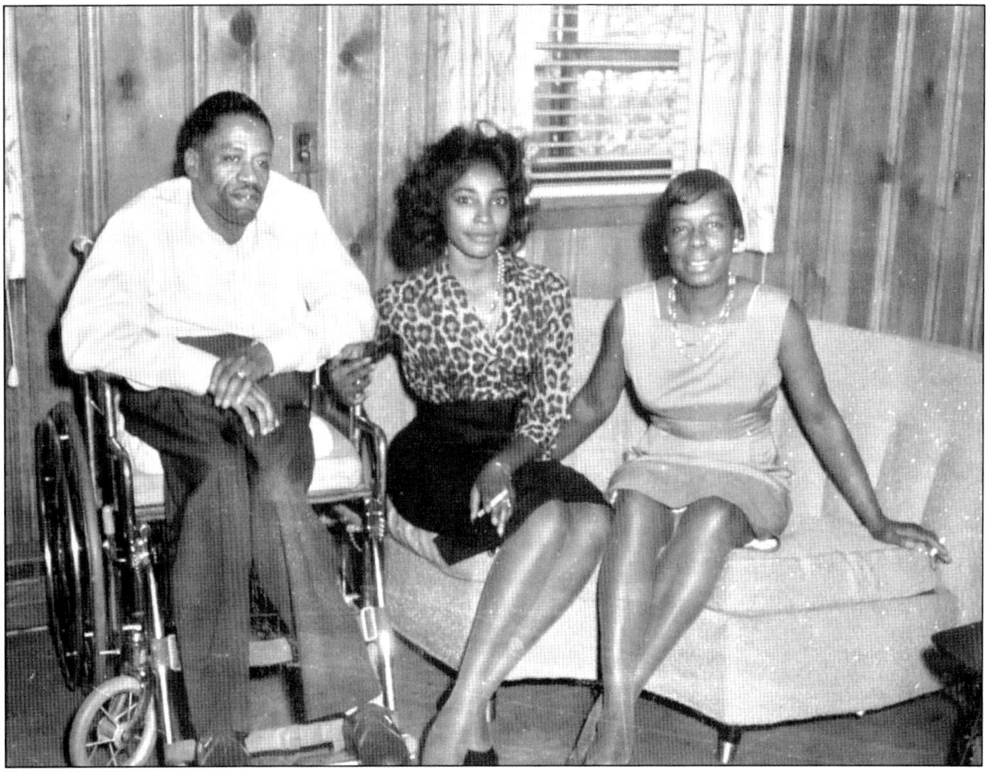

Mr. William Wisher (left), an unidentified friend (center), and Mrs. Sue Wisher relax in the family room of the Wisher home in the 1950s. The couple lived on Rogers Road.

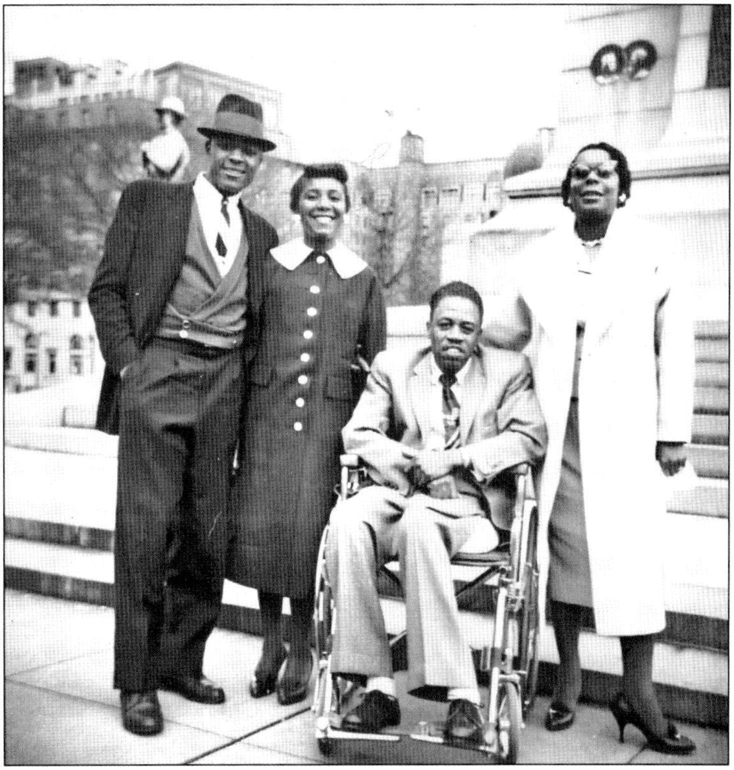

Pictured here from left to right are two unidentified friends, Mr. William Wisher, and Mrs. Sue Wisher. The picture was taken in the 1950s.

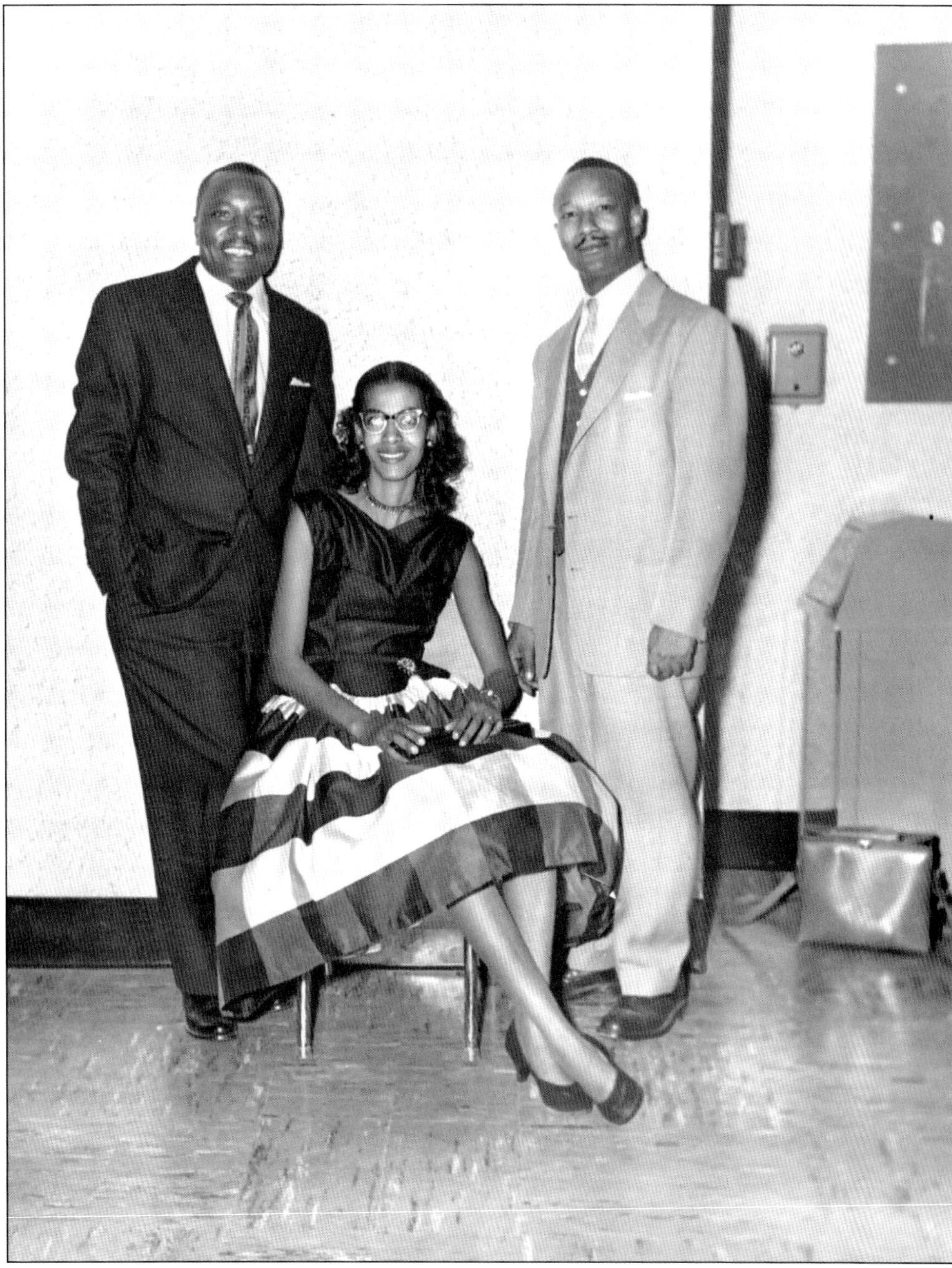

This is a picture of James Orr (left), Mrs. Dorothy Orr (center), and William Shipley in the Dunleith Community School cafeteria at a dance in the 1950s. (Dorothy Orr collection.)

Pictured here in the 1940s is Mr. James Orr.

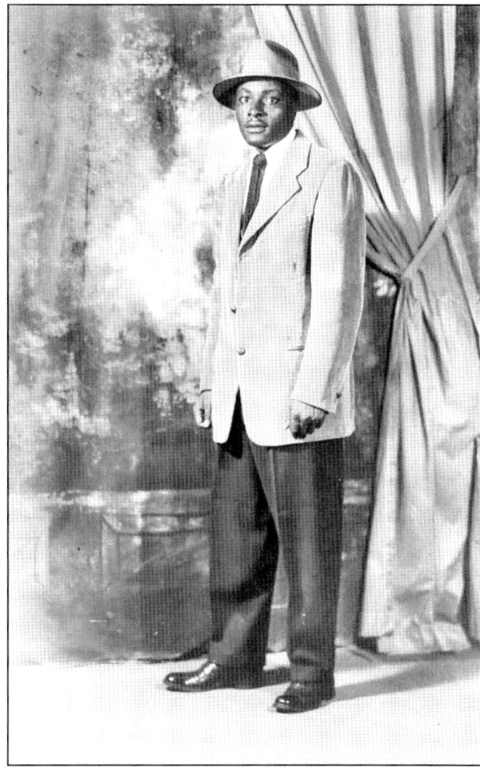

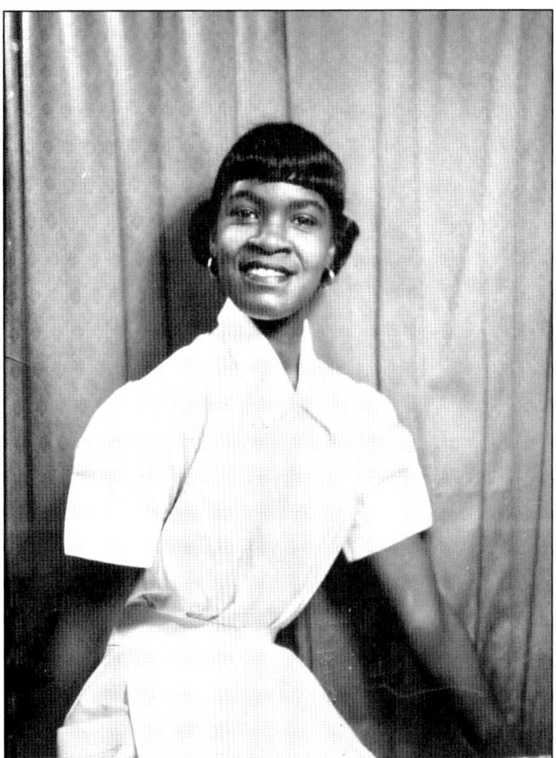

Mrs. Hazel Quarles is pictured here in her hospital kitchen uniform. Mrs. Quarles worked in the Veterans Administration cafeteria in the 1950s.

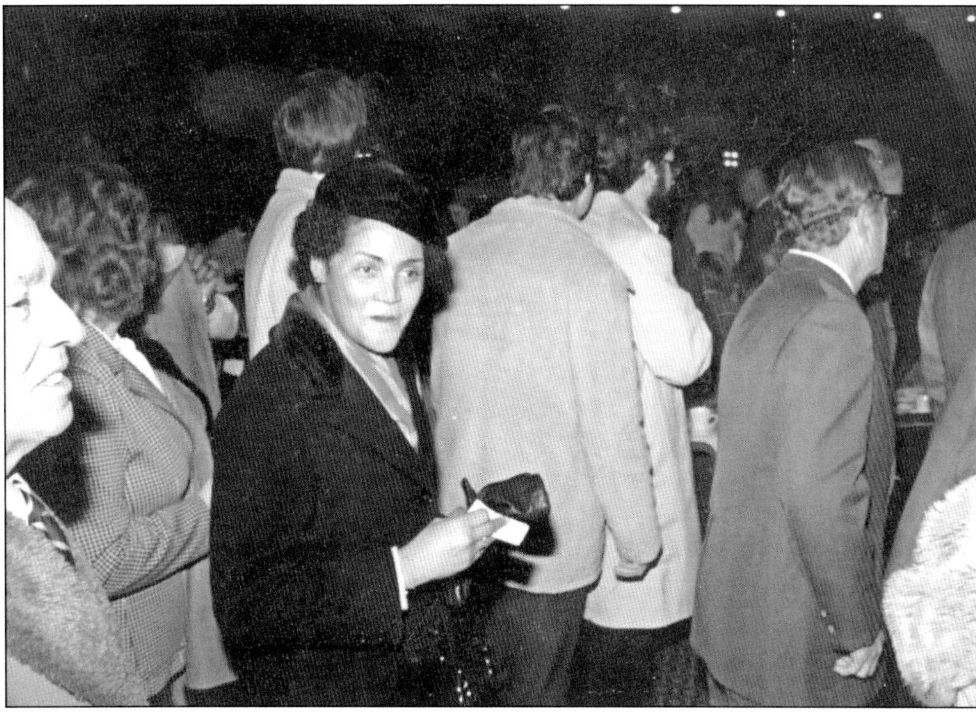

Mrs. Marion Perkins is on her way to work in the Hercules Corporation lobby in the 1970s. The Hercules Corporation was a chemical company specializing in raw materials.

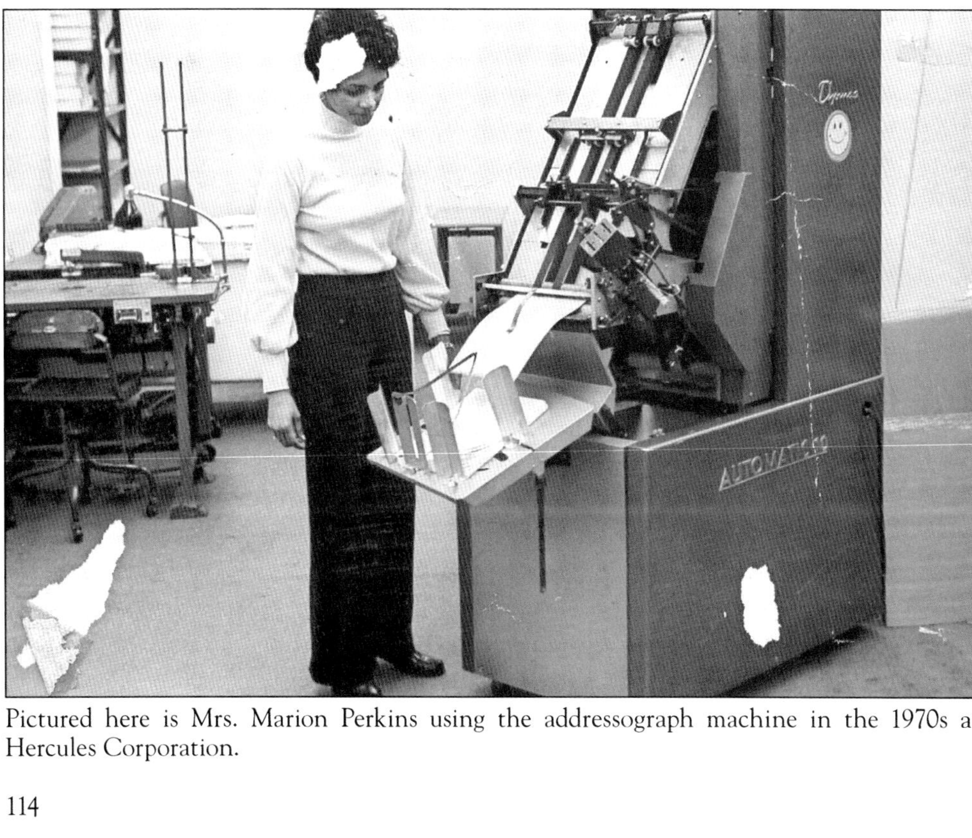

Pictured here is Mrs. Marion Perkins using the addressograph machine in the 1970s at Hercules Corporation.

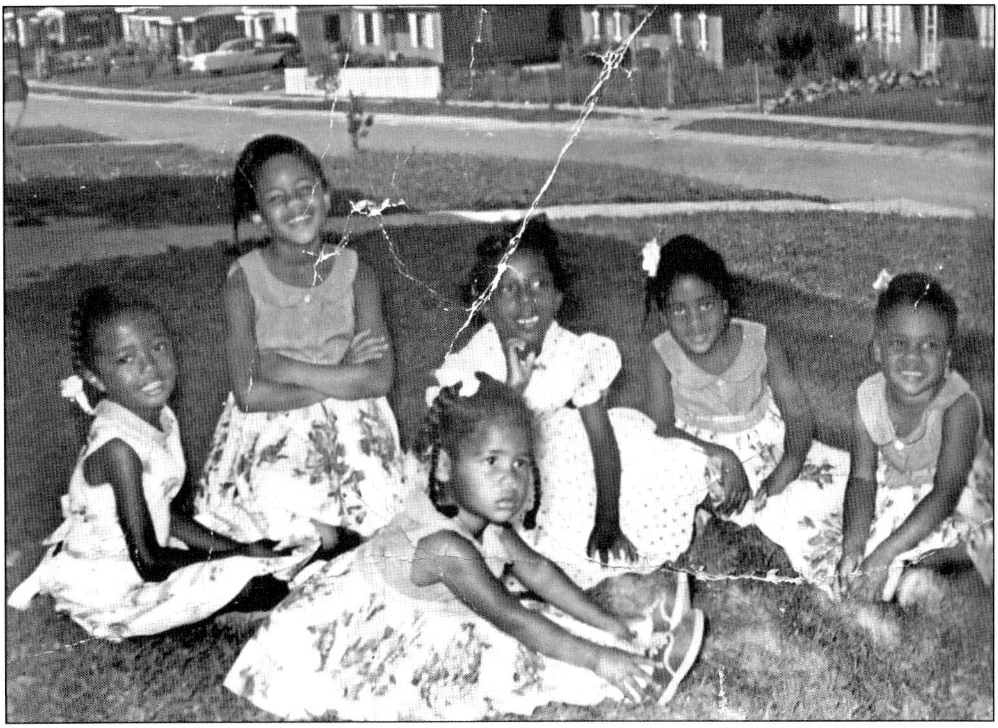

Neighborhood girlfriends gather on a Talladega Drive lawn in 1956. From left to right are Carmita Hightower, Vicky Perkins, Virginia Congo, Penny Perkins, and Barbara Perkins. Joyce Perkins is in front.

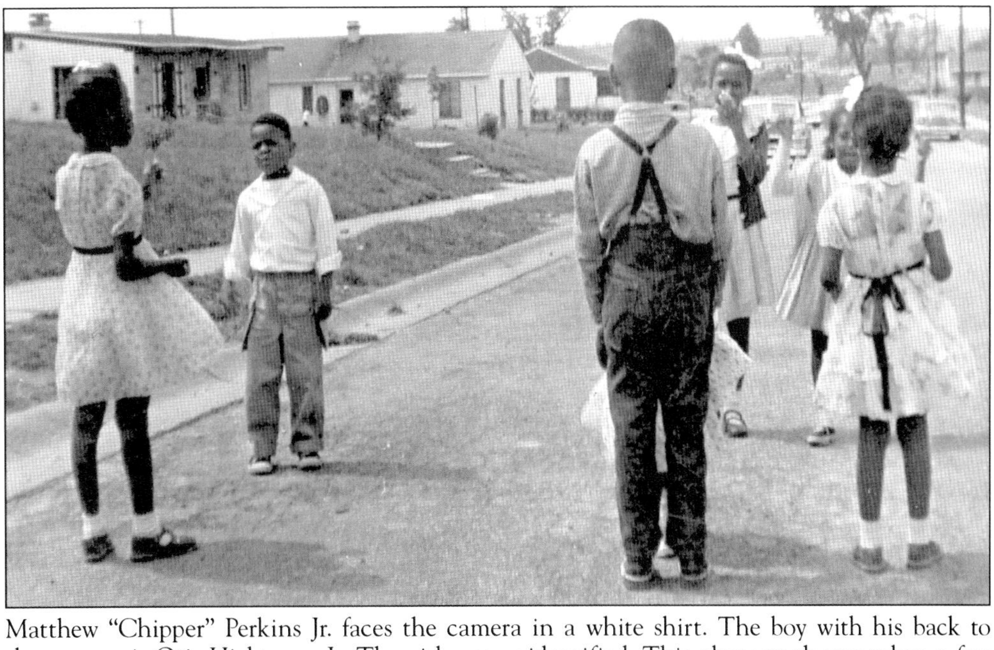

Matthew "Chipper" Perkins Jr. faces the camera in a white shirt. The boy with his back to the camera is Otis Hightower Jr. The girls are unidentified. This photograph was taken a few months before the death of Chipper in 1956. Chipper and Otis were crossing Rogers Road when Chipper was hit by an unidentified driver. He died on the scene.

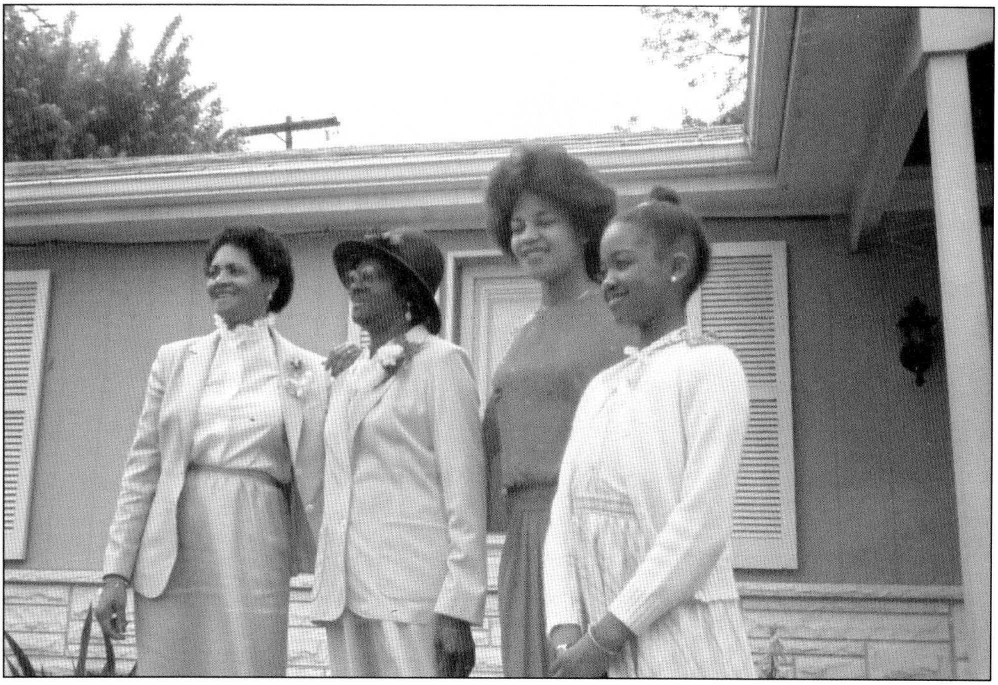

This picture of four generations was taken in the 1960s. From left to right are Marion Perkins; her mother, Marcella Dryden; Vicky Perkins; and Evette James.

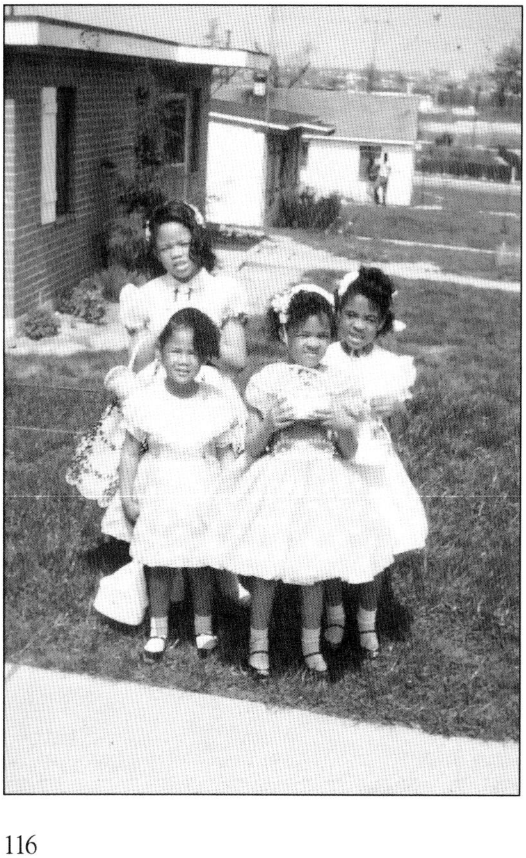

This photograph, taken at Easter time, shows, from left to right, (first row) Joyce, Barbara, and Penny Perkins; (second row) Darlene Perkins. The picture is taken with a view of the Howard family home on Talladega Drive in the 1950s.

Bernard (left) and Bill Orr enjoy a snow day in the 1950s. This picture was taken in the Millside community area.

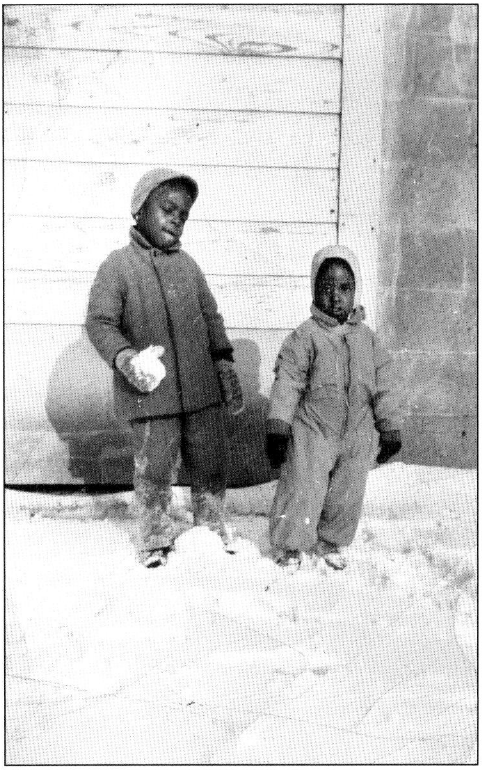

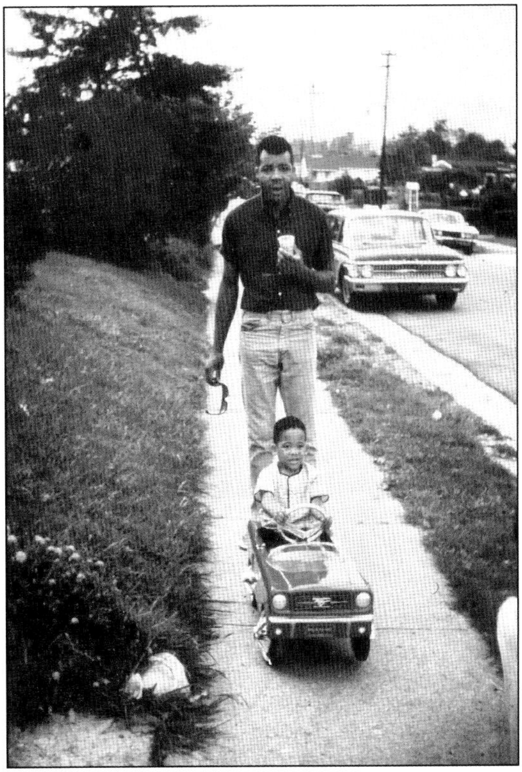

Matthew Perkins is out for a stroll through Dunleith with his son, Robert, in the 1960s.

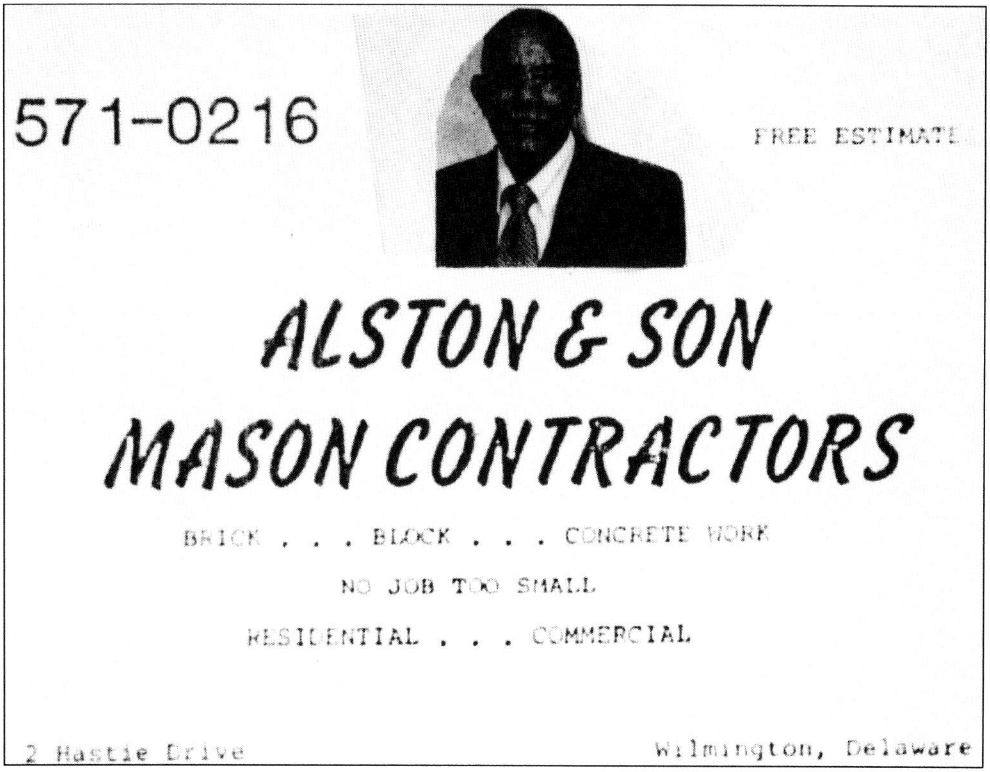

Mr. William Alston advertises his mason contractor's business in the late 1950s. He specialized in masonry work. Alston built the brick wall in the front of Coleman Memorial Methodist Church. He also helped to construct rooms in the church.

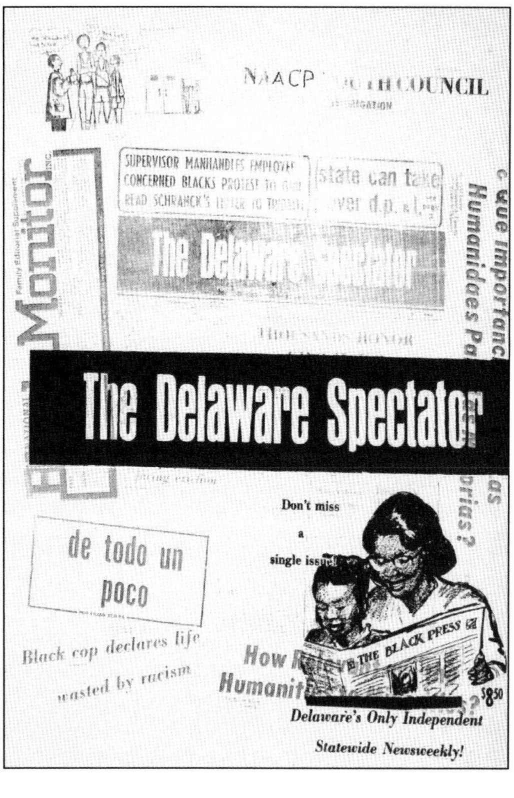

The *Delaware Spectator* was a newspaper that was widely read by black people in the 1950s.

Eight

CELEBRATIONS

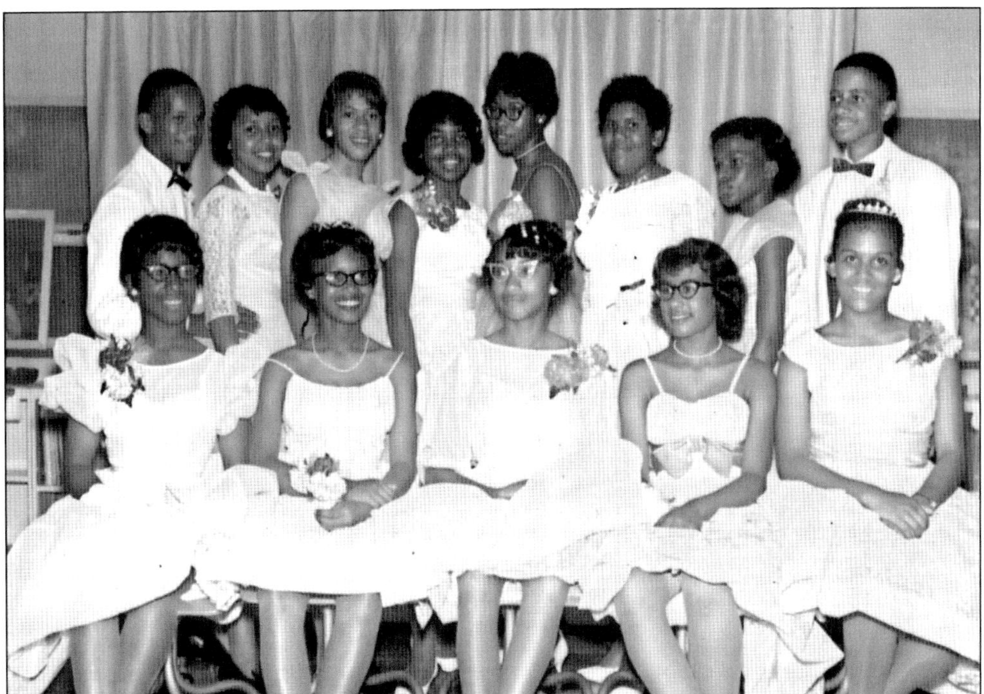

The Coleman Memorial Methodist Youth Fellowship Group dressed up for this evening in the early 1960s. Shown from left to right are (seated) Barbara Thomas, Sheena Quarles, Patricia Murphy, Cecila Spencer, and Sydella Davis; (standing) Ronald White, Emma Barnes, Jackie Ridgeway, Clara Thomas, Beverly Holland, Betty Horsey, Cynthia Dickerson, and David Ruth.

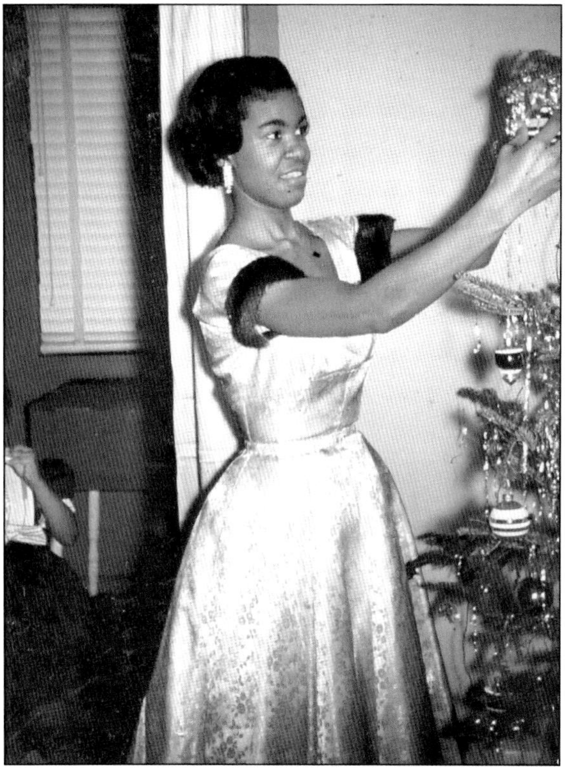

Mrs. Hazel Quarles celebrates Christmas in her home in Dunleith in the 1950s.

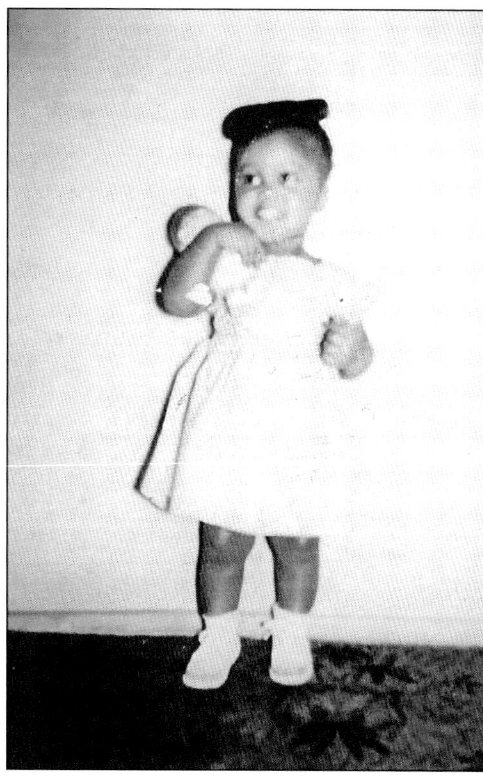

Sheena Quarles is shown here in the 1950s with her new toy doll.

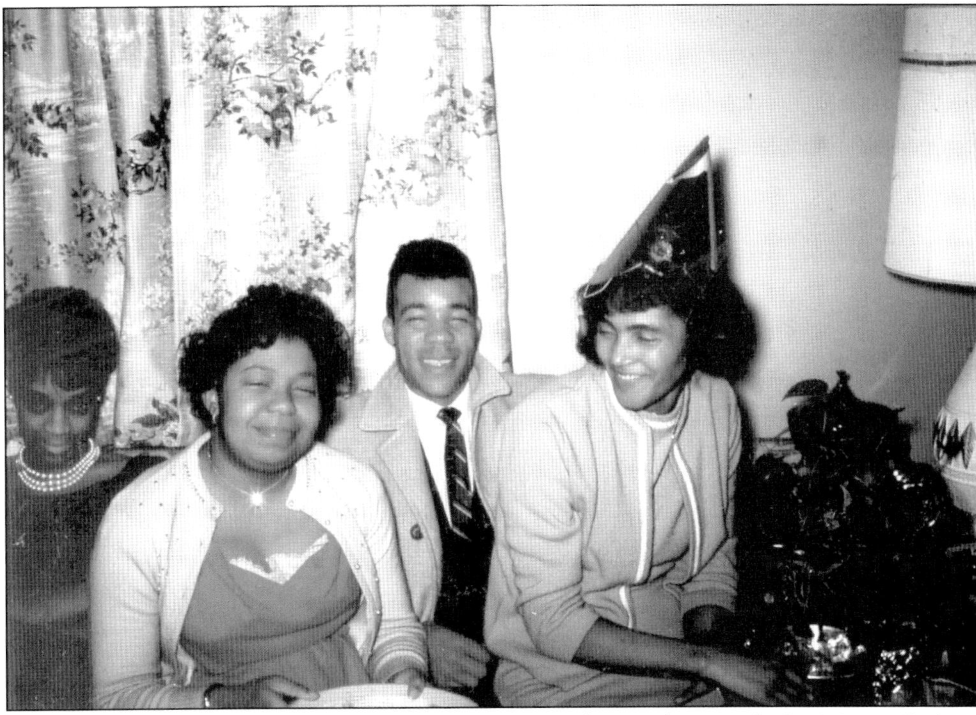

From left to right are unidentified, Margie Perkins, Matthew Perkins, and Mrs. Marion Perkins. The celebration was a birthday party for Margie Perkins in the 1950s.

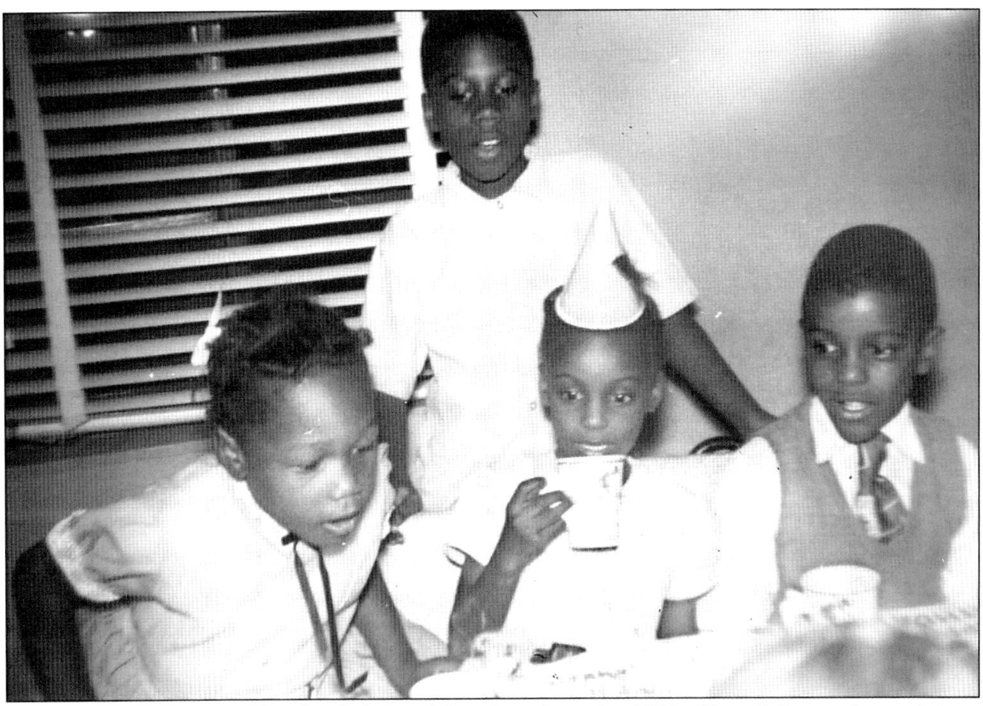

Brenda Emory celebrates her birthday with her friends in the 1950s. From left to right are Marie Trapp, Richard Trapp, Brenda, and Bernard Emory.

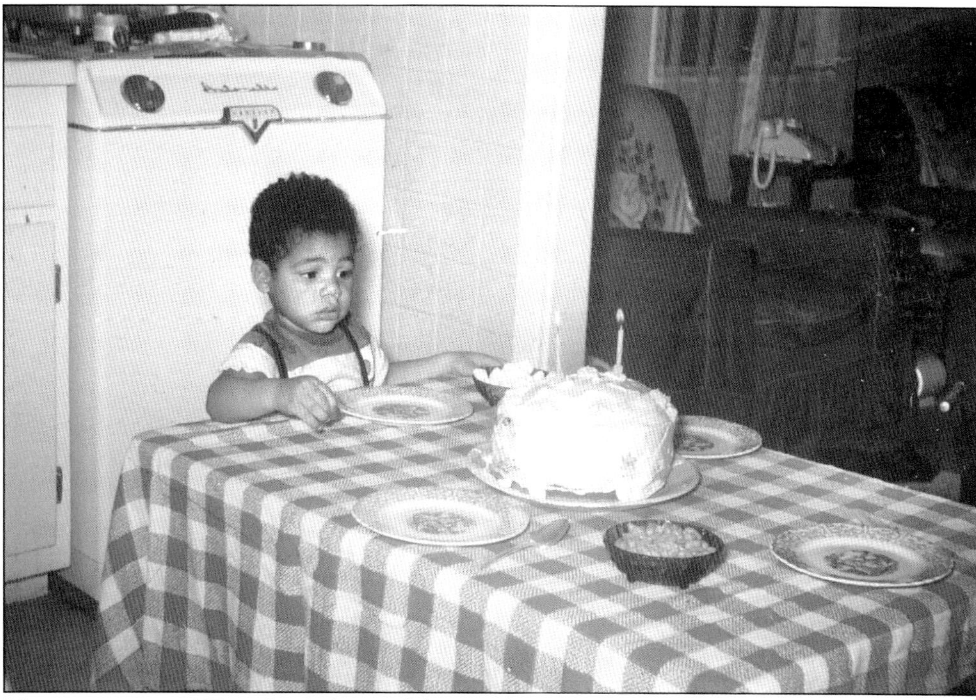

This is a picture of Timothy Perkins celebrating his second birthday at the family kitchen table in 1957.

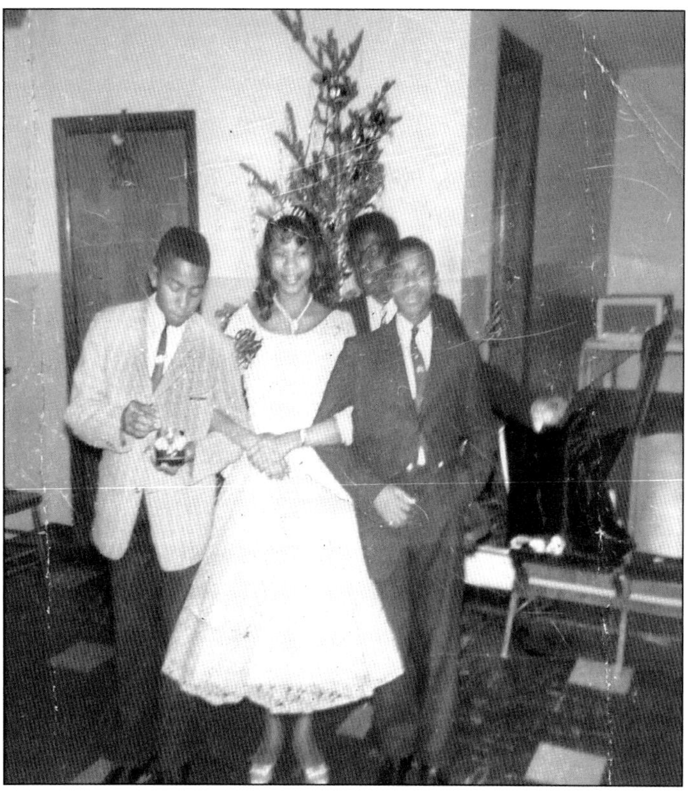

Bible school friends celebrate at Christmas in the 1950s. From left to right are Daniel Ridgeway, Margarite Quinn, Phillip Garnett, and Woodrow Ivy. (Hazel Quarles collection.)

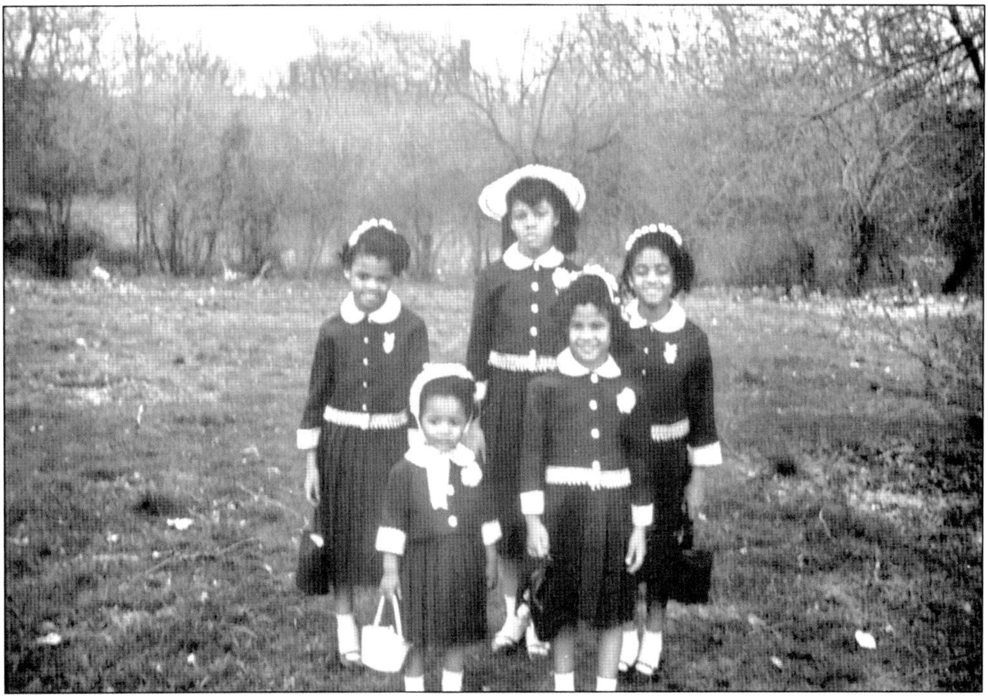

The Perkins sisters are dressed in their Easter bonnets on an outing at the Eden Park in Wilmington, Delaware, in the 1950s. Pictured from left to right are (first row) Lynn and Joyce; (second row) Barbara, Darlene, and Penny.

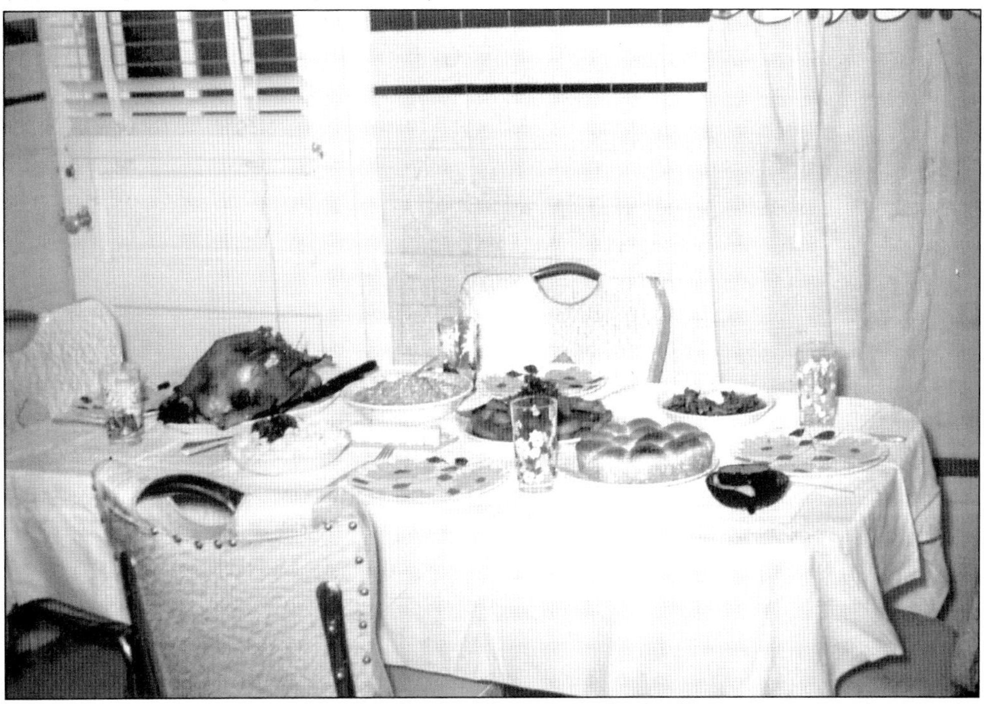

This table was set for a Thanksgiving feast in the 1950s. The food preparation was done in the home of Marion Perkins. She prepared many traditional favorites for her family to feast on.

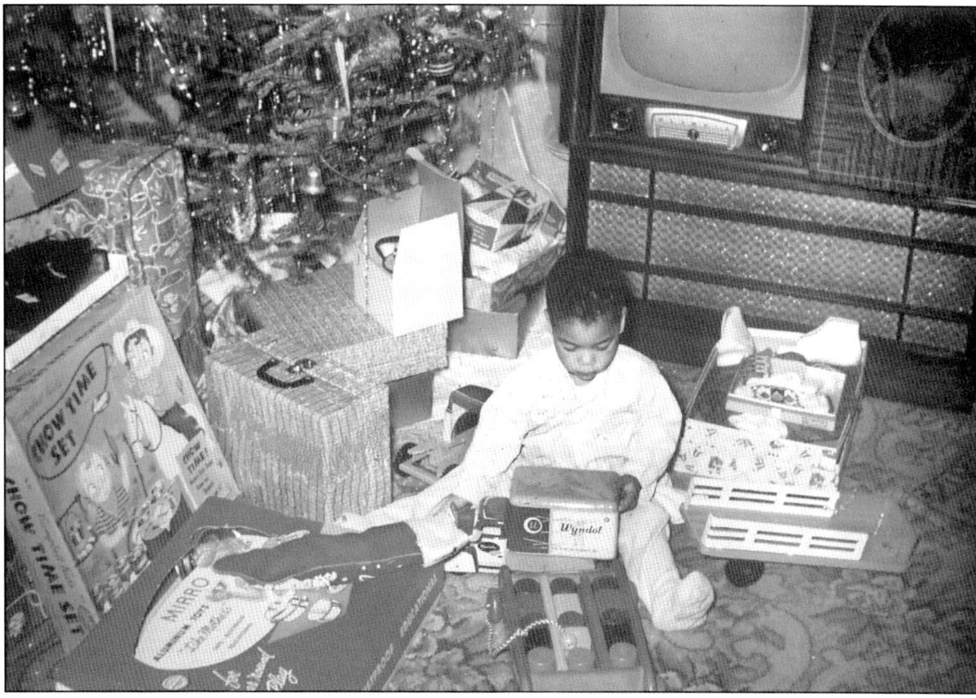

This is a picture of Timothy Perkins on Christmas day in the 1950s. Timothy is having fun unwrapping his Christmas presents.

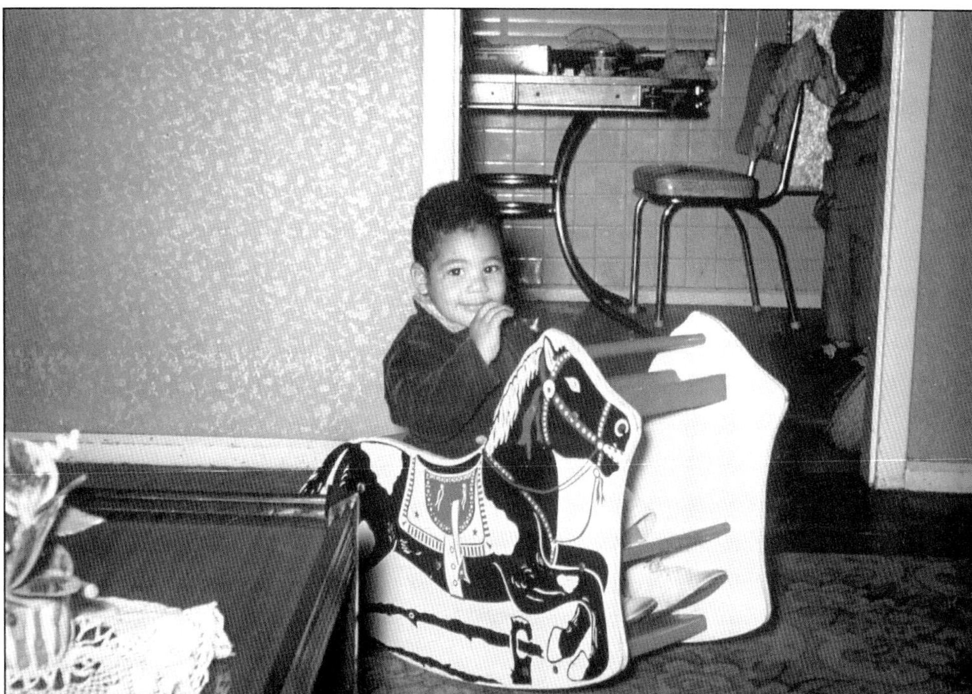

Timothy Perkins enjoys his wooden rocking horse in the 1950s. The toy had a wide seat in the center. The small bar in between was made for the child to hold on to while rocking.

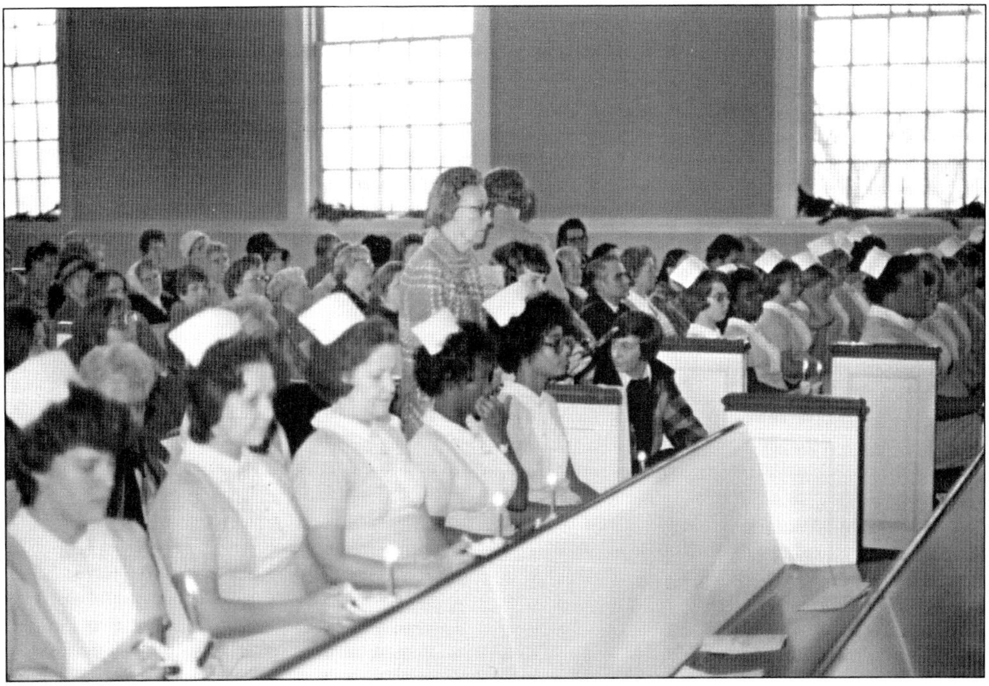

This is a picture of Ruth Perkins (fifth from the left) during her graduation ceremony for nurses. The capping ceremony took place at the Immanuel Church on Pennsylvania Avenue in Wilmington, Delaware, in the 1970s.

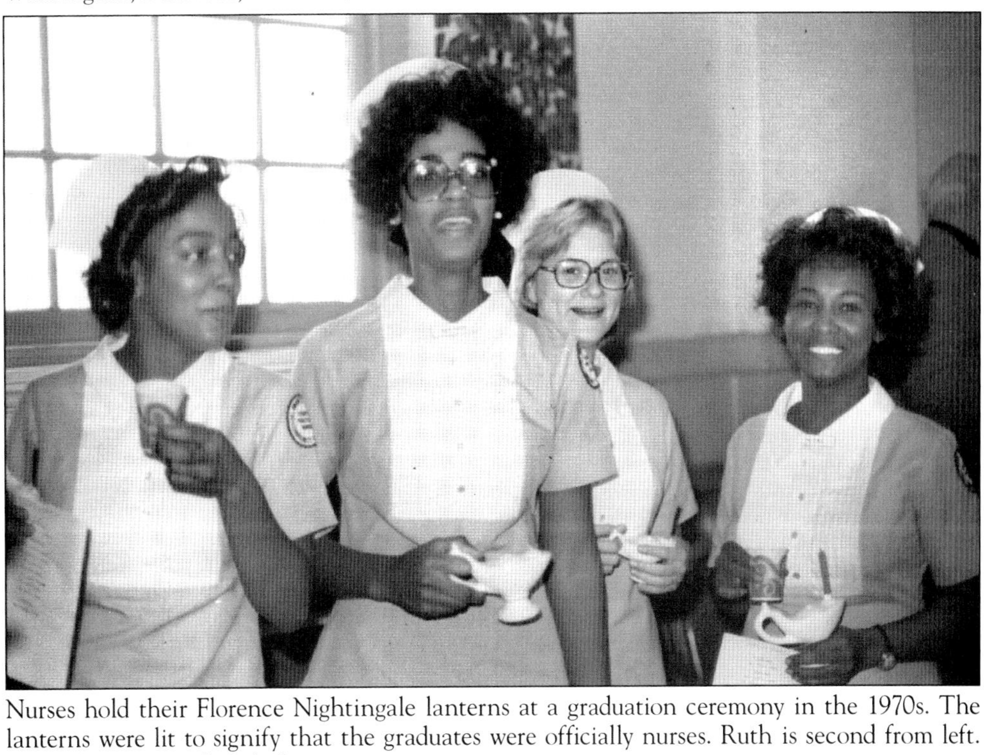

Nurses hold their Florence Nightingale lanterns at a graduation ceremony in the 1970s. The lanterns were lit to signify that the graduates were officially nurses. Ruth is second from left. The others are unidentified.

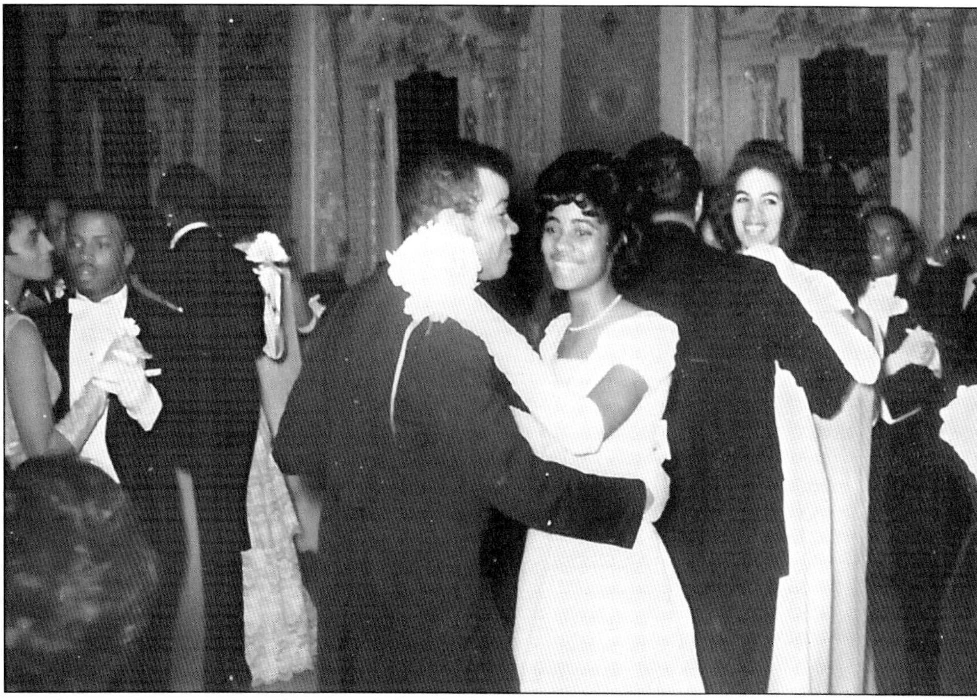

Matthew Perkins enjoys a dance with his daughter Ruth. The Debutante Ball was celebrated in the du Barry Room at the Hotel du Pont in 1969.

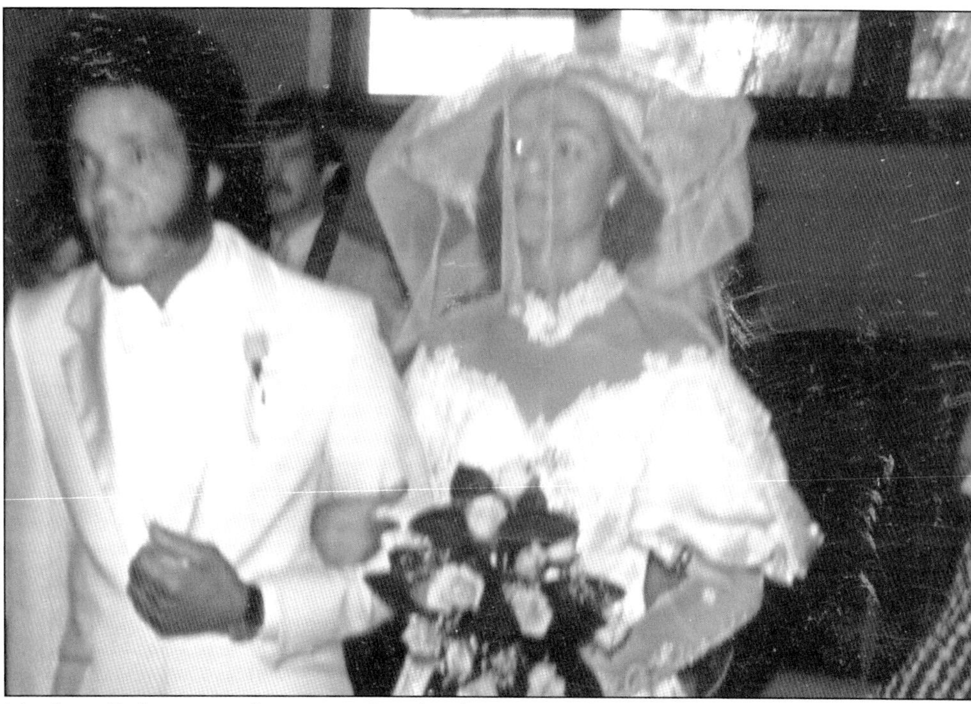

Matthew Perkins proudly escorts his daughter Lynn down the aisle. The joyous wedding celebration took place at the Waterfall Banquet and Conference Center in Wilmington, Delaware, in the 1970s.

Barbara Perkins poses for a pre-prom picture before the arrival of her date in the 1970s.

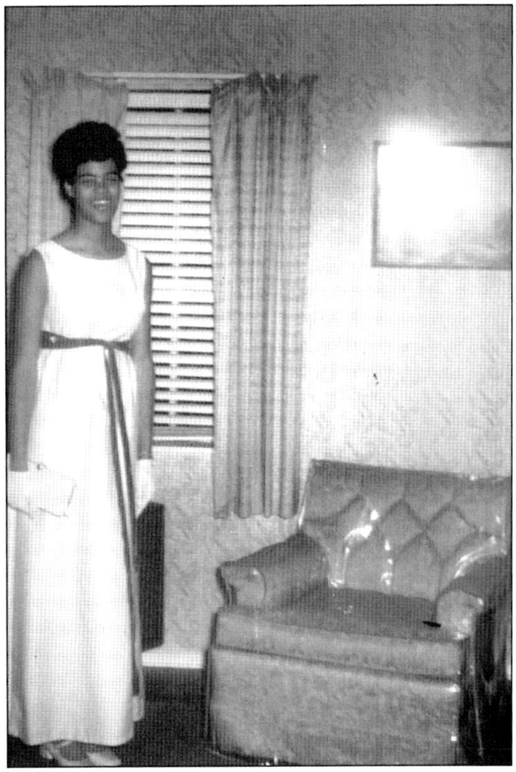

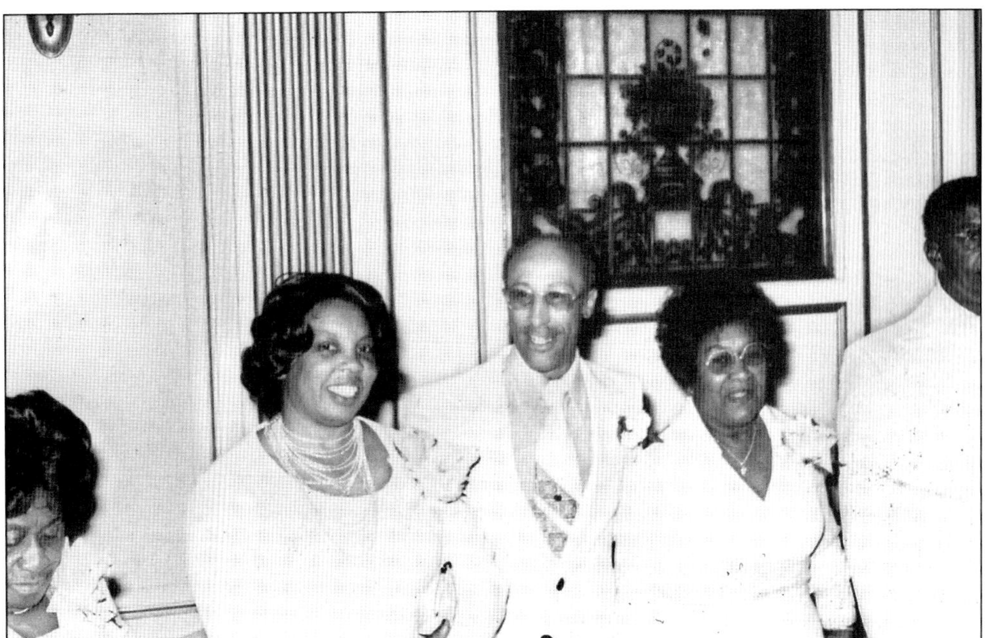

This is a picture of a gala 25th-anniversary reception-dinner for Coleman Memorial United Methodist Church in 1979. The celebration was held in the Gold Ballroom of the Hotel du Pont in downtown Wilmington, Delaware. From left to right are unidentified, Nancy Gaines, Henry Spencer, and Violet Jenkins.

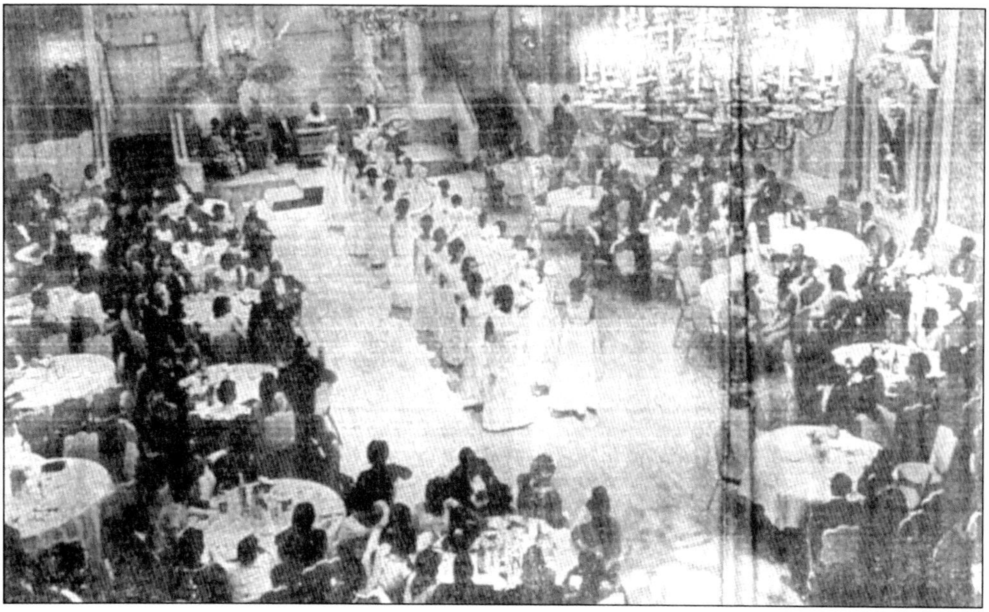

This is a picture of Dunleith debutante Ruth Perkins's coming-out ball. She was one of 26 girls honored for contributing in community service. The 20th annual ball, sponsored by the Zeta Omega Chapter of Alpha Kappa Alpha sorority, was held in the du Barry Room at the Hotel du Pont in Wilmington, Delaware, in 1969.

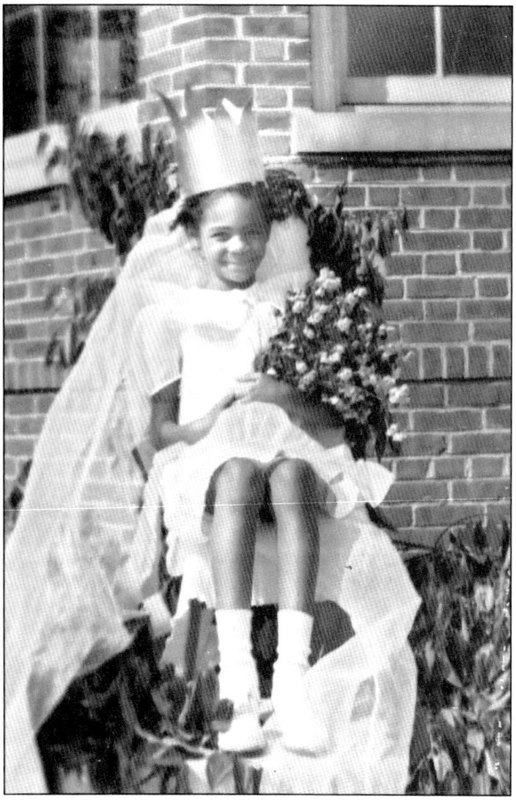

Marion Dryden was one of eight girls who participated in this May Day celebration held at the Elbert School in Wilmington in the 1940s. Marion was declared the winner, and she was crowned May Day queen.